CALUMET
BEGINNINGS

KENNETH J. SCHOON

Indiana University Press
Bloomington & Indianapolis

This book is a publication of

Indiana University Press
601 North Morton Street
Bloomington, Indiana 47404-3797 USA

http://iupress.indiana.edu

Telephone orders 800-842-6796
Fax orders   812-855-7931
Orders by e-mail iuporder@indiana.edu

*The paper used in this publication meets the minimum
requirements of American National Standard for Information
Sciences—Permanence of Paper for Printed Library
Materials, ANSI Z39.48-1984.*

MANUFACTURED IN THE UNITED STATES OF AMERICA

Library of Congress Cataloging-in-Publication Data
Schoon, Kenneth J.
   Calumet beginnings: ancient shorelines and settlements at
the south end of Lake Michigan / Kenneth J. Schoon.
       p. cm.
Includes bibliographical references and index.
   ISBN 978-0-253-34218-8 (alk. paper)
   1. Calumet Region (Ill. and Ind.)—History.   2. Calumet
Region (Ill. and Ind.)—History, Local.   3. Calumet Region
(Ill. and Ind.)—Geography.   4. Human settlements—Calumet
Region (Ill. and Ind.)—History.   5. Land settlement—Calumet
Region (Ill. and Ind.)—History.   I. Title.
   F547.C7S365 2003
   977.2'99—dc21
                                            2003000619

5   6   7   8   9   13   12   11   10   09   08

CONTENTS

PART ONE
The Physical Setting

PART TWO
The Human Touch

PART THREE
Community Beginnings

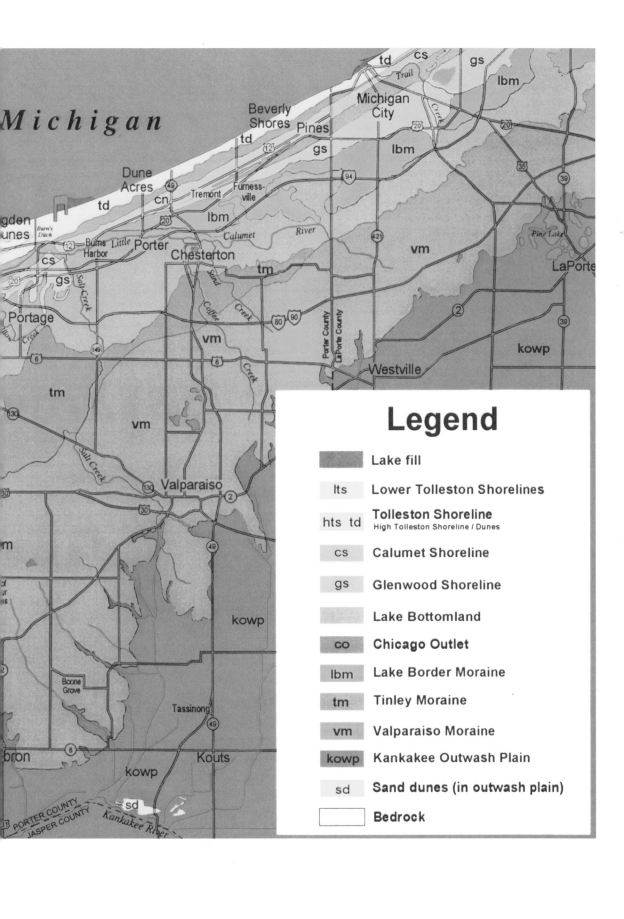

CALUMET
BEGINNINGS

Ancient Shorelines and Settlements at the South End of Lake Michigan

Preface

This book is about the land that is called the Calumet Area, located at the southern tip of Lake Michigan. It describes how the land was created and how it has affected human settlement. Likewise, it describes how human activity has altered the land.

Part One, "The Physical Setting," is a discussion of the natural forces that created this place. Chapter 1 discusses the geological history before and during the Ice Age. Chapter 2 focuses on Lake Michigan, its origins, its changes, its ancient shorelines, and the sand dunes that were formed near it.

Part Two, "The Human Touch," is a history of the human settlement and the subsequent use of the land that is the Calumet Area. It begins in chapter 3 with a discussion of the Native Americans who were here before European exploration and is followed by a discussion of that exploration by Europeans and the earliest settlement of the area. Chapter 4 describes the establishment of the initial farms, villages, and early cities. Because the Calumet Area has always had several transportation routes going through it, I discuss the role of the land, especially the ancient shorelines, in determining the routes for Indian trails, stagecoach routes, and modern highways. The railroads' profound effect on settlement is described in chapter 5.

The Calumet Area does not look the way it did in 1800. Thus chapter 6 concerns itself with how human activity has altered the natural features of the area. Rearranging the natural shape of the earth's surface is an old habit, and it was done extensively in this region. Each action turned some "inhospitable" parcel of land into something believed at that time to be more useful.

Part Three, "Community Beginnings," describes the geology and the settlement of each of the cities, towns, and villages of the Calumet Area. Many of the community descriptions end with a few sentences called postscripts, which describe interesting public historic buildings or museums in that community.

Because not all parts of the Calumet Area have been physically altered, and one can still find places that look similar to what the Potawatomi and the first settlers may have seen, the book ends with an epilogue entitled "Preserved Natural Areas."

ERRATA

Unfortunately, much local history material contains errors, and it would be presumptuous to assume that this book has eliminated them all and has no errors of its own. Readers are therefore encouraged to send corrections to the author at kschoon@iun.edu or by mail to 3400 Broadway, Gary, Indiana 46408. Please be specific and, if possible, include some way that I can confirm the correction. A current list of errata will be displayed at www.iun.edu/~edukjs/calumetbeginnings. A copy of the footnoted manuscript is held at the Calumet Regional Archives, Indiana University Northwest, and is available for researchers.

Acknowledgments

My sincere thanks to the following people who assisted with the preparation of this book: geologists Steve Brown, Mike Chrzastowski, Lyndon Dean, Tim Fisher, Ardith Hansel, and Todd Thompson; naturalists Kim Holson, Paul Labus, and Noel Pavlovic; anthropologist Clarke Johnson; archivist Steve McShane, and librarians and researchers: Scott Bocock, Janet Burden, David Hess, Lois Heiser, Lynne Ingersoll, Pat Walker, Jane Walsh-Brown, Nancy Vaillancourt, Jim Rodgers, and others whose names I don't know.

For history information and verification: Shirley Anderson, Harold and LaVerne Barkow, Virginia Bushong, Elin Christianson, Ross Ettema, Tyrone Haymore, Ed Hedstrom, Marvin Jacobs, Loretta Johnson, Karen Kulinski, Marge Loitz, Suzanne Long, Peter McCarthy, Bunty MacDonald, David Nellans, Cynthia Ogorek, Joyce Parrish, Paul Petraitis, James Rogers, Rod Sellers, Richard Schmall, Fern Schultz, Paul Schultz, Janice Slupski, Kathleen Sonntag, Art Schweitzer, John Swenson, Jim Thiel, William Tuley, Cindy Watson, Roger Wiers, Ann Wood, Bruce Woods, Jim Wright, Peter Youngman, Dorothy Humpfer Zacny, David Zandstra, Anne Zimmerman, and dozens of church and governmental secretaries and historians whose names I don't know.

For illustrations: Lyle Adley-Warrick, Harold Barkow, Ray Borgia, Tony Borgo, Daniel Bruhn, Elin Christianson, Father Tom Conde, Brad Cook, curator at the Indiana University Archives, Glen Eberly, Helen Eenigenburg, William Farrand, Roland Fabian, Matt Figi, Alton Goin, Mark Hoenke, Tyrone Haymore, Ed Hedstrom, Barbara Iverson, Mike Janko, Gayle Faulkner Kosalko, Linda Kus, Debbie Lamoureux, Suzanne Long, Elaine Olson, Joyce Parrish, Lester Schoon, Jill and Mike Schrage, Art Schweitzer, Rod Sellers, Janice Slupski, Ed Smith, Kathleen Sonntag, Shirron Soohey, John Spinks, Jim Thiel, Roger Weirs, Bruce Woods, and Anne Zimmerman. For use of their artwork, Robert Ramsey Smith, Edward M. Verklan, and the family of Carol Cameron.

For reviewing the manuscript and making invaluable suggestions: Lee Botts, Steve Brown, Tim Fisher, Larry McClellan, Paul Petraitis, Ron Robbins, and Peter Youngman.

And to Peg Schoon for finding books, articles, and miscellaneous information, copyediting probably two dozen versions of the manuscript, compiling the index, and putting up with four and one-half years of my hogging the family computer.

The author and IU Press also thank the John W. Anderson Foundation for its financial support, which allowed for a larger page size, additional illustrations, and the color end sheets.

CALUMET
BEGINNINGS

Prologue

The Calumet Area

The Calumet Area is a geographical region of Illinois and Indiana at the southern end of Lake Michigan that surrounds three rivers: the Grand Calumet River, which rises at a lagoon in Marquette Park in Gary, the Little Calumet River, which rises in the hills of western LaPorte County, and the Calumet River, a channel in South Chicago that has connected the Grand and Little Calumet Rivers to Lake Michigan since about 1805. The Calumet Area thus extends from southern Cook County, Illinois, through Lake, Porter, and LaPorte Counties in Indiana.

It is generally agreed that the name Calumet is a French substitution for the Indian name for the river. What that word was or what it meant has been debated for over 150 years. Early maps had more than a dozen spellings in French and English.

In 1945, geographer Alfred Meyer noted that it may have meant "little reed" or "pipe of peace." (Pipe stems were made of reeds.) Father Marquette described peace pipes called calumets in his journal for 1673. Others ascribe Calumet as a corruption of another Indian word meaning "a deep, still water."

More recent scholarship has uncovered another meaning. In a 1696 manuscript written by Jesuit missionary Jacques Gravier, researcher John Swenson found that the oldest recorded Indian name for the river was Kinoumiki, meaning "ship that draws a lot of water." Had the Indians seen a European ship on the Calumet River? It's possible, says Swenson. The Calumet River was much larger in the days before various drainage ditches diverted much of its waters. And the French explorers certainly had the means to build ships. LaSalle himself had one built on the Great Lakes in 1678–79. Called *Le Griffon,* during its brief life, it sailed on Lakes Erie, Huron, and northern Lake Michigan.

Acquiring a Sense of Place

My grandfather, Jacob Schoon, was born in 1873 in a small rented farmhouse along what is now Ridge Road in Munster but what was then a small farming community of Dutch immigrants. One hundred and one years later, he was laid to rest in a cemetery along the same Ridge Road, a few miles east of his birthplace. During his lifetime, the Calumet Area changed from a quiet, primitive, and rural area to one of the world's greatest manufacturing centers, and Ridge Road changed from a sandy, one-lane path to a busy four-lane roadway.

Jacob Schoon was a product of the Calumet Area. As expected, he traveled along Ridge Road to get to church services in Lansing. As expected, he finished just three years of school and then began working on the farm. Then often, as expected, he accompanied his father to Chicago to sell their produce. Later in life, as expected, he married a Dutch girl, Kate Koedyker, who lived on the farm next door. And as expected, they established their own farm near those of his brothers and sisters. However, twenty-three years later, he quit farming and moved with Kate and their ten sons (one more to come later) to the new city of Gary. There he found employment at the U.S. Steel plant and later with the EJ&E Railroad. Like thousands of others, he became part of the country's fastest growing urban area. The Calumet Area was always his home, as it has been for my father and was for my mother and her family since 1916.

The Calumet Area is also my home. I have lived in four of its communities. I have worked with cultural and educational organizations in Cook, Lake, and Porter Counties. And although I have lived here practically all of my life, I am always learning new things about this extraordinary region. With my roots in the Calumet Area, degrees in geology and education, a fascination with history, and decades of teaching experience, I feel uniquely qualified to combine the geology and early history of this special place into one integrated story.

Figure 1. Sand dunes along Lake Michigan. Calumet Regional Archives.

*　　　*　　　*

The Calumet Area extends roughly from Blue Island to Michigan City and hugs the southern rim of Lake Michigan. Eons ago, when mid-America was below sea level, tiny animals built up coral reefs such as the one at Thornton. Much later, the area was populated by dinosaurs and later still by woolly mammoths. Fresh-water clams and fish lived here when ancestral Lake Michigan covered much of the area.

Great physical forces helped shape the Calumet Area. Movements of the earth's crust raised and lowered the land, causing huge seas to slowly recede, return, and recede again. Mighty glaciers invaded from the north—not once but perhaps dozens of times. Powerful waves in the early ancestral Lake Michigan pounded the shoreline, eroding sand from places farther north and depositing it here. Beaches, sand bars, and sand and gravel spits were formed. Strong westerly winds picked up beach sand and shaped enormous sand dunes. When Lake Michigan was first formed, it extended farther south than it does today. In places, remnants of its original shoreline can still be seen. As the lake lowered in elevation, other shorelines formed as well. Many of the area's early trails, highways, and settlements were built along these ancient shorelines.

The Calumet Area is a headwaters region, meaning that every stream or river in the area begins, if not within this area, then nearby. In addition, the Eastern Continental Divide, which separates all the rivers and streams that flow north from those that flow south, runs through the Calumet Area. Thus some of its rivers flow into Lake Michigan and onward over Niagara Falls to the north Atlantic Ocean through the St. Lawrence River. Other waterways rise in the Calumet Area and flow south to the Kankakee River, then west to the Illinois and Mississippi Rivers, emptying into the Gulf of Mexico.

What makes the Calumet Area special, however, is more than just the happenstance of physical forces. It includes the effects of its human population. Here, Indians built mounds so long ago that the Miami and Potawatomi knew nothing about them. Indians hunted game, built their villages, braved the elements, and raised their families. Here, Father Jacques Marquette encamped along the lakeshore in the 1670s and spent some of the last days of his remarkable life. Here, for 100 years, French voyageurs explored the rivers and forests. Here, in 1780, Spanish soldiers marched on their way from St. Louis to British-held Fort St. Joseph. Here, in 1822, Joseph and Marie Bailly established their home and trading post in the wilderness.

Hundreds of settlers from the south and east came to live in the Calumet Area in the 1830s. Unfortunately, most historical accounts give only the names of male settlers and businessmen. One of my goals has been to find the names of the pioneer women who came to this area, helped clear the land, work in the fields, and run the stores, as they established households and raised the first generation of Calumet Area children.

Stagecoaches began traversing this place in the 1830s, but they disappeared soon after the railroads arrived in the early 1850s. Building the rail lines was an undertaking that altered the shape of the land itself and changed its settlement patterns. The railroads brought more people and prosperity to the area, and they employed hundreds of its citizens. The communities of Markham, Whiting, Griffith, and Miller were named for railroad employees. One of the lines, popularly called the South Shore Railroad, promoted the area

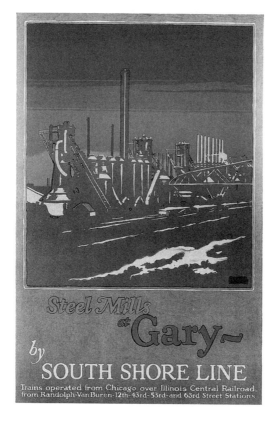

through its advertising posters and was instrumental in the establishment of Indiana Dunes State Park.

Lake Michigan has also had a profound influence upon this place, and its waters are valued by the residents and industries of the region. Its beaches are crowded in the summer. Its very size and shape, and its location in the center of a great inland plain, dictated that many travelers would have to go around its southern end, making transportation an important industry. Its current and ancient shorelines provided many of the routes for these cross-country movements.

Soon after the Dunes Highway (U.S. Highway 12) in Porter County was built in 1922–23, it became Indiana's busiest roadway. At that same time, the most celebrated section of concrete highway in the world was the "Ideal Section" of the Lincoln Highway, built between Dyer and Schererville, also in 1922–23. This one and a third mile section was four lanes wide and made of ten inches of reinforced concrete. Such care was taken in building this highway that no traffic was allowed for thirty days after it was poured. (Indiana historical markers are posted at each end of this highway segment.) The Ideal Section also had sidewalks, landscaping, and electric lights. In fact, it was one of the first highways to have street-

Figure 2. South Shore advertising posters: *Steel Mills at Gary by South Shore Line* was a 1925 lithograph by Norman Erickson, and *Indiana Dunes State Park by South Shore Lines* was a 1929 lithograph by Raymond Huelster. Calumet Regional Archives.

Figure 3. The Ideal Section of the Lincoln Highway between Dyer and Schererville in 1923. Lincoln Highway Association, 1935.

lights, and all wiring was underground. "Motorists were surprised and delighted to find they could drive this section at night, without headlamps on their cars."

Both roadways were built along ancient shorelines of Lake Michigan: the Dunes Highway on the Calumet Shoreline, and the Ideal Section on the older Glenwood Shoreline.

The industrial might of the Calumet Area adds to the specialness of this place. Superlatives are easily used in describing the impact of industry. The Pullman Company had what was for many years the largest railroad passenger car manufacturing plant in the country. Thornton had the world's largest commercial limestone quarry. U.S. Steel's Gary Works was the largest integrated steel mill in the world when it was built. Standard Oil's refinery in Whiting was the world's largest refinery. Universal Portland Cement at Buffington Harbor was the world's largest cement plant.

Such achievements have not come without cost. In the early days, to "improve the land" meant to drain the wetlands or to clear the forests. Many early Calumet Area residents saw the area and its natural resources as property to be used or things to be exploited. Beginning in the 1840s, first timber, then sand were exported at prodigious rates. By the 1870s pollutants from agriculture, industry, and households were being released into the air or dumped into rivers and lakes.

However, in the 1890s, a new understanding of the Calumet Area was beginning to emerge. In 1897, geologist Frank Leverett

Figure 4. Excavating sand at Dune Park, ca. 1909. Ed Hedstrom collection.

pieced together evidence about the formation and early history of Lake Michigan. He gave the names Glenwood, Calumet, and Tolleston to the three former shorelines of Lake Michigan. At the same time, University of Chicago botanist Henry Chandler Cowles used his studies in the Indiana Dunes, the Blue Island Ridge, and the Gibson Station area to develop his theories about ecology. His dissertation on plant succession was published in 1899.

The Indiana Dunes

There are few places on our continent where so many species of plants are found in so small compass as within the [dunes area].

It is not so well known as it should be that the dunes of Lake Michigan are much the grandest in the entire world. Not necessarily the highest, though some of them reach up 400 feet and more above the lake, but more than any other anywhere, our dunes show magnificent and contrasting types of plant life, everything from the bare dunes to magnificent primeval forests. No other dunes than ours show such bewildering displays of dune movement and struggle for existence, such labyrinths of motion, form, and life. They are without a parallel.
—Henry Chandler Cowles, 1917

The 20th century saw preservation of significant and beautiful parts of the bistate area become a priority for conservation-minded citizens. The Forest Preserve District of Cook County, Illinois, was established in 1914, and by 1922 it had purchased more than 20,000 acres of undeveloped land. In the 1890s, artists, poets, and

Figure 5. Carr's bathhouse and dance pavilion at Miller Beach, July 4, 1917. Calumet Regional Archives.

writers began to take note of the Indiana Dunes, and many Chicagoans came to the dunes by train. By 1912, the Prairie Club of Chicago began efforts to create a Sand Dunes National Park. In July 1916, a group of Chicago and Calumet Area citizens formed the National Dunes Park Association to encourage the creation of a park along the lakeshore. Although it would be fifty years before the national lakeshore would be a reality, Indiana Dunes State Park was established in 1927.

After World War II, the conflict between conservation and development intensified. The Save the Dunes Council, created in 1952, carried on efforts for a national park. An agreement was finally reached which allowed in 1966 for the formation of the Indiana Dunes National Lakeshore as well as for development of the Port of Indiana between properties owned by the Midwest and Bethlehem steel companies.

The controversial attitude of the mid-twentieth century has given way to a new spirit of cooperation. Today, broad coalitions of citizens including captains of industry, environmentalists, and educators are spearheading efforts to advance the causes of commerce, recreation, and conservation. Both industrialists and environmentalists want to enhance the quality of this area. It is now recognized that the Calumet Area requires good stewardship of its resources and preservation of its natural areas as well as historically important buildings and civic spaces.

The Calumet Area is no longer a virgin wilderness. It is home and workplace to more than a million people. The area has changed and today reflects the contributions of its citizens, both past and present. Yet, with citizen pride and involvement, respect and resourcefulness, it can be a delightful place in which to live.

PART ONE

The Physical Setting

If a person could rise in a balloon so as to get a bird's-eye view of this plain . . . he would see that it comprises three distinct belts or regions, each with well-marked surface characteristics. The region on the north and the one on the south would each be seen to be lower, and comparatively much more level than the one intervening. Along the upper margin of the northern region would be noted, however, a narrow strip covered with numerous hills and ridges of sand.

"The surface of the middle region [the moraines], comprising more than half of the entire area, would in some parts be seen to be high and undulatory, in others more even and regular, but on the whole much more rugged and broken than either of the other two."

—Willis S. Blatchley, Indiana state geologist, 1897

Seas, Sediments, and Glacial Ice

FORMING THE LANDSCAPES

W hen **Willis Blatchley** wrote the above fantasy about floating over the Calumet Area, he was probably not aware of the experiments in human flight that had occurred in this very region within the previous year. In the summer of 1896, South Chicagoan Octave Chanute and a small group of foolhardy experimenters arrived at Miller Beach to try out his biwinged and multiwinged gliders. After many failures and a few partial successes, his group returned six weeks later to try again. This second trip to the Indiana Dunes resulted in several hundred successful flights of up to 350 feet in length.

Chanute liked the dunes. They were tall and windy enough for taking off, and the sand provided a soft landing. After his experiments, he visited and shared his results at the dunes with Orville and Wilbur Wright, who made their first flight at Kitty Hawk, North Carolina, six years later. When airplanes began to fly over the area, people could finally see what Blatchley imagined: three very distinct regions at the south end of Lake Michigan.

A story about Calumet Beginnings must include a description of how this landscape was formed. But it must also go farther back in history to the formation of the bedrock that underlies the area.

Figure 6. Willis S. Blatchley, Indiana state geologist, 1895–1910. Indiana University Archives, Bloomington.

For it was these rocks which actually dictated where Lake Michigan and the Calumet Area would eventually be placed. To find that history, one must look downward.

The bedrock under the soil and sediment of the Calumet Area is composed of dozens of nearly horizontal layers of limestone, sandstone, shale, and dolomite, all of which form underwater. Each type of rock forms in a different way. As a result, bedrock layers tell us something about the environment at the time they were formed. For instance, most sandstone forms underwater but near a shore, whereas shale, limestone, and dolomite may form far from shore. Shale is made from clay or mud that has settled at the bottom of a sea. Limestone is made from seashells or other calcium-carbonate materials. Dolomite is a form of limestone that was chemically altered after deposition.

The layers of bedrock are nearly horizontal except to the east in Porter and LaPorte Counties, where they slope gently downward to the northeast. They then reappear near Niagara Falls, more than 400 miles away. Layers of dolomite and limestone under the Calumet Region are the same layers of rock that form the rock shelf over which the Niagara River flows at Niagara Falls. This hard rock is also found parallel and next to the Lake Michigan shore in Wisconsin and Illinois and may have acted to restrain numerous glacial advances and thus helped create the Lake Michigan basin.

Unfortunately, very little of these rock layers can easily be seen locally. There is a rock outcrop at Thornton that now is the site of one of the planet's largest limestone quarries. Further south, bedrock can be seen at Turkey Run State Park near the appropriately named Rockville, Indiana. It can also be seen to the west at Starved Rock State Park and at Rock Island, both in Illinois, as well as at Baraboo, Wisconsin, and along the Dells of the Wisconsin River.

Even though underground and not visible in the Calumet Area, surprisingly, bedrock does have important economic value. The Northern Indiana Public Service Company (NIPSCO) uses the porous sandstone south of the Calumet Area to store natural gas, and some Calumet Area industries have disposed of waste acids in the deep bedrock rather than dump them into Lake Michigan. In northeast Illinois, as part of the Deep Tunnel flood-relief project, huge tunnels have been carved out of the bedrock to create rainwater reservoirs.

No igneous or metamorphic rocks can be found in the Calumet Area except for the huge mass of granite that underlies all of these sedimentary rocks and the pebbles, cobbles, and boulders (up to ten feet in diameter) that lie near the surface. One such boulder (the largest yet seen by the author) is next to the Revelli Bandshell at Festival Park on the banks of Lake George in Hobart. These rocks, called erratics, are native to Canada and upper Michigan and were carried here by glaciers during the recent Ice Age.

The Rock-Recorded History

The sedimentary rocks underneath the Calumet Area are about 4,000 feet thick. As is typical with sedimentary rock, the rock layers farther down are older than the layers closer to the surface. This is because new sediment, which may later turn into rock, is laid upon existing material. Figure 7 illustrates the bedrock that underlies the Calumet Area. Above the bedrock is between 15 and 270 feet of glacial till and lake sediment.

Devonian rocks form the top layer of rock in LaPorte, Porter, and Lake Counties. They show that during the Devonian Period this area was covered by seawater. The uppermost layer is a rock called shale (#5). Below that is limestone. Because the shale is the uppermost layer of bedrock, if any rocks were formed at later times, they have been completely eroded away.

Silurian rocks form the top layer of rock in Cook and western Lake Counties. During this period, there was deposition of much limestone that later was altered to dolomite (#4). This includes the coral reef dolomite mined at the Thornton Quarry. In New York and Ontario, Silurian rocks include the dolomite at Niagara.

Ordovician rocks were formed at a time when the continent apparently rose and fell, allowing the sea to alternately invade and recede from this area. Uplift resulted in the rock and sediment layers being eroded by rain and rivers. When the sea returned, more sediment was deposited. Rocks formed during this period include some shale, sandstone, limestone, and much dolomite (#3).

Cambrian rock, the oldest sedimentary rock layer in the area, is primarily sandstone (#2). The fossils in this layer indicate that this area was then at the bottom of a shallow sea.

Pre-Cambrian rock, the oldest rock in the area, is the granite

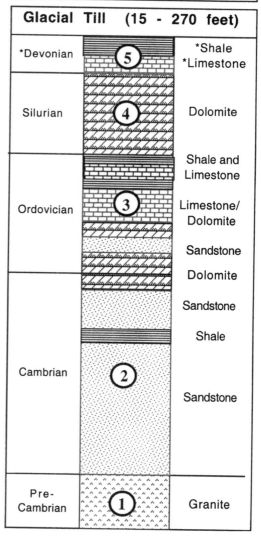

* Devonian rocks not present in the northwest portion of the Calumet Area.

Figure 7. Summary of bedrock layers beneath the Calumet Area.

shown at the bottom of the diagram (#1). Granite is formed by the slow cooling of magma deep within the earth. The upper part of this rock mass has been eroded, showing that it was at one time at the surface of the earth.

Today, the Calumet Area is 700 miles from the nearest sea and varies from 580 to more than 900 feet above sea level.[1] No major sedimentary rock layers are being formed here or anywhere else on the great plains of the American Midwest. Rather, the agents of erosion are slowly carrying away its soils to new resting places at the bottom of Lake Michigan or the Gulf of Mexico where the sedimentary rocks of the future are being made.

Limestone Quarries

A notable landmark in the Calumet Area is the huge quarry that is bisected by Interstate Highway 80/294. One of the largest commercial limestone quarries in the world, it has been in operation since the mid-nineteenth century. Much smaller quarries (since filled in) once operated in South Chicago in the area around South Chicago Community Hospital. Once an island in ancestral Lake Michigan, it is now a mile-long hill along Ninety-second and Ninety-third Streets called Stony Island. Just south of the Calumet Sag Channel was once a small stone quarry at 135th and Claire Boulevard in what is now Robbins. There were also, in the nineteenth century, two small quarries near the intersection of Cottage Grove Avenue and U.S. Highway 30 in what is now Ford Heights. These rock areas are all remnants of tropical coral reefs formed long before the North American continent looked the way it does today.

The Thornton and most of the other reefs are roughly circular, unlike the unusual "dumbbell" shape of the reef at Stony Island. It is likely that Stony Island's long dumbbell shape may have been the result of two reefs merging.

Although called limestone quarries, the rock mined at these locations is an exceptionally pure rock called dolomite, a rock similar to limestone. The rock mining industry often refers to both as limestone. This dolomite does not have the beauty or strength of the much more famous Indiana limestone mined in southern Indiana and thus is not used for building. Rather, much of it is crushed and used as bedding for roads, railroads, and building foundations.

During the Silurian period, this rock formed as several huge coral reefs were growing in a warm, shallow sea environment. A coral reef is composed of the shells of coral animals. These animals build their shells attached to the shells of other corals. Over

1. The lowest elevation in the Calumet Area is at the Lake Michigan beach. The highest elevations are in the moraine in an area from just north of Valparaiso to just north of LaPorte.

Figure 8. The
Thornton Quarry.

thousands of years, these coral colonies can grow, as did the Thornton reef, to be more than a mile in diameter. Coral reefs today grow best in seas with temperatures of 73° to 80° Fahrenheit, so it is likely that the Silurian water temperatures also were in that range. Corals feed on algae in the water, and since algae require shallow water so that sunlight can penetrate, geologists have surmised that the sea in which this coral grew was warm and shallow. Besides coral fossils, there are fossils of trilobites, cephalopods, brachiopods, and crinoids at Thornton.

There are about 125 of these reefs in the Chicago/Calumet Area. They are generally much higher than the surrounding bedrock and thus the only bedrock in the region that is visible at the surface.

Dinosaurs and Other Extraordinary Animals

Dinosaurs probably lived in the Calumet Area during the Jurassic, Cretaceous, and Triassic Periods. The land was above sea level and so would have hosted the plants and animals of the time. However, with all the wind and rain since then, their fossils have eroded. Finally, during the much later Ice Age, huge glaciers invaded the area and removed all remaining evidence of the dinosaurs having ever been here.

Several large mammals did populate Indiana and Illinois during

Figure 9. Mural at the Indiana University Bloomington Department of Geology.

and after the Ice Age. Among these were the American mastodon, Jefferson's mammoth, Harlan's musk ox, the stag moose, saber-toothed tiger, and giant beaver. All of these animals are now extinct.

Mastodons became extinct 10,000–12,000 years ago. Their bones are rare, but a few have been found in the Calumet Area. One set can be seen today at the Old Jail Museum in Valparaiso. Another can be seen at Gibson Woods in Hammond.

Evidence for the Ice Age

The theory that ice once covered much of the earth originated in Switzerland, where geologists were familiar with landforms made by glaciers in the Alps. In 1821, Ignatz Venetz was the first to suggest that Swiss glaciers had once been much larger and that they had created the nearby European landscapes that were identical to those found closer to the Alps. A critic of this theory, Louis Agassiz, began to gather evidence to discredit the idea. He soon realized that his evidence not only supported it but also suggested that widespread glaciation had resulted in landforms over much of Europe and Britain. In 1837, he suggested the possibility of a "Great Ice Age." A lecture he gave that year is regarded as the birth of glacial theory. Soon North American geologists realized that Agassiz's theory could explain the origin of many American landscapes.

This evidence includes the widespread distribution of a type of sediment called till that can be seen near glaciers today. Till is a mixture of clay, silt, sand, pebbles, and even boulders that has been deposited directly by glaciers. When glacial ice melts, it releases the material that it has been carrying. If the material is simply dumped on the ground as the ice melts back, the till forms an uneven but generally flat landscape called a till plain. Although often dismissed as boring scenery, large vistas of prairie or cultivated fields can be a beautiful and awesome sight. These great plains of the Midwest serve as a "breadbasket" for the world.

If, however, the glacier had for many years been in equilibrium (so that the amount of ice brought forward equaled the amount that melted each year), the released sediment along the edge of a glacier might form a ridge called a recessional or end moraine, a long line of hills, much higher and often steeper than is typical of a till plain. Thus end moraines mark the location of the edge of the glacier when the moraine was formed. Because the glaciers receded from south to north, the moraines to the south were formed first and the northernmost moraines were formed last.

Large granite boulders called erratics often lie on till plains and within moraines. Kettle lakes, which form when huge separated blocks of buried ice finally melt, also are found in moraines. In a process similar to rough sandpaper being rubbed over a smooth, soft surface, boulders dragged by a glacier can create large striations (deep scratches) in the bedrock beneath it, usually parallel to the direction that the glacier had moved.[2]

Striations, erratics, kettle lakes, till plains, and moraines are formed today only by glaciers. Yet thousands of similar moraines and lakes exist far removed from glacial ice. Geologists were at a loss to explain these formations until 1837 when Agassiz's theory was developed. The evidence for an ice age was so overwhelming that opposition to the idea, at first widespread, largely disappeared by the 1890s.

The Great Pleistocene Ice Age

THE FORMATION AND SPREAD OF GLACIERS

At the beginning of the Ice Age, the earth began to cool. Why this happened is not fully understood. Reasons offered have included a lowering of energy given off by the sun and an increase in volcanic dust in the atmosphere. In 1941 Serbian mathematician Milutin Milankovitch suggested that changes in the earth's orbit might be responsible. The cooling may only have been 6–10° Fahrenheit, but it was enough to greatly reduce the amount of snow that melted in high mountainous areas as well as subarctic areas of North America

2. Exceptions can occur in circumstances such as when a moving glacier pushes an oddly shaped slab of hard rock, causing it to rotate.

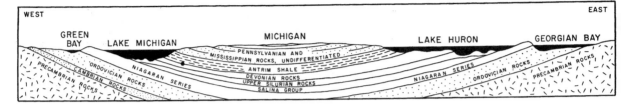

WEST   EAST

GREEN   MICHIGAN   GEORGIAN BAY
BAY   LAKE MICHIGAN   LAKE HURON

Figure 10. Cross-section showing sedimentary rock layers from the west side of Lake Michigan to Niagara Falls, Ontario. From Hough, 1958.

and Eurasia. With less melting, more and more snow remained on the ground throughout the increasingly cooler summers. Geologists used to think that perhaps thousands of years were required for glaciers to grow. Recent studies have shown that at times glaciers can advance more rapidly.

The Ice Age was not a time of perennial winter. Even during times of great ice advance, there were still seasons, including summer. However, the climate was a little cooler and so summers were not as warm as they are now. Even so, vast amounts of glacial ice melted each year. Geologists don't know exactly how long parts of Indiana and Illinois were covered by ice, but there is evidence that the ice advanced and retreated many times.

As the glaciers moved southward, they appear to have been greatly influenced by the very durable layers of Silurian dolomite. Figure 10 shows how Calumet Area bedrock slopes down to the northeast. The dolomite then reappears on the north and east sides of Lake Huron. Wherever this dolomite is at the surface, the ground is higher, and where the shale appears at the surface, the ground surface is lower because shale is more easily eroded.

Map 1 shows how this Niagaran dolomite forms the outer boundaries of Lakes Michigan and Huron. It separates Green Bay from Lake Michigan and Georgian Bay from Lake Huron. This same-aged rock can be seen at the Thornton Quarry and at Niagara Falls. When the glaciers slowly headed south into the current Great Lakes region, they eroded the softer rock layers alongside this dolomite. The glaciers scooped out some very deep holes. Lake Michigan is more than 900 feet deep near its north-central section, a depth that is more than 300 feet below sea level! Lake Superior has even deeper sections, with places more than 700 feet below sea level. Lake Huron has sections up to 600 feet deep—a mere 170 feet below sea level.

DIVISIONS OF THE PLEISTOCENE ICE AGE

The Ice Age occurred during a period called the Pleistocene. Until recently, it was believed that there were four great advances of ice. In 1894 geologist T. C. Chamberlin named the last two major advances the Illinoian and the Wisconsin. The first two were named Nebraskan and Kansan. However, there is now evidence for many ice advances before the Illinoian, and because it is difficult to date

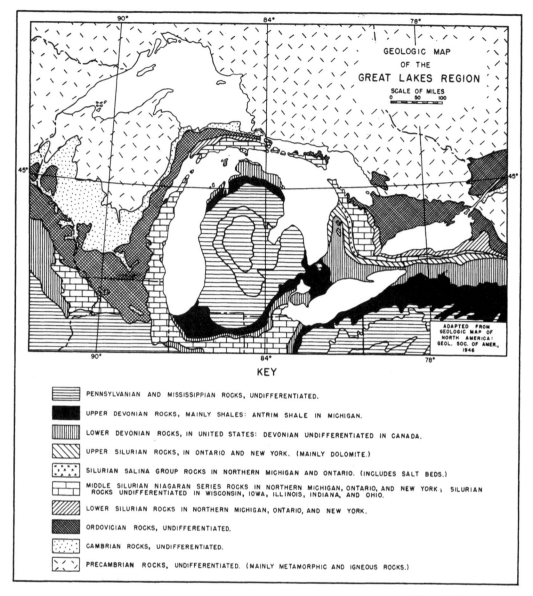

GEOLOGIC MAP
OF THE
GREAT LAKES REGION
SCALE OF MILES
0   50   100

ADAPTED FROM
GEOLOGIC MAP OF
NORTH AMERICA:
GEOL. SOC. OF AMER.,
1946

KEY

	PENNSYLVANIAN AND MISSISSIPPIAN ROCKS, UNDIFFERENTIATED.
	UPPER DEVONIAN ROCKS, MAINLY SHALES: ANTRIM SHALE IN MICHIGAN.
	LOWER DEVONIAN ROCKS, IN UNITED STATES: DEVONIAN UNDIFFERENTIATED IN CANADA.
	UPPER SILURIAN ROCKS, IN ONTARIO AND NEW YORK. (MAINLY DOLOMITE.)
	SILURIAN SALINA GROUP ROCKS IN NORTHERN MICHIGAN AND ONTARIO. (INCLUDES SALT BEDS.)
	MIDDLE SILURIAN NIAGARAN SERIES ROCKS IN NORTHERN MICHIGAN, ONTARIO, AND NEW YORK; SILURIAN ROCKS UNDIFFERENTIATED IN WISCONSIN, IOWA, ILLINOIS, INDIANA, AND OHIO.
	LOWER SILURIAN ROCKS IN NORTHERN MICHIGAN, ONTARIO, AND NEW YORK.
	ORDOVICIAN ROCKS, UNDIFFERENTIATED.
	CAMBRIAN ROCKS, UNDIFFERENTIATED.
	PRECAMBRIAN ROCKS, UNDIFFERENTIATED. (MAINLY METAMORPHIC AND IGNEOUS ROCKS.)

Map 1. The Relationship of Niagara dolomite and Lakes Michigan and Huron. From Hough, 1958.

and correlate all of these earlier glacial advances, these earlier stages are now simply called pre-Illinoian.

Not much evidence for the earlier glaciations in Indiana and Illinois would be expected because any till deposited by the earlier glaciers would have been removed or rearranged in the later glaciations. However, south of this area, there are a few deposits of subsurface glacial till that appear to have been left during pre-Illinoian stages. They are widely scattered and located under more recent deposits. Thus it is quite likely that the pre-Illinoian glaciers once covered the Calumet Area.

The Illinoian glaciation was the largest of them all (at least in this part of the country). Glaciers during this stage advanced all the way south to the Ohio River. During the Illinoian advance, most of Illinois and all of Indiana except for the portion of the state south from Martinsville and Bloomington to the Ohio River probably were covered by glacial ice. (That part of Indiana looks so different from the rest of the state because it was never glaciated.)

After the Illinoian glaciation ended, there was a long period with climates similar to ours today. Then the Wisconsin glaciation began. During the latter part of this period, glaciers extended south past what is now Indianapolis. It was during the Wisconsin glaciation that much of today's landscapes of northern North America were shaped, especially the area around the five Great Lakes.

Moraines, Kettle Lakes, and the Kankakee Outwash Plain

One of the most visible differences between Wisconsin and Illinoian deposits is the presence of end moraines formed during the late Wisconsin glaciation. Illinoian till has few remaining end moraines with steep hills, probably because, being so much older, there has been enough time for rains and rivers to erode them down.

The ending of the Pleistocene Ice Age was marked by numerous glacial advances and retreats, with most retreats followed by an advance not quite as extensive as the previous one. The last of these advances that invaded the Calumet Area occurred during the Crown Point phase, a 2,400-year period that began about 15,200 years ago.[3] By this time, the Lake Michigan lobe of the glacier was thin enough that as it grew it was restrained by the regional topography, including the hard layers of dolomite shown in Map 1. Thus the lobe was relatively confined to the width of the Lake Michigan basin. The Valparaiso, Tinley, and Lake Border (including the Park Ridge) Moraines were built during this time period.

At the beginning of the Crown Point phase, the curved southern edge of the Lake Michigan lobe of the glacier extended from eastern Wisconsin through northeast Illinois (west of Chicago), northwest Indiana, to western Michigan. Huge amounts of sediment from this lobe were piled up along its edge into long curved ridges and hills known as the Valparaiso Moraine. It is the largest and highest of the three moraines in the Calumet Area and together with the smaller Tinley/Lake Border Moraine forms the dominant landscape in much of the outlying Calumet Area. The moraines shown on the end sheets of this book in shades of brown extend from Wisconsin,

---

3. The Crown Point phase was named by Ardith Hansel because of the deposits made at that time at Crown Point, Indiana.

THE PHYSICAL SETTING

Figure 11. Isaac and Kate Suman's Porter County residence on the Valparaiso Moraine, as drawn for Hardesty's 1876 *Illustrated Historical Atlas of Porter County, Indiana.* Hobart Historical Society Museum.

south through Lake, McHenry, DuPage, western and southern Cook, and Will Counties in Illinois, through central Lake, Porter, and LaPorte Counties in Indiana, and northeast into southwestern Michigan. Unlike most moraines, which are made entirely of till, the Valparaiso Moraine is basically a long, curved ridge of sand covered by glacial till. It gets its name from Valparaiso where the moraine is narrower, higher, and steeper than in places farther west.

In 1883, Chamberlin said of the Valparaiso Moraine that it "may be likened in a general manner to an immense 'U' embracing the Great Lake [Michigan] between its arms . . . over two hundred miles in length. . . . The parallelism of the Moraine to the lake shore is one of its most striking features." Chamberlin and other early writers did not differentiate between what are now called the Valparaiso, Tinley, and Lake Border Moraines.

After the Valparaiso Moraine was formed, the Lake Michigan lobe of the glacier retreated some distance north and then readvanced and built the Tinley/Lake Border Moraine[4] on the lakeward flank of the Valparaiso Moraine. The boundary between the Tinley and Valparaiso Moraines is a roughly linear low area. In Cook County this low area was the site of several small glacial lakes. In Lake and Porter Counties, portions of Bull Run (in St. John), Main Beaver Dam Ditch, and Deep River (in Crown Point and Merrillville) flow through it. The Tinley/Lake Border Moraine is narrower and

4. The name Lake Border was given (by Frank Leverett in 1897) to the more northern till, and the name Tinley Moraine was given (by J Harlen Bretz in 1939) to the more southern of the two. Recent research has shown that there was no major retreat and readvance of the glacial ice between the two.

Figure 12. The gentle slope of the Tinley Moraine near the state line at Sauk Village. This photograph is of George Kloss hauling a manure spreader. The view is looking north on Torrence Avenue toward Sauk Trail. Fr. Tom Conde and St. James Catholic Church.

not as high as the older Valparaiso Moraine. Roughly the northern four to seven miles of the moraines in Lake and Porter Counties belong to this Tinley/Lake Border Moraine sequence. In addition, the Blue Island Ridge and Hobart Island (the low ridge at about 56th and Broadway in Merrillville) are part of this last moraine, as is a narrow band of till near Lake Michigan in Porter and LaPorte Counties.

The combined moraines are fifteen miles wide at the Illinois-Indiana state line and narrow to about eight miles at the Indiana-Michigan state line. Characterized by a haphazard "swell and swale" (hill and lowland) topography, the moraines today comprise just a small percentage of the land area of Cook and LaPorte Counties, but more than half of the land area of Lake and Porter Counties.

Several nearby cities and villages have names that are descriptive of their location in the Valparaiso and Tinley/Lake Border Moraines. These include Palos Hills, Country Club Hills, Hickory Hills, Orland Hills, Crest Hill, Glendale Heights, Palos Heights, Chicago Heights, South Chicago Heights, Ford Heights, Woodridge, Burr Ridge, Westmont, Crown Point, and Blue Island.

Although many other moraines were created by glaciers in what are now Indiana and Illinois, the Valparaiso and Tinley Moraines are significant because they form part of the Eastern Continental Divide, which separates the rivers that flow north and east to the North Atlantic from those that flow west and south to the Gulf of Mexico.

Kettle lakes are formed when huge blocks of glacial ice near the

Figure 13. Flint Lake near Valparaiso. Historical Society of Porter County Old Jail Museum.

edge of a glacier separate from the main mass and are buried by till or outwash (sand and gravel deposited by water from the melting glacier) as the glacier melts. As the buried ice block thaws, the sediment on top of it collapses and a large hole is formed. The larger the block of ice, the larger the hole. In many cases, these holes are filled with water and are called kettle lakes. Kettle lakes tend to be rather deep for their size and are named for the large round-bottomed black kettles that early settlers used to cook soups and stews over open fires. Flint Lake in Porter County is sixty-seven feet deep; most of the others range from thirty to thirty-five feet in depth. There is a concentration of kettle lakes in Lake County, Illinois, northwest of Chicago. Two concentrations can be found in northwest Indiana, one north of Valparaiso, the other at LaPorte.

Cedar Lake, the largest natural lake in northwest Indiana, appears to have been formed by glacial meltwaters that eroded a large north-south channel under the ice through what are now Hanover and West Creek townships. Traces of this channel can still be seen between the lake and the Kankakee River to the south.

Even as early as 1897 it was recognized that these lakes are gradually diminishing in size. For years, sediments have been washed into the lakes during rainstorms while surface water outlets have eroded their channel bottoms. The first action raises the level of the lake bottom; the second lowers the surface level of the lake water. These processes have been accelerated by the clearing of forests and the plowing of fields, both of which have increased the amount of soil being eroded into area rivers and then deposited into the lakes.

Contrary to folklore, Crown Point's Fancher Lake is not bottomless and does not have an underwater connection to Cedar Lake.

Local legend has it that some time ago a man drowned in Fancher Lake and that his body washed ashore at Cedar Lake. If true, then surely foul play was involved!

South of the Valparaiso Moraine is the large, expansive Kankakee Outwash Plain, which once carried meltwaters away from the glacier. These waters eroded valleys through the moraine as they emerged from subglacial tunnels or cascaded off the top of the ice, carrying with them tons of sand and mud. As the waters moved beyond the moraine and the slope of the ground leveled out, the water lost speed and began depositing the coarse sand to form the nearly flat outwash plain. The fine mud was carried downstream out of the area. The Kankakee Outwash Plain is the result of this large-scale deposition of sand. It extends across seven Indiana counties and Kankakee County, Illinois. The meltwaters escaped from the area through the Kankakee River flowing westward from Indiana into Illinois where it merged with the Des Plaines River and flowed southward to the Mississippi River and onward to the Gulf of Mexico.

Before settlement and its subsequent draining, the Kankakee Marsh was one of the largest freshwater marshes in the country. It formed an effective barrier to north-south transportation and thus hindered early settlement of the Calumet Area. In later years it was well known for its good hunting and fishing. Since then, a large system of ditches has converted about 87 percent of that area into farmland.

Many people are surprised to learn that there are more sand dunes in the Kankakee Outwash Plain than along Lake Michigan. Some of these dunes are small, but others are more than twenty-five feet high. These hills are (or at least were) great places to find spearheads and arrowheads as, before settlement, they were high and dry locations where for centuries Native Americans placed their camps and villages. The Potawatomi name for the river was Aukiki, meaning "beautiful river."

The Kankakee River valley is bounded by the Valparaiso Moraine on the north, the Iroquois Moraine on the south, and the Maxinkuckee Moraine on the east. The river today rises near South Bend in St. Joseph County, Indiana, flows westward—often through manmade channels—and after about 200 miles joins the Des Plaines River near Wilmington, Illinois. Because of the low gradient of the river (just twelve inches of drop per mile), the Kankakee's water moves slowly. As a result, following heavy rainfalls or quick melting of snow, the river often overflows its banks and floods nearby areas.

Our route lay in a semi-circle of 100 miles round the end of the lake. It was almost a perfect circle; no bays, outlets, capes, promontories, or islands interrupt its regularity; only now and then a small river enters, and so sandy and fluctuating is the beach that it is nothing uncommon for the mouths of the streams to be completely stopped by sand thrown up by the surf and remain so till the accumulated waters force their way into the lake again.

All the streams form an extensive shoal at a considerable distance from the mouth; this is the reason there is not a single good harbor even for the smallest craft anywhere in the southerly part of the lake.

—Pioneer traveler, Reland Tinkham,
August 23, 1831

Water and Wind

INTERPRETING LAKE MICHIGAN'S HISTORY

Early Interpretations of Ancient Shorelines

No one will ever know who first recognized that the long sand ridges that parallel Lake Michigan were former shorelines of that great lake. The Miami and Potawatomi, among others who established trails on these ancient shorelines, knew the features of both the lake and the higher ancient shorelines. However, many of these trails were very narrow paths, often through dense forest, offering little in the way of panoramic views. The Indians and the earliest settlers may have noticed clues impossible to see today, such as the sand/pebble beaches, the nearly undisturbed shoreline features and dunes, and even shells and bones of fish.

In 1838, Charles Shepard, a physician and professor of chemistry, published "Geology of Upper Illinois" in the *American Journal of Science*. The first geological report on the Chicago/Calumet area, it proposed that Lake Michigan must have been higher in the past and that the sand ridges that lie parallel to the lake must be "ancient beaches." He described them as "a succession of ancient beaches

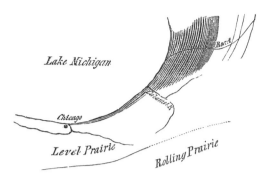

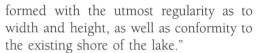

Map 2. Charles Shepard's 1838 depiction of the lower Tolleston sand ridges, the first map showing the area's dune and swale topography. On this map, north is to the left. *American Journal of Science,* 1838.

formed with the utmost regularity as to width and height, as well as conformity to the existing shore of the lake."

Crown Point pioneer Solon Robinson in 1847 described the northern part of Lake County as a "succession of sand ridges and marshes . . . conforming with the bend of the Lake Shore." He did not speculate (in that writing anyway) about how they were formed. In 1868, Henry Bannister expanded on the theory in "Geology of Cook County": "At a comparatively recent period, subsequent to the Glacial epoch, a considerable portion of Cook county was under the waters of Lake Michigan, which at that time found an outlet into the Mississippi valley through the present channel of the Des Plaines." He described one of the ancient shorelines, the Calumet, which "runs in a general east and west direction, [and] is well seen on the road between Thornton station [Homewood] and the village of Old Thornton . . . crossing the State line at Lansing station."

Timothy Ball, a Baptist minister and early Lake County historian, may have been one of the first local residents to recognize the origin of these ridges. This remarkable man, who wrote extensively about religion and history, was very proud of Lake County, through which he traveled a great deal. In his 1873 history, he described the southernmost ancient shoreline of Lake Michigan: "The appearance near Dyer is as though the waters of Lake Michigan, a number of years ago, washed this ridge and dashed its waves upon this sand, finding here its south-western limit, then retiring northward, ridge by ridge, reached its present bounds, leaving its old beach to show where once its free waves dashed their spray."

The next year (1874), G. M. Levette, an assistant to the Indiana state geologist, wrote, "That these successive ridges were, in turn, the shore lines of the lake, is clearly inferable, when we see the winds and waves repeating the same process at Michigan City, at the present time." These conclusions were easily accepted by Calumet Area residents. In 1882, historian George Garard commented, "Almost unquestionably, all that is now North Township [then also including what is now Gary] was at no distant date, geologically considered, the bed of Lake Michigan."

There is much visible geographic evidence for three major phases of Lake Michigan that were higher and larger than today's lake. These phases each developed beaches and some sand dunes, remnants of which can still be seen throughout the Calumet Area. The oldest is not only the highest but also the furthest from today's lakeshore.

In 1897, Frank Leverett of the U.S. Geological Survey proposed the names Glenwood, Calumet, and Tolleston for the three ancient

Figure 14. Calumet Area historian Timothy H. Ball (1826–1913). Calumet Regional Archives.

shorelines and the name Lake Chicago for all the early phases of ancestral Lake Michigan that discharged through the Chicago Outlet. Although the name Lake Chicago has fallen out of favor (because it really is the same lake as Lake Michigan—so now many geologists simply call it ancestral Lake Michigan), his names for the three shorelines remain in use today.

Over time, geologists have added new pieces to the lake history puzzle. The three major ancient shorelines can easily be seen in many locations, but when and how they were formed, and how long the waters remained at each level, are less easily determined. The ages of the various shorelines were finally determined using radiocarbon dating. By this method, the age of pieces of buried organic matter (e.g., bones or driftwood) could be estimated. In addition, the study of the various layers of sand and clay along the former shorelines and lake bottomland gave new insights to their formation. Geologists are still adding to what we know about the lakeshore and trying to unravel the secrets of the ancient shorelines.

Figure 15. Frank Leverett (1859–1943). It has been said that no one contributed more to our understanding of the origin of Midwestern landscapes than Leverett. Department of Geological Sciences, University of Michigan.

Ancient Shorelines and Beaches of Lake Michigan

A gift of the glaciers was an abundant supply of clay, sand, and pebbles in and along ancestral Lake Michigan, so extensive sand and pebble beaches were formed in places where waves could develop. For most of the history of the lake, sand has been moved southward by lake currents on both sides of the lake.

Sandy beaches do not form along all lake or ocean shorelines. They are landforms created by the action of waves and lake currents and thus form only in bodies of water large enough to have waves. These waves bring sand up to the shoreline and deposit it on the land. Prevailing winds may then blow the sand away from the shoreline to form dunes.

Sand dunes formed along each of the ancient shorelines of ancestral Lake Michigan. In the same way that wind can blow dry snow into drifts, it blows sand into dunes. In the south Lake Michigan area, the largest sand dunes are located east of the lake because the prevailing wind direction is from the west. Thus these western winds blow beach sand on the west side of the lake (from Hammond northward) into the lake while they blow beach sand on the east side (from Gary northeastward) away from the lake into dunes.

The three ancient shorelines of Lake Michigan, the Glenwood, Calumet, and Tolleston, once had characteristics similar to the present shoreline. However, even though natural and man-made processes have greatly altered them, portions of these former shorelines can still be recognized by the careful observer.

THE GLENWOOD SHORELINE

Lake Michigan was formed toward the end of the Ice Age about 14,000 years ago when the Lake Michigan lobe of the glacier retreated from the Tinley/Lake Border Moraines. Much of its meltwaters were then trapped between the ice to the north and the U-shaped moraine on the west, south, and east.[1]

As more ice melted, the ponded waters overflowed the moraine at its lowest point near Palos Park, Illinois, at what Frank Leverett (in 1897) named the Chicago Outlet. As can be seen from Map 3, this outlet consisted of two channels, the Des Plaines and the Calumet Sag channels, which flowed around Mount Forest Island and then merged and flowed southwestward to the Illinois River.[2] The best view of the Chicago Outlet is south of the Calumet Sag Channel along LaGrange Road in Palos Park.

This earliest phase of ancestral Lake Michigan is called the **Glenwood phase** (14,000–12,200 years ago), and at an elevation of 640 feet (about 60 feet higher than the present level of Lake Michigan), the Glenwood is the highest of Lake Michigan's ancient shorelines.[3] This shoreline was somewhat uneven with several inlets, peninsulas, and offshore islands. Where the shoreline was smooth, with enough sand, deep offshore water, and enough open water for good-sized waves to develop, wide sandy beaches with accompanying dunes formed, similar to the beaches and dunes along Lake Michigan today. The first beaches that formed in ancestral Lake Michigan were probably at Dyer and Schererville near the Illinois-Indiana state line where these conditions were met. As late as 1939, the Glenwood age sand dunes in the Dyer area were said to be 30 to 40 feet high. Few of these exist today. Perhaps the best remaining dune is south of U.S. Highway 30 at Castlewood Drive in Dyer.

In other places, beach sand was not deposited and dunes did not form, making it difficult to identify these old shorelines without careful analysis. During the Glenwood phase, a few sand spits formed alongside the shoreline. Today, these spits form some of the best remaining ancient beaches.

In 1897 Frank Leverett named this beach the Glenwood Shore-

1. There is evidence that earlier stages of Lake Michigan existed after the Valparaiso Moraine was formed. However, the first lake stage to leave a recognizable beach (the Glenwood) began as glacial ice receded from the Tinley/Lake Border Moraine.

2. In 1968, A. F. Schneider proposed that initially, and for a short time, lake drainage may have been through a gap in the moraines west of Valparaiso where Salt Creek is today. Chrzastowski and Thompson (in 1994) noted that this might have been because an ice block dammed the entrance to the Chicago Outlet or that erosion of the moraine was required before the waters of the lake could flow through that outlet.

3. The elevations given here are the classic levels based on shoreline features. The actual elevation of the lake water that created these features is debatable and is still being studied. Chrzastowski and Thompson have suggested that the water level may have been several feet lower than these figures.

Map 3. The Glenwood Phase. After Chrzastowski and Thompson, 1992.

South Cook County: Diagonal line from Palos Park to Homewood, then south to Chicago Heights and Ford Heights. The Glenwood Spit extends from Glenwood to Lynwood.

The mainland shoreline (at the north edge of the Tinley Moraine):

Homewood—south and west of the intersection of Dixie Highway and 175th Street and at the intersection of Ridge Road and Halsted Street. The cemeteries east of Halsted Street are located on a short sand spit that once extended into the lake.

Chicago Heights—Shoreline features not well developed.

Ford Heights—Cottage Grove Avenue, ¼ mile north of U.S. Highway 30.

Blue Island: the obvious slope north of the Calumet Sag Channel extending north on both sides of the ridge into the Chicago community of Beverly. Mt. Hope, Olivet, and Greenwood Cemeteries on the west; Longwood Avenue on the east.

The Glenwood Spit (parallel to the mainland):

Glenwood—East of town along the Glenwood-Dyer Road is perhaps the best preserved section anywhere. It contains the tiny Glenwood Island east of Illinois Highway 394 as well as the spit. South of the road are four low sand ridges that were extensions of the spit. The spit separated Chicago Heights Bay from the rest of Lake Michigan.

Lynwood—Glenwood-Dyer Road, except near the state line

Lake County:

The mainland shore

Dyer—U.S. Highway 30–Best seen from the front of St. Joseph's Church.

Schererville—U.S. Highway 30 west of its intersection with Joliet Street. Some beach and dunes are well preserved along parts of Joliet Street.

Merrillville—North of, and roughly parallel to 73rd Avenue, but not well developed.

The Griffith Spit

Griffith—The low sand ridges on the south side of town in areas such as that east of Broad Street at the grand junction.

Glen Park—45th at Grant Street, 43rd at Broadway

Hobart—Liverpool Road south of 37th Avenue (Old U.S. Highway 6)

Lake Station—New Chicago—South of Deep River between Riverview Park and River Forest High School.

Hobart Island from about 56th Avenue at Broadway in Merrillville to 40th Avenue at Wisconsin in Hobart.

Porter County: In the western part of the county, part of this shoreline is buried by dunes of the Calumet Shoreline.

Portage—A sand spit from Salt Creek (south of its junction with the Little Calumet River) past the new Crisman Elementary School area to Garyton.

Porter/Chesterton—Generally between U.S. Highways 12 and 20, and from Wagner Road east-northeast to Furnessville.

LaPorte County: Michigan City—From Greenwood Cemetery south to the intersection of U.S. Highway 20 and Indiana Highway 421.

line because one of the best-preserved beaches of this old shoreline can be seen along the Glenwood-Dyer Road just east of the village of Glenwood, Illinois. The Glenwood Shoreline is the only ancient shoreline of ancestral Lake Michigan that has the moraine on one side and lake bottomland on the other.

At the beginning of the Glenwood phase, Lake Michigan was fed by meltwaters from the glacier to the north, rainwater that fell directly into the lake, and several creeks and rivers. Some of these were Thorn Creek, Deep River, Salt Creek, Trail Creek, and the (Little) Calumet River. All of these streams then flowed off the higher moraines and north directly into the lake.

During the Glenwood phase, there were several islands in Lake Michigan (see Map 3). Part of the Lake Border Moraine, they included Mt. Forest Island, Blue Island, and tiny Glenwood Island all in Cook County, Hobart Island in Lake County, and various small islands in Porter and LaPorte Counties in Indiana.

Mt. Forest Island was located at the outlet of the lake with the Des Plaines Channel to its north and the Calumet Sag Channel to its south. Blue Island was a narrow island six miles long. Its east side, which faced the open lake, was a steep wave-cut cliff. Its west side had the Chicago area's largest sand deposit. The city of Blue Island is at the southern end of this former island. North of that city are today's Chicago neighborhoods of Beverly, Morgan Park, and Mount Greenwood.

During the Glenwood phase, lake currents and waves built up long spits, or sandy peninsulas on the down-current sides of these islands. The Glenwood Spit, southeast of the original Glenwood Island (and along today's Glenwood-Dyer Road) now forms one of the best visible portions of the Glenwood Shoreline. The combined Glenwood Island and its spits created Chicago Heights Bay between them and the moraine to the south.

Hobart Island is the hill in the Hobart/north Merrillville area. The Griffith Spit, formed north of Hobart Island, was the largest of the Glenwood era spits. At its west end are the low sandy ridges now within the town of Griffith. Generally, the northern slope of the spit is much more noticeable than the southern slope because it faced the lake and thus was shaped by its powerful waves. The spit was connected to the Lake Border Moraine north of Chesterton forming a long peninsula parallel to the shore (see Map 3). This peninsula separated the open lake from the quiet waters south of them—Hobart and Chesterton Bays, now the locations of Turkey Creek, Lake George, and Deep River, and in Porter County, the Little Calumet River. These islands and spits acted as a breakwater and prevented waves from developing a sand beach on much of the mainland shoreline. Thus it is difficult today to find evidence of the mainland Glenwood Shoreline around Merrillville, south Hobart, or Chesterton.

Figure 16. Joliet Street on the ancient Glenwood Shoreline, about 1909. Ancestral Lake Michigan was to the north (left) of the road. Schererville Historical Society.

North of the shoreline slope at the edge of the Glenwood beach is the flat bottom of ancestral Lake Michigan containing extensive deposits of clay left by the glacier. The clay was discovered by early settlers and was often mined to make bricks. Although none of their plants are still in existence, Blue Island, Pullman, Roseland, Dolton, Riverdale, Lansing, Munster, Hobart, Porter, and several other communities had brickworks. Amber Lake in Hobart, the lakes in and near Lakewood Park in Munster, and those of the Lansing Country Club are all leftover clay pits.

During the Glenwood phase, the Lake Michigan glacial lobe continued to move, sometimes retreating, sometimes advancing. At one point (between 13,000 and 13,500 years ago) the glacier retreated past the Straits of Mackinac at the northern end of the lake. The lake level then fell because the Straits were lower than the Chicago Outlet and thus Lake Michigan water could flow out of the lake by means of this lower Mackinac Outlet. However, the glacier then returned, blocking the straits, and the lake's waters returned to the Glenwood beaches. Later in the Glenwood phase, the lake level began to drop gradually, perhaps as the Chicago River slowly eroded its valley. Then about 12,200 years ago, the lake level dropped by a large amount as the glacier again retreated past the Straits of Mackinac.[4] The Glenwood phase was over.

The **Two Creeks phase** (12,200–11,800 years ago) was characterized by an undetermined low level of Lake Michigan. Evidence for this level, discovered about 1905, consisted of the remains of a

4. For a more detailed description, see the 1992 and 1994 articles by Chrzastowski and Thompson.

buried spruce forest just west of the Lake Michigan shore near the town of Two Creeks, Wisconsin. Radiocarbon dating later showed that this forest, at an elevation lower than the Calumet Shoreline, was older than the Calumet. The forest was destroyed and buried when the glaciers readvanced at the end of this stage.

In 1982 Allan Schneider and Mark Reshkin reported the first evidence of deposits of this age in Indiana at Liverpool (Lake Station). Then, just a few years later, the remains of another spruce forest were found south of U.S. Highway 20 near the town of Pines (southwest of Michigan City). All the partially decayed spruce trees identified in this area, many still upright, were found to be of the same age as those at Two Creeks. Because spruce trees do not grow on the lake bottom, the ground on which these trees grew had to be free of lake water at that time.

After about 200 years, the glacier readvanced and again blocked the Straits of Mackinac. The lake then rose and flooded this ancient Calumet Area forest. The trees died and were buried in sand and clay.

THE CALUMET SHORELINE

During the **Calumet phase**, the level of ancestral Lake Michigan was again higher than Lake Michigan is today, but about 20 feet lower than the original Glenwood Shoreline.[5] The renewed lake began to develop a new beach along its new shoreline, 620 feet above sea level. Named after the nearby Little Calumet River, the Calumet Shoreline has a large number of sand dunes along its southern side, but not nearly as many as there were before settlement.

Timothy Ball wrote in 1884, "From Highlands, a grand sand ridge extends westward to Lansing, and eastward for some miles towards Hobart. . . . From its summit near the state line the view extends, without obstruction, southward to Dyer, and off as far as the eye can reach upon the prairie region of Illinois." Unfortunately, the dunes are not as high today as they were in Ball's time. In the early days, farmers used horse and mule power to remove sand from the tops of the dunes to fill in the nearby wetlands. (This was back in the days when wholesale filling in of wetlands was considered a civilizing and productive action.)

The Calumet beach has a much smoother coastline than the Glenwood beach. In southwest Chicago, two sand spits, Washington Heights and Stewart Ridge, were formed from sand eroded from

---

5. There are different theories about the causes of the various levels of ancestral Lake Michigan. One suggestion is that the Chicago Outlet had been eroded down twenty feet by the end of the Glenwood Phase and that this level determined the elevation of the Calumet Phase. In 1988, Hansel and Mickelson proposed that the Chicago Outlet was fully eroded all the way down to the present level during the Glenwood Phase. They explain the differing water levels since then as simply being a result of differing amounts of water in the lake.

Map 4. The Calumet Phase. After Chrzastowski and Thompson, 1992.
In South Cook County:
   Blue Island Ridge area—Oak Hill Cemetery on the west; Vincennes Avenue
      on the east. Washington Heights spit near Mt. Vernon Park and
      Stewart Ridge spit near West Pullman Park.
   Hazel Crest/East Hazel Crest—The intersection of Interstate Highways 80 and
      294 and east
   Thornton—Around the limestone reef
   Lansing—Thornton-Lansing Road west of Torrence, Indiana Avenue east of
      Torrence, Ridge Road near the state line
In Lake County: From Munster to Griffith, it was a sand spit with the North
Creek Lagoon south of it. From Glen Park to Lake Station, it was a mainland
beach.
   Munster/Highland/Griffith/Glen Park (Gary)—Ridge Road
   Lake Station—North of Deep River and on Central Avenue east of Ripley
      Street.
In Porter County: In places, the Calumet dunes bury parts of the Glenwood
Shoreline.
   Portage–U.S. Highway 20 from the B&O tracks to Willow Creek and at the
      intersection of Interstate Highway 94 and Crisman Road.
   Burns Harbor—U.S. Highway 12 at the east edge of the town
   Porter/Tremont/Pines—U.S. Highway 12 and the Calumet Bike Trail
In LaPorte County: Michigan City—South and southwest of the Indiana State
Penitentiary and at Franklin Street and Eleventh Street.

the newly combined Mt. Forest–Blue Island. At the eastern end of
the Calumet Area, the Calumet Shoreline developed close to the
older Glenwood Shoreline. In places, Calumet dunes even bury
those of the Glenwood. Closer to the Illinois/Indiana state line
where the ground wasn't as steep, the Calumet Shoreline formed
several miles north of the Glenwood. What is today Ridge Road in
Lansing, Munster, and Highland is part of the Calumet Shoreline,
but it developed not as a mainland beach but as an offshore peninsula or spit. Thus it is higher in elevation than the ground either
north or south of it. North of this beach ridge were the open waters
of ancestral Lake Michigan, while to the south was the North Creek
Lagoon (see Map 4.) now occupied by Cady Marsh Ditch (from
Glen Park to Highland), Schoon Ditch (in Munster), and North

Figure 17. Calumet Beach scarp south of LaPorte Street, perhaps near Kennedy Avenue, about 1895. From Blatchley, 1897.

Calumet Beach near Highland, Lake County, Indiana.

Creek (in Lansing). The Calumet beach, like the higher Glenwood beach, was used by Indians as a convenient, flat, high, and dry route to traverse the area. When European American settlers came to this area, this part of the Calumet beach became a stagecoach route and later U.S. Highway 6.

The Calumet phase lasted about 600 years. It ended about 11,200 years ago, when the glacier retreated past the Straits of Mackinac for the last time and the lake level dropped about 28 feet to an elevation of 592 feet above sea level. The Calumet phase was over.

Algonquin phase beaches can be found farther north along Lake Michigan, but there are few beach deposits of this age at the south end of the lake. Geologists Michael Chrzastowski and Todd Thompson suggested that this lack resulted from a combination of the short period (300 years) when the lake was at this level and little sand being transported to the southern shores of the lake.

However, with the weight of much of the glacial ice removed, the crust of the earth was slowly rebounding (returning to its original level before it had been depressed by the glacial ice). This rebounding raised the level of the lake. Chrzastowski and Thompson suggest that the lake then eroded the shoreline, creating the rather steep slope a bit north of Ridge Road in Lake County. Thus the Algonquin Shoreline in the Calumet Area is an erosional scarp rather than a beach.

This scarp extends with few interruptions from Munster to Glen Park. It can be seen most easily in Munster along Ridgeway and Alta Vista Avenues, through Wicker Park and south of LaPorte Street near Kennedy Avenue in Highland, and in Glen Park, between

Thirty-fifth and Thirty-seventh Avenues. (This feature can be seen better along side streets, where there has been less smoothing off of the land, than at the major thoroughfares.)

The **Chippewa phase** began with an extreme drop in the lake level about 10,000 years ago, when the retreating glacier uncovered a very low outlet for the upper Great Lakes to the Atlantic at North Bay, Ontario. The lake level at this time was perhaps as low as 381 feet above sea level.[6] (Today's level averages 580 feet.) At this point much of the lake plain dried up. Lake Michigan's two deepest parts, an area that begins about thirty miles north of today's southern shore and a larger basin father north, still had water.

The Chippewa low-level phase lasted about 4,000 years—the longest of any of the lake phases. However, throughout that phase, as during the Algonquin phase, the crust of the earth continued rebounding. This rebounding slowly raised the level of the North Bay Outlet and with it the level of Lakes Huron and Michigan.

THE HIGH TOLLESTON SHORELINE

The **Nipissing phases**[7] began about 6,300 years ago, when the lake rose slowly past the level it is today. Then beginning about 4,700 years ago, when the lake's water levels reached 603 feet, a third major shoreline was formed in the Calumet Area.

In 1897, Frank Leverett named this the Tolleston Shoreline because it was so prominent in the village of Tolleston, now a part of the city of Gary.[8] This shoreline goes through Chicago, Calumet City, Hammond, Gary, Ogden Dunes, Dune Acres, Beverly Shores, and Michigan City.

Like parts of the Calumet and Glenwood beaches, the High Tolleston beach in Lake County was first a long spit/barrier beach. It separated the lake from the quiet Calumet Lagoon to its south (see Map 5).

SEARCHERS FOR LAKE MICHIGAN SHIPWRECKS FIND PREHISTORIC FOREST

In June 1989, salvage operators were searching for shipwrecks along the bottom of Lake Michigan about ten miles northeast of East Chicago where the lake was about eighty feet deep. Instead, divers found a drowned and partially buried forest of more than fifty trees.

The largest tree stump had a diameter of about 30 inches. Most of the stumps are cone-shaped, apparently the result of subsurface erosion. Radiocarbon analysis showed that these oak and ash trees lived approximately 8,100 years ago—exactly the period of the low-water Chippewa phase. What had been found were the remains of a forest that had been growing in a low land area. As the waters of Lake Michigan rose at the end of the Chippewa phase, the forest was drowned and the trees died. The upper trunks and branches have all been broken off, but the trunks and their roots remain—dramatic evidence of the low water stage of ancestral Lake Michigan.

---

6. How low the water level fell during the Chippewa phase is uncertain. Estimates have ranged from an elevation of 381 feet (about 200 feet below today's level) down to 230 feet (about 350 feet below today's level).

7. The name Nipissing was chosen because a former shoreline from this phase is prominent at present-day Lake Nipissing in Ontario (near Lake Huron).

8. The "High Tolleston Shoreline" is here defined as that shoreline formed as ancestral Lake Michigan was at its highest post-Chippewa level. It is the same "Tolleston Shoreline" as described by early geologists such as Leverett, Cressey, and Bretz. Chrzastowski and Thompson called it the early Tolleston Beach.

Figure 18. A diver investigates one of the fifty drowned tree stumps found under eighty feet of water. From Chrzastowski et al., 1991.

About 3,800 years ago, as the lake level began to decline, the Calumet Lagoon was largely drained and became the floodplain of what is now the Little Calumet River. In 1928, George Cressey noted that the dunes of the Tolleston Shoreline were generally taller than any of the older and higher shorelines. However, most were removed years ago, with much of the sand being used to raise ground levels elsewhere.

The High Tolleston Shoreline, at an elevation of 605 feet, is 15 feet lower than the Calumet Shoreline, but still 25 feet higher than Lake Michigan is today. It can easily be seen today east of Michigan Avenue in the Roseland area of Chicago (between 100th and 127th Streets). From Calumet City to Michigan City, the High Tolleston Shoreline was a long sand spit parallel to the mainland shore. The shoreline was once well developed, and although much sand mining has obliterated parts of it, it still can be seen in places along the Michigan City Road in Calumet City and along 169th Street in the Hessville neighborhood of Hammond. In Gary it is located between Seventeenth and Twenty-first Avenues in Tolleston and midtown; then it extends northeast through Aetna and Miller. In Porter and LaPorte Counties, the Tolleston dunes are near the lakeshore.

Because in Indiana much of the shoreline was a spit, there was water on both sides of it. North of it was ancestral Lake Michigan, and south of it was the long, narrow, and quiet Calumet Lagoon

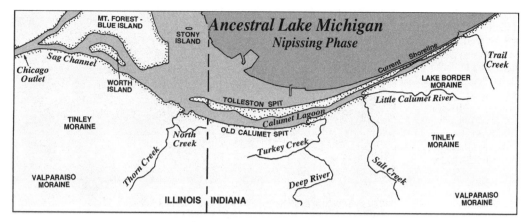

Map 5. The Nipissing Phase showing the High Tolleston Shoreline. After Chrzastowski and Thompson, 1992.

South Cook County:

Roseland—East of Michigan Avenue

Dolton/Calumet City—Lincoln Avenue and the Michigan City Road

Lake County: A sand spit that separated the Calumet Lagoon (now the course of the Little Calumet River) from the rest of the lake.

Hammond—About 165th Street at Hohman Avenue; 169th Street through Hessville.

Gary—Through the southern part of Tolleston, crosses Broadway about 21st Avenue, through Aetna and the southern edge of Miller.

Porter County: Just south of the recent dunes along the lakefront from the West Beach area, through Dune Acres and Beverly Shores. South of these dunes are low areas that once were lagoons.

LaPorte County—North of the Indiana State Penitentiary in Michigan City and the South Shore tracks.

(see Map 5). The site of this lagoon is still a low wetland area. From Riverdale, Illinois, to Portage, the former Calumet Lagoon is now the site of the Little Calumet River and its floodplain. From the Bethlehem Steel Mill in Burns Harbor to Michigan City, the lagoon is now occupied by Cowles Bog, the Great Marsh, and Dunes Creek.

THE LOWER TOLLESTON SHORELINES

When the Tolleston Shoreline was first formed, the upper Great Lakes had three outlets: the North Bay Outlet near Georgian Bay, the Port Huron Outlet past what is now Detroit, and the Chicago Outlet. With continuing crustal rebound up north, the northern-most North Bay Outlet was soon raised higher than the two southern outlets and thus could no longer carry water out of the lakes. Then erosion along the Port Huron Outlet slowly lowered it and with it the level of Lakes Huron and Michigan so that the Chicago Outlet, with its floor of bedrock, dried up.

About 3,800 years ago, during the **Algoma phase**, the lake level dropped to its current level, but it did so in a pulsating manner. Lowered water levels resulted from a combination of erosion at Port Huron and dry weather conditions, while higher water levels were

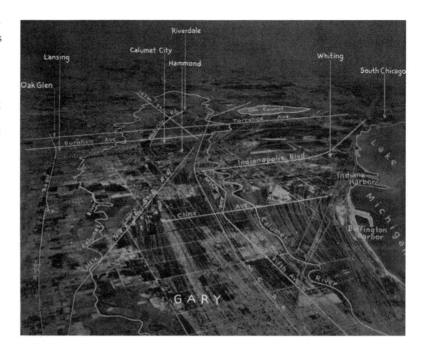

Figure 19. The lower Tolleston beach ridges can be seen in this aerial photograph taken about 1937. Ridge Road at the far left is on the Calumet Shoreline; Michigan City Road in Calumet City is on the High Tolleston Shoreline. From Bretz, 1939.

caused by periods of greater rainfall. This pulsating pattern resulted in a series of more than 150 small beach ridges, all roughly parallel to the lake and all located north or east of the High Tolleston beach. Between the ridges were long, low swales that often contained standing water. Geologist J Harlen Bretz called these ridges the lower Tolleston beaches. Originally they ranged in height from 5 to 12 feet and averaged about 150 feet in width. Although most of them were leveled as southeast Chicago, Gary, Hammond, and East Chicago were developed, several can still be seen in Miller and the Tolleston/Brunswick areas of Gary. Gibson Woods in Hessville has the longest of these narrow dune ridges still remaining.

Although the water level of Lake Michigan continues to rise and fall, it reached its current level about 1,500 years ago.[9] However, since that time the currents of Lake Michigan have continued to move sand southward along the shores and deposit it at the southern end of the lake. About 1,500 years ago, a sand spit grew south of Stony Island (by then a bedrock island in the lake) and enclosed an open bay, creating Lake Calumet. About 400 years later a similar spit closed off Wolf Lake, straddling the Illinois/Indiana state line.

The change of seasons and rainfall and drought will still cause the lake level to rise and fall by small amounts. During the course of a typical year, the lake level may rise more than a foot from its late winter low level to a summer high and then back down to its

9. Lake Michigan water levels still fluctuate. Thompson, Fraser, and Hester (1991) reported geological evidence for high water levels 2,300, 1,700, 1,175, and 600 years ago.

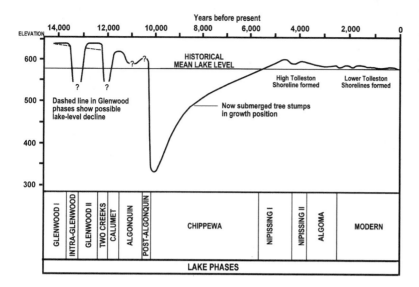

Figure 20. The changing elevation of Lake Michigan. After Chrzastowski and Thompson, 1992.

late winter low level again. Since the 1990s, concerns about global warming spurred the development of research on possible relationships between global warming and lake levels.

Although it is assumed that the lake level will again drop a significant amount, it probably will not do so for several thousand years. This is because the level of Lakes Michigan and Huron is somewhat determined by the level of Lake Erie into which they flow. The waters from Lake Erie then flow over a cliff of very durable Niagara dolomite at Niagara Falls. Until the falls erode that dolomite back to Lake Erie, Lake Erie's elevation will stay about where it is now. Thus the elevation of Lake Huron and Lake Michigan will, too.

There were sand dunes formed along Lake Michigan's ancient shorelines as well as along its current shoreline. However, the largest expanse of Calumet Area sand dunes is in Porter County, which has the tallest remaining dunes. Mt. Tom, Mt. Holden, and Mt. Jackson, all in Indiana Dunes State Park, gave the Tremont area its name (a corruption of the French for "three mountains"). Mt. Baldy, in LaPorte County near Michigan City, is a migrating dune; it moves southeastward at a rate of four to six feet a year.

THE GRAND AND LITTLE CALUMET RIVERS

Between the ancient shorelines and Lake Michigan flow the Grand and Little Calumet Rivers. Before 1805, much of these two rivers were one long river. (See Map 6d.)

This river first formed in Western LaPorte County when the glacier retreated from the Calumet Area and Lake Michigan was formed. It then carried ground and rain waters northwestward a few miles and emptied into the lake south of where Michigan City

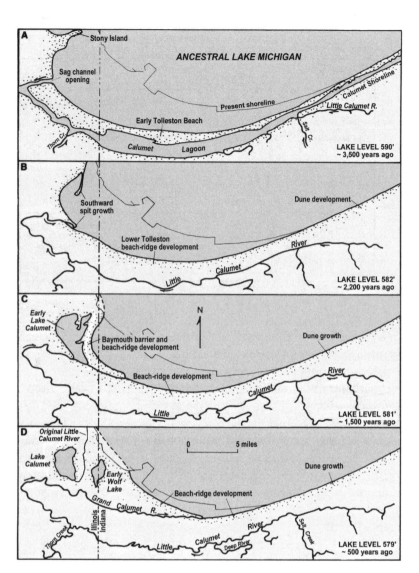

Map 6. The development of the Calumet Rivers, Lake Calumet, and Wolf Lake. After Chrzastowski and Thompson, 1992.

is today (Map 3). During the Calumet phase, the river grew in length, soon emptying into the lake near its current intersection with Salt Creek in Porter County (Map 4). During the Tolleston phase, the long Tolleston shoreline/spit prevented the river from flowing directly to the lake. Instead, it forced the rivers' waters to enter the quiet Calumet Lagoon behind the beach and flow all the way into Illinois before they could reach the open waters of the lake (Map 5). As the spit grew in length, eventually the river began emptying directly into the Chicago Outlet (Map 6a). However, as the lake level receded about 2500 years ago, the river made its hairpin turn south of the present site of Blue Island (Map 6b). Then drifting sands slowly forced its mouth twenty-two miles eastward past what are now Riverdale, Hegewisch, and Hammond, to Miller Beach (Maps 6c and d).

Figure 21. The Little Calumet River in flood stage at South Holland. The First Reformed Church, since 1848 just south of the Little Calumet River, has often been threatened by high waters. South Holland Historical Society Museum.

Until 1805, the original Little Calumet River, today the Calumet River, was truly a little river (extending only between what are now Hegewisch and South Chicago) draining Lake Calumet. The Little and Grand Calumet Rivers appear on some early maps as the west and east Kalamick Rivers. They remained separate until 1805 when a spring freshet caused the Grand Calumet to overflow its banks and surge into the Little Calumet. Historian Timothy Ball claimed in 1872 that he had been told that Indians had used their canoe paddles to open this channel. It at least is possible that Indians or early European explorers had lowered the north bank of the Grand Calumet River while portaging between the two rivers, thereby aiding the breach that occurred in 1805.

Antoine Deschamp, a Mackinac-based fur trader, was apparently the first to notice the change in drainage. He described the change to his apprentice, Gurdon Hubbard, who then told the story to Jonathan Periam, who later repeated it to Chicago historian Albert Scharf. Unfortunately Scharf died before publishing his book on early Chicago, but Chicago Historical Society librarian Caroline McIlvane secured the manuscript from his widow. Over 20 boxes of Scharf's materials were cataloged in the 1960s and collated by historian Paul Petraitis who then discovered the long-hidden story. George Brennan's *Wonders of the Dunes* uses a copy of an 1812 map of the Chicago/Calumet area as an end sheet. It shows the Little and Grand "Killomick" Rivers with a canal connecting them.

The Grand Calumet River today flows slowly westward from the Marquette Park Lagoon to the junction with the Little Calumet River at Hegewisch. It is also connected to Lake Michigan by the Indiana Harbor Ship Canal at East Chicago. This river today, in a manmade channel, has no natural tributaries and has been considerably cleaned up since the 1980s National Geographic Society named it one of the nation's top 10 ecological disasters.

Today's Little Calumet River is unique in that it has three outlets: one through Burns Ditch in Porter County, a second at South Chicago, and a third where the river empties into the Calumet Sag Channel—and in that parts of it flow east while other parts flow west. West of Highland the water flows west into Illinois; east of Highland the water flows east toward Burns Ditch. In between these sections is a portion of river where the water sometimes flows east and at other times flows west, depending on how much and where water enters into the river. Because of its nearly flat gradient, much of the Little Calumet has always been flood-prone. It is an easily ignored part of the landscape except after heavy rains.

PART TWO

The Human Touch

The Calumet
Area before
1833

Indiana became a state in 1816, and Illinois in 1818, but the Calumet Area had few permanent settlers on either side of the state line until after 1833. Even after the Potawatomi Indians relinquished their control of northwestern Indiana and northeast Illinois, the related problems of poorly drained soils and difficult transportation contributed to its late settlement.

Before it was dredged, the Kankakee River in Indiana was a vast marshland, three to five miles wide with waters only one to four feet deep. Except when frozen in the winter, it was too wet to walk through and contained too much vegetation to get a boat through. The Calumet Rivers flooded as well, and the low areas parallel to the Glenwood, Calumet, and High Tolleston Shorelines were marshy and nearly impassable. Traversing this region was extremely difficult in those early days. With these vast marshlands and wide flood-plains, the shorelines became natural, sandy highways connecting points east and west. From the many arrowheads and tomahawks found along the ridges, we know that the Sauk, Potawatomi, and other tribes made much use of these natural passageways.

The landscape was rich and varied with dune ridges, rivers and floodplains, former beaches, and abundant marshes. This diversity provided environments for a rich variety of plants and animals; the woodlands teemed with wildlife. The rivers and creeks were full of crystal-clear water. For about 200 years, the Calumet Area was a hunter's paradise.

Harry Eenigenburg, who was born in 1859 in a log cabin in Oak Glen (Lansing), Illinois, reported that in the early days, "Wild deer roamed in droves. The woods teemed with animals and birds. The river and creeks were full of clear water that often overflowed their banks. It really was the most beautiful country in the Middle West with all its streams, high sand ridges, big trees, meadows, and marshes."

Overhunting and loss of habitat have greatly reduced the diversity of animals in the Calumet Area. There were once great numbers of American bison in Indiana and Illinois, but they were gone by 1830. Once plentiful beavers were gone by then as well. Historian Alfred Andreas referred to an 1836 bear sighting in the South Chicago area, and George Garard described sightings of bears in 1836, 1838, and 1850. Elk, panthers, and bears were practically gone by 1850. The bald eagle had left the area by 1897. The river otter was gone by 1900. The last passenger pigeon was seen in 1902, the last timber wolf in 1908. The bald eagle, however, has since returned. It and the peregrine falcon, both once common along the lakeshore, have been successfully reintroduced by the Indiana Department of Natural Resources. In 1997 Kenneth Brock noted that they were by then commonly seen along the lakefront—particularly on windy days.

Native American Occupation

Archaeologists have been able to identify four "traditions" or eras of Native Americans. They were the Big Game Hunter or Paleo-Indian Tradition (more than 10,000 years ago), the Archaic Tradition (from 10,000 to 3,000 years ago), the Woodland Tradition (from 3,000 to 1,100 years ago), and the Mississippian Tradition (beginning 1,100 years ago).

Very little is known about the first two traditions. Stone spearheads from the Paleo-Indian Tradition have been found with skeletal remains of mastodons and woolly mammoths. Glaciers at that time still covered much of the northern United States and Canada. The Archaic Tradition saw the use of more specialized tools and trade of raw materials. This period was marked by a warmer climate, the growth of the hardwood forests, and the extinction of the large game animals.

During the late Woodland Tradition, the bow and arrow became common (beginning about 1,200 years ago). In addition, Indians made pottery and created thousands of burial mounds. To do this, they obtained loose soil from riverbanks and carried it in baskets to higher places where it was placed on top of the deceased. In this way burial mounds were slowly built up. It appears that mounds were built for the Indians' chiefs or leaders. Some mounds contained a single skeleton; others were built over several bodies.

In many cases pottery, weapons, and copper ornaments were buried along with the dead. It is possible that some mounds were built for defense purposes; a few certainly made it possible to see greater distances than one could see from the natural ground level. Mounds ranged from 2 feet to more than 20 feet in height. The most noteworthy local mounds were probably a group of ten mounds east of Boone Grove in Porter County.

A. F. Knotts reported that there were still a few mounds in Lake County in 1918. Unfortunately, many were considered nuisances to the pioneer farmers, who plowed right over them or hauled the soil away in order to flatten their fields.

Figure 22. Indian points collected by Neil Tanis on his Ridge Road farm in Munster. Munster Historical Society Museum.

The prehistoric mound builders do not seem to be related to the Indian tribes that inhabited the area in the 1670s when the first French explorers arrived. The Potawatomi, Miami, and Sauk Indians who met the French, British, and American explorers were of the fourth culture, the Mississippian, which was marked by village life and by the cultivation of plants. These Indians raised turkeys and cultivated corn, beans, squash, peppers, potatoes, grapes, melons, and sunflowers. It has been estimated that more than half of the agricultural wealth of the world today comes from plants that were first cultivated by American Indians and thus were unknown to residents of the Old World until Columbus' "discovery" of the New World in 1492.

Before the French exploration of Lake Michigan, Potawatomi lived in what is today southwestern Michigan. During the Iroquois Wars in the latter part of the 1600s, they were forced north and westward to the Upper Peninsula/Green Bay area. There they met the first of the French explorers and missionaries. Claude Allouez described the Potawatomi as warlike but friendlier than any of the other tribes.

Miami Indians were living in the Calumet Area when French explorers first came to northern Illinois and Indiana in the 1670s. With the Iroquois wars over (after 1701), many Potawatomi moved back to the south Lake Michigan area, and the Miami Indians moved southeastward to the Wabash and Maumee River valleys.

Figure 23. Stone tomahawk found by then Munster resident John Haimbaugh. Munster Historical Society Museum.

In 1830, there were thirty-six Potawatomi communities in northern Indiana and forty in northeast Illinois with a combined population of about 6,100. One of the largest was McGwinn's Village, south of Turkey Creek in what is today Merrillville (near Broadway at Seventy-third Avenue), where there were areas for wigwams, ceremonial dancing, and burials. It was said that sixteen Indian trails converged there.

The Potawatomi culture, similar to most American Indian cultures, was complex, one whose traditions created a sense of closeness to nature. The Potawatomi were both hunters and farmers. However, since they had no steel axes or plows, they could not clear forests or cut through the thick prairie sod. So the Potawatomi often planted their seeds along the soft soils of streams and riverbanks. After germination, they would leave the young plants when the tribes went on hunting expeditions, returning in late summer to harvest their crops and set aside a certain percentage for the next spring's plantings. Through the simple act of selecting and planting seeds from the best corn plants, the North American tribes bred new varieties of corn plants that had fewer side branches and fewer, but larger and probably better tasting, ears of corn.

Fishing provided much of the food. Simon Kaquados remembered:

Fish nets were made of basswood bark cord with stones attached to keep it properly suspended. Spears had long handles, with stone points and deer horn points. . . . Canoes were made of pine dug out, or fashioned of birch bark. With these they fished all night. . . . The kinds of fish secured were trout, white fish and sturgeon. In spring time, the middle of May, sturgeon came to shore. The fish were smoked and stored in summer. Fish hooks were made of barbed deer bones. Caught pike, pickerel, and bullhead with these hooks.

We cultivated our garden with stone hoes and wooden shovels. In our gardens we raised squashes, pumpkins, beans, potatoes, wild corn and onions. We pounded corn into a cornmeal in a wooden dish with a round stick. . . . We made corn soup of bear and deer meat.

Many of the Potawatomi villages were located alongside the rivers and lakes of the Calumet and Kankakee areas where a supply of fresh water was available. The Potawatomi spent the winters near the Kankakee River, away from the snow belt and the harsh weather near Lake Michigan.[1]

1. According to Alfred Meyer, Lake Michigan's name came from the Indian word *Mitchawsagiegan*, meaning "great water."

Gary Mitchell, a historian of the Prairie Band Potawatomi Tribe, wrote that his people tended to make wigwams with the bark of elm or birch trees. He added: "Inside these dwellings, the Potawatomi kept extra clothing, storage vessels and cooking utensils. Potawatomi women made baskets and bags from cedar or linden bark, while other containers were manufactured from birch, elm, hickory bark, and animal skins. Winter was a time of hardship, with food often scarce, but it was also a time when tribal stories and traditions were shared by family members crowded around a fire."

For the Indians, just as it was for the settlers, the geography of the area dictated transportation routes. Because of the east-west orientation of rivers, shorelines, and moraines south of Lake Michigan, north-south travel across them was difficult at best. East-west travel was easier. For this the Indians used the lakeshore and the ancient shorelines. Some trails were routes used originally by deer or bison. Others likely started as a line of least resistance for one person or a small group of people and were used again by others until some of them were very well defined. These Indian trails were then used by explorers, hunters, missionaries, soldiers, mail carriers, and finally settlers.

Valparaiso University geographer Alfred Meyer identified the five major Indian trails shown on Map 7:

- The Calumet River Trail, which followed the Grand Calumet River from Illinois to Gary, where it merged with the Lake Shore Trail.
- The Dunes Trail, which followed the high Tolleston Shoreline through what are now south Hammond, Hessville, Tolleston, Aetna, and then east to Michigan City. Because of the abundance of east-west trending ridges in the Hammond—Hessville—Tolleston area, there was never just one route in use.
- The Calumet Beach Trail, which followed the north edge of the Calumet Shoreline dunes from Thornton through Lansing, Munster, and Highland (Ridge Road) to Vermont Street in Gary. It then headed northeast through Liverpool, across Deep River, through

A BOY'S MEMORIES OF WITNESSING INDIAN LIFE

"I had an opportunity to visit the Indian wigwams on the shore of Lake Michigan in the summer and fall of 1837—to see the women at their work, the children at their play, the fires in the centers of their frail structures, and the hunters as they returned from a successful chase. I saw their roasted venison and had an opportunity to partake of it. I saw their large birch-bark canoes and the Indian boys of my own age spearing fish. I often saw parties of Indian men riding on their ponies one after the other in true Indian file; and I saw some of them in the attitude of mourners beside some graves at a little Indian burial ground.

"A similar life, with some quarrels and strife, some scenes perhaps of war and bloodshed, we may suppose the Red Men to have passed for the last 200 years. For them the Calumet Area must have been peculiarly attractive as furnishing so many muskrats and mink for fur, so many fish and water fowls for food."

—Attributed to Timothy Ball[2]

2. J. W. Lester, historical secretary of the Lake County Old Settlers Association, confirmed (1924) that the young boy paraphrased above was historian Timothy Ball, who as a child in 1837 spent seven months living in City West on the Lake Michigan shoreline.

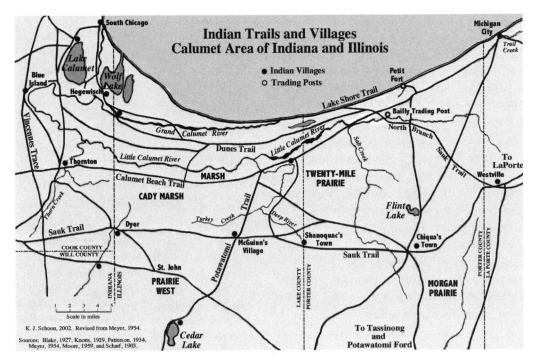

Map 7. Indian trails
of the Calumet Area.

Lake Station and Portage to the area where Bailly was to establish his trading post, and then eastward along the Dunes Highway to Michigan City.

- The Sauk Trail, the most famous of the old trails, which ran from Rock Island, Illinois, eastward to Detroit. The Illinois portion of the trail, preserved by the Sauk Trail road goes through South Chicago Heights and Sauk Village. In Indiana, it followed the Glenwood Shoreline from Dyer to Merrillville, crossed Deep River at Wood's Mill, and then went east to Valparaiso and LaPorte. The route later was chosen for the Lincoln Highway, the first coast-to-coast highway (Old Lincoln Highway in the Schererville/Merrillville/Hobart area). A northern branch of the Sauk Trail split from the main trail at what is now Westville and ran through Baillytown to Lake Michigan.
- The Vincennes Trace, a north-south route which connected Lake Michigan to the Wabash River at Vincennes. It avoided crossing the Little Calumet River by passing to the west of its hairpin curve. Much of this trail is today's Illinois Highway 1. A branch of this trail passed through Thornton.

The Potawatomi Trail is a name informally given to many Calumet Area Indian trails on both sides of the state line. In one sense, all the trails were Potawatomi trails. The most famous extended from

Buchanan, Michigan, through LaPorte, Baillytown, Portage, Lake Station, McGwinn's Village, and west to Dyer and Patterson, Illinois. At times they followed the Calumet Beach Trail, and at other places they followed the Old Sauk Trail.

Another route by that name crossed the Indiana/Illinois state line at the southern edge of the Valparaiso Moraine (just north of the Kankakee marshes). It then passed about two miles south of Lowell and went east toward Porter County. One fork went northeast to about a mile east of Valparaiso where it joined the Sauk Trail. The other fork continued east to an Indian town about two miles southeast of Hebron. The Vincennes Trace is, in some records, also called the Potawatomi Trail.

Many Indian trails became wagon and stagecoach routes. Years later, when the new counties needed to build roads through the area, the first routes chosen often followed these trails. Albert Scharf noted that the Indian trail became "first a bridle path, then a public highway, stage and mail route along which the main streets of many towns were subsequently laid out."

Unfortunately, the routes of many of the smaller Indian trails are lost forever. The government surveyors in the 1830s only made notes where the trails crossed section lines—and these lines were all one mile apart. Between these mile markers the surveyors either ignored the trails or simply guessed where they might run. Meyer gave much credit to "enthusiastic and enterprising pioneers" whose interest in discovering and recording facts of local geography gives us a great deal of information that otherwise would have been lost.

French Exploration and the Fur Trade

Although Jacques Cartier claimed the entire St. Lawrence Valley for France in 1534, actual North American colonization by the French did not begin until Samuel de Champlain established the city of Québec in 1608. In the decades to come, French voyageurs slowly moved up through the Great Lakes toward Lake Michigan and the Calumet Area—the extreme southwestern limit of the St. Lawrence Valley.

In 1634, Jean Nicolet became the first known French explorer to explore Lake Michigan. It seems unlikely that for the next thirty-nine years no French explorer or missionary visited the southern end of the lake, but there are no records of such trips, and in 1667, Father Claude Allouez referred to the "yet unexplored" Lake Michigan.

It is probably impossible to identify the first Europeans to visit the Calumet Area. Although the first records of exploration were written by French missionaries, it is believed that many of the first Europeans to visit the upper Great Lakes were French voyageurs

Figure 24. Father Jacques Marquette at the entrance of Gary's Marquette Park. This sculpture by Henry Hering of New York was dedicated in 1932.

and fur trappers. In the late seventeenth century, dozens of voyageurs, also called *coureurs de bois* (runners of the woods), headed into the Great Lakes region. These hardy folks, in pursuit of beaver furs and other fine pelts, tended not to keep written records of their trips the way the Jesuit missionaries did. However, it is likely that the Calumet Area, with its wealth of wildlife, would have been known to these French adventurers. Two voyageurs met Father Jacques Marquette in December 1674 when he encamped at Chicago.

Father Marquette is by far the best known of the French missionaries who explored the south Lake Michigan area, and his visit in 1673 is the earliest for which there are any written records. That summer, Marquette and Louis Jolliet found and explored the Mississippi valley from Wisconsin to the Arkansas River. On their return trip, they came up the Illinois River, crossed the Chicago portage, and canoed down to the mouth of the Chicago River. Marquette was evidently pleased with his reception by the Illinois Indians, and he promised that he would return.

In the autumn of the following year, Father Marquette did return. He and two companions spent the 1674–75 winter camped at the portage of the Chicago and Des Plaines Rivers.[3] Marquette had been very ill during much of this trip, but by March he was well enough to travel down the Illinois River and to preach to the Illinois Indians at the village of Kaskaskia (near modern Utica). However, by April he was much worse and soon lost almost all of his strength. As Marquette wished to return to his mission at the Straits of Mackinac, he cut short his trip and, accompanied by many of the Illini, paddled up the Illinois and Des Plaines Rivers, then up Hickory Creek. There they parted from the Indians and made a short portage—most likely to Butterfield Creek, downstream to

3. The exact location of Marquette's encampment is unknown. Several sites in Chicago have been suggested. A bronze relief commemorating Marquette's visit is attached to the Damen Avenue Bridge where it crosses the Chicago Sanitary and Ship Canal. Another can be found where Damen Avenue crosses the Chicago River. Major Henry Lee insisted that the encampment was at Hegewisch. The route of Marquette's return trip has also been the subject of much debate.

Thorn Creek, then down to what is now the Little Calumet River, around the big bend and east down the Grand Calumet River to its mouth, where Marquette Park at Miller Beach is today. This was all possible because the Calumet Area rivers and creeks were deeper and wider in the seventeenth century than they are today. And the high April level of these creeks would have made this trip much easier still than at other times of the year.

It is believed that in late April 1675 Marquette and his two aides disembarked at the mouth of the river and camped there. The small group then continued eastward and northward along the lake. Father Marquette, only thirty-eight years old, didn't make it to the mission. He died a couple of weeks later and was buried near what is now Ludington, Michigan, along the banks of the river now known as the Pere Marquette. Although the French left very little behind when they traversed this area, historians George Brennan and Powell Moore reported that a small sixteenth-century silver baptismal font and lid were found in the beach sand of Miller Beach, near the former mouth of the Grand Calumet River.

In December 1679, Robert Cavelier de la Salle and his group of twenty-seven voyageurs skirted the Calumet Area when they paddled up the St. Joseph River from Lake Michigan and then crossed overland (at the site of South Bend) to the Kankakee River. From there they went downstream into Illinois. In 1682, La Salle traversed the Mississippi River to its mouth and claimed the entire Mississippi River valley for France, naming it Louisiana, in honor of Louis XIV.

In 1850, a steel nail was found inside the trunk of a huge oak tree growing near Cedar Lake. According to Timothy Ball, the nail was of fine workmanship and was covered by 170 annual rings. That would date the nail's insertion into the tree to about 1680. Thus it is easy to speculate that La Salle, or other explorers, camped in the area and used the nail to post a map or some other information to the tree so that other explorers would find it. In any event, in the words of Timothy Ball, "Of the presence here of La Salle . . . or of some other Frenchman, let us infer that it bears witness."

The fur trade was very profitable for the French, who supported and protected that trade with a series of forts built between Montreal and New Orleans. The most important of these near the Calumet Area was Fort St. Joseph, built about 1689 on the banks of the St. Joseph River, north of the present city of South Bend. This strategically placed fort controlled traffic along the portage between the St. Joseph and the Kankakee Rivers. A similar fort was built on the Chicago River to control access to the Chicago portage. Le Petit Fort, built about 1750, was at what is now Indiana Dunes State Park. A smaller fort, commanded by Lieutenant Nicolas d'Ailleboust (1693–96), was apparently built near the south end of

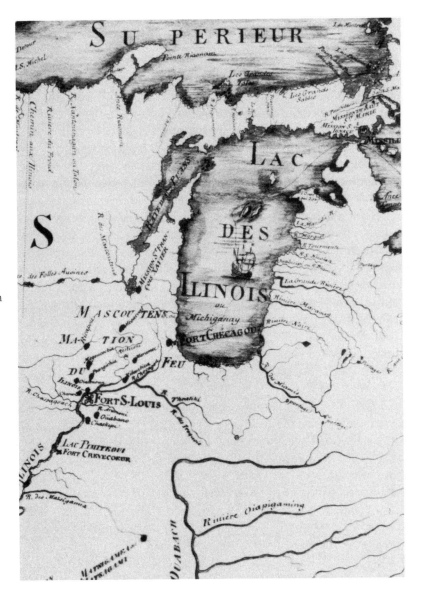

Figure 25. The Lake Michigan area from a 1688 map drawn by Jean-Baptiste Louis Franquelin. Franquelin was the first cartographer to place Chicago on a map. Wisconsin Historical Society.

Lake Michigan, perhaps at the mouth of the Grand Calumet River (now Gary's Marquette Park). John Swenson noted that this fort might have been the same as Le Petit Fort.

These forts allowed the French to control the fur trade in the rich Calumet and Kankakee River areas. It is hard to say exactly where any of these were located, as nothing of them remains today. In 1923, George Brennan claimed to have located the site of Le Petit Fort on a high dune about half a mile from the beach.

The French contact with the Potawatomi permanently changed their way of life. Before the Europeans came into the Great Lakes region, the Indians were self-sufficient. The Potawatomi did trade excess corn to tribes from the north, but they did not depend on trade for needed supplies. However, French traders wanted furs, which the Indians could easily provide, and the Indians soon wanted the metal utensils, guns, gunpowder, and alcohol that the French were willing to give them. Although the trade for European items made their lives easier, it also caused the Potawatomi to lose their self-sufficiency.

The French and Indian War (1754–63) ended French control of northern North America. With the defeat of French armies at Québec, France ceded its North American lands east of the Mississippi to Britain. Thus British soldiers graduallly replaced French soldiers in many of the forts throughout the Midwest.

Scattered reminders of the French period exist today throughout the Calumet and surrounding areas. Marquette Park, several Marquette Streets, and Marquette Schools commemorate the most famous of the missionaries. The city of Joliet sits on the Des Plaines River. Several Calumet Area communities have Joliet Streets. Local railroads have used both Marquette and Joliet in their names. LaPorte ("the door") refers to the passageway in the old forests that leads to the Calumet Area.

The British Period

After Great Britain was given control over the lands north of the Ohio River in 1763, George III decreed that these lands would not be open to settlement but instead would be reserved for the Indians. Thus American settlers were discouraged from moving west of the Alleghenies, while the French settlers already here continued their fur trade but under new British rules. Records show that as late as 1781 and 1783, the British government at Montreal issued licenses for traders to work along the Grand Calumet River at the south end of Lake Michigan.

During the American Revolution, a few British troops were stationed at Fort St. Joseph. The less significant Petit Fort in the dunes apparently was occupied for a short time but then abandoned about 1779.

The Calumet Area's only skirmish during the Revolution came as a result of a raid on Fort St. Joseph by French adventurers under the command of Jean Baptiste Hamelin. In the raid, provisions and furs belonging to the Potawatomi were stolen. The fort's commander, British lieutenant Dagneau de Quindre, was away from the fort at the time. However, he quickly gathered a group of Potawatomi braves and gave chase. Hamelin's group was at or near Le Petit Fort near Lake Michigan when the warriors caught up with them. The battle at the fort, in which de Quindre and the Potawatomi were victorious, occurred on December 5, 1780. A historical marker near the pavilion at Dunes State Park commemorates Le Petit Fort and the battle that took place there. However, historian George Brennan believed that this battle took place near Trail Creek in what is today Michigan City. Thus a similar marker commemorating the same battle stands at Krueger Park in Michigan City.

A few weeks later, Don Eugène Pouré, a French militia commander in Spanish service, led a force of 125 Europeans and Indians up the Illinois River until the river ice forced them to continue on land. They then marched east (probably on the Sauk Trail) for twenty days and captured Fort St. Joseph. (Once again, de Quindre was absent.) The Spanish flag flew over the fort that day, and Pouré claimed the entire upper Midwest for Spain. However, the Spanish force left within twenty-four hours and returned to St. Louis. So as quickly as Spanish troops entered the region, they were gone.

The Northwest Territories

Map 8. Evolution of the Northwest Territories. U.S. Northwest Territory Celebration Commission, 1937.

After the Revolution, the Spanish government entered a claim for the entire Mississippi River valley. As justification, it noted the conquest of Fort St. Joseph. The British, however, gave this "Northwest Territory" to the new United States and gave Florida to Spain. The new nation then extended from the Atlantic Coast to the Mississippi River. Nevertheless, British troops remained at Michilimackinac (at the north end of Lake Michigan) until 1796.

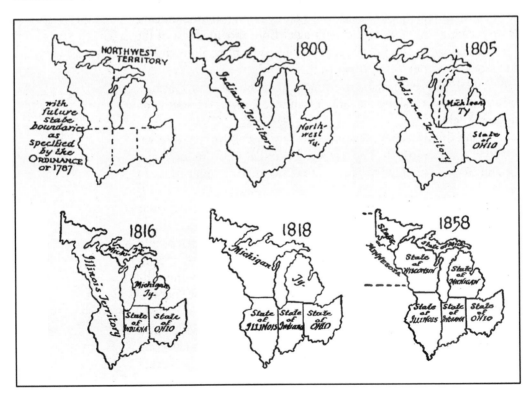

THE HUMAN TOUCH

In 1787, Congress passed the Northwest Ordinance, which provided that three to five new states would be created from this new territory. The ordinance also prohibited slavery, provided that land could not be acquired by settlers until after it had been purchased from the Indian tribes, established means of surveying and selling land, and provided for free transportation on navigable waterways.

Once land had been purchased from the Indians, the policy of the federal government was to sell the land cheaply to those who would settle on it. For special purposes, the government would donate land to fund projects that it could not afford otherwise.[4] Through "land grants," the government created roads, canals, railroads, and universities. For land to be distributed, however, it first had to be subdivided. So the Northwest Ordinance set up the surveying system that defines counties, townships, roads, and properties even today. Section boundary roads, both east-west and north-south, one mile apart, gave the area a grid appearance that in many cases took no heed of the natural contours of the land.

In 1800, the Indiana Territory (then also including what is now Illinois, Wisconsin, and Michigan) was created with its capital at Vincennes. Five years later, when Michigan became a separate territory, its southern boundary was set at the southern tip of Lake Michigan. Thus what are now the Indiana Dunes and Michigan City were all part of Michigan. In 1809, the Illinois Territory was separated from Indiana and the Indiana-Illinois boundary was set as a line north of the Wabash River, extending due north from Vincennes to Lake Michigan.

In 1816, Indiana was admitted to the Union as a state. Because the northern boundary of the Indiana Territory was the southern edge of Lake Michigan, it had virtually no frontage on the lake. Recognizing the value of Lake Michigan, Indiana's leaders convinced Congress to move the state boundary ten miles north, giving the new state forty miles of frontage on Lake Michigan. When Illinois became a state two years later, it took Indiana's lead and set its northern boundary about sixty miles north of the southern edge of the Lake.[5] This allowed the mouths of both the Calumet River and the Chicago River to be in Illinois—an important consideration because plans were already in place to connect Lake Michigan to the Mississippi River by means of a canal.

4. Wellington noted (1914) that in 1825 New York senator Rufus King proposed that funds derived from the sale of lands be used for the emancipation of the slaves.
5. The northern boundary of Illinois is set at 42°30' north latitude.

The Calumet Area before 1833

Fort Dearborn

American military presence at Chicago can be traced back to 1794, when General Anthony Wayne, acting for President George Washington, signed the Treaty of Greenville. The treaty gave the U.S. government about thirty-six square miles of land surrounding the mouth of the Chicago River. In 1803 President Thomas Jefferson directed Captain John Whistler to build Fort Dearborn there.[6] Two years later, a trading post was established, and soon traders, farmers from downstate, and speculators found their way to the area. The nearest post office to Fort Dearborn was at Fort Wayne. Two or three soldiers were sent monthly to carry the mail between these two outposts. The road, the northern branch of the Sauk Trail, passed through what are now LaPorte, Westville, and Chesterton before heading to the lakeshore. It was then only a pathway, not wide enough for carriages or stagecoaches.

In 1827, Illinois representative Daniel P. Cook convinced Congress to give Illinois sufficient land along the proposed route of the Illinois and Michigan Canal that the state could afford to build the canal—a waterway originally proposed by the French explorer Louis Jolliet in 1673. In August 1830, a plat for the town of Chicago was drawn at what would become the northeastern end of the canal. Three years later, on August 12, 1833, Chicago was formally incorporated as a town with a population of about 350.

The Calumet Area was among the last regions in both Indiana and Illinois to be relinquished by the Indians. In 1826, the Potawatomi ceded the northeastern part of it in what was called the Ten Mile Purchase. The southern boundary line of this purchase is marked appropriately today by Indian Boundary in Miller and the Indian Boundary Road in Chesterton. Beam Street and Woodlawn Avenue in Porter also are on this line, which was the boundary between the Indiana and Michigan Territories. In 1832, the Potawatomi ceded most of their remaining lands in Indiana, and in 1833 they gave up their Illinois and Michigan holdings. They then began the long, slow trek to Kansas. James Monahan saw the Potawatomi during their forced removal as they walked westward, probably in 1838 at the Gibson Inn along the Chicago–Detroit Road. He wrote, "It certainly was a sad sight. The Indians loved their homes as well as we loved ours. They sat around in their blankets looking sorrowful and dejected. Some, even the bravest, broke down and sobbed."

---

6. The soldiers heading out from Detroit to build Fort Dearborn (named for Jefferson's secretary of war) followed the Sauk Trail to what is now LaPorte, then followed Trail Creek up to the lakeshore and headed along the beach to the mouth of the Chicago River.

THE HUMAN TOUCH

Not all the Potawatomi left the Midwest. Some migrated to northern Wisconsin and the Upper Peninsula of Michigan. Potawatomi today live all across the United States. Many live on reservations, but, according to the Potawatomi web site, most do not. Active groups of Potawatomi can be found in Kansas, Michigan, Ontario, and Wisconsin. Closest to the Calumet Area is the Pokagon Band of Potawatomi Indians in southern Michigan and northern Indiana. They were awarded federal recognition in 1994.

The Last Trading Posts

The first known non-Indian resident in the Calumet Area and the first settler and founder of what would be Chicago was the black pioneer and trader Jean Baptiste Point de Sable,[7] a French and Algonquin-speaking British subject. Between 1775 and 1779, Point de Sable and his Potawatomi wife, Catherine, ran a fur trading post on the Rivière du Chemin (Trail Creek) at the present-day site of Michigan City. Alfred Andreas and other early historians maintained that Point de Sable's post was at the mouth of the "Chicagou" River, but letters written by explorers at the time clearly show that the settlement was at the Trail Creek location. During the Revolution, Point de Sable was accused of being an American sympathizer, and in 1779 he was arrested by British forces. He was taken to Michilimackinac where, cleared of all charges, he served as a member of the British Indian Department.

Between 1784 and 1788, Point de Sable and his wife built a log cabin (or perhaps moved into an already existing one) and established a farm on the north bank of the Chicago River near its mouth where years before there had been a French trading post. In doing so, they became the first residents of the permanent settlement that became the city of Chicago. For many years, they were the only residents of the area. Slowly, however, they were joined by other French-speaking settlers. By 1800, their settlement had become an important outpost. In 1803, U.S. soldiers built Fort Dearborn at the mouth of the Chicago River. The fort remained a military post until 1836.

A temporary American trading post was established at Tassinong in southern Porter County sometime before November 1824.

---

7. This book uses the original spelling of the name. According to John Swenson (2000b), Jean Baptiste Point de Sable was not known as "du Sable" until long after his death.

Figure 26. Log cabins at the Bailly Homestead before reconstruction. Calumet Regional Archives.

Very little is known about the post, and it was gone by the time the first American settlers arrived about 1835.

The last trading post in the Calumet Area was established by French Canadians, Joseph and Marie (Monee) Bailly. In 1822, they built a home on the north bank of the Little Calumet River at the south edge of the Lake Border Moraine, near where the ancient Calumet Shoreline and thus the Potawatomi Trail crossed the river. In this strategic location they could be reached by canoe or by foot. After their home was badly damaged by flooding, they moved to higher ground but remained close to the river. There they also established an inn and a trading post.

Bailly had a successful business with the Indians. He received large quantities of furs, which he traded for items that he could get from Mackinac and Detroit. Marie, whose mother was of French and Ottawa Indian descent, was as familiar with Indian ways as she was with French customs. This undoubtedly helped them in their dealings with the Potawatomi. Within a decade, Bailly had six to eight cabins for his French employees. For ten years, the Bailly settlement was the only one in the Calumet Area.

The Bailly homestead was rather isolated, and for that reason the inn became a particularly welcome sight for the occasional travelers going to or from Detroit to Fort Dearborn and other points west. Ottawa and Potawatomi Indians were the most frequent visitors. The site, with several log buildings and Bailly's home, built in 1833, has now been restored and is operated by the National Park Service at the Indiana Dunes National Lakeshore.

Joseph Bailly died in 1835. Marie moved to Illinois, but later returned to the homestead, where she died in 1866. It is believed that Monee, Illinois, is named for her.

The Pioneer and Stagecoach Period, 1833–1858

The early settlers in the area followed the various Indian trails as they moved into, through, and about the Calumet Area. Two of the first groups, the William Ross and Solon Robinson families, entered the area by way of the Sauk Trail. Even though some of these trails were quite famous, Timothy Ball noted that an Indian trail might require "a pioneer's eye, or an Indian's sagacity, to enable one to follow it safely." Solon Robinson described how, in 1833, a Mrs. Farwell and her family were trying to follow the old Sauk Trail (now Seventy-third Avenue in Merrillville). The trail was so hard to detect (probably as it passed through the summer prairie) that the family lost its way and ended up spending the Fourth of July somewhere in the vicinity of what was to become Crown Point.

Even as late as 1913, when the Lincoln Highway, the country's first transcontinental highway, was designed, the route chosen for it through the Calumet Area was along old Indian trails. From LaPorte, through Valparaiso, Merrillville, Schererville, and Dyer to South Chicago Heights, it followed the Sauk Trail (which in Lake County was the ancient Glenwood Shoreline). Then it turned north and followed the Vincennes Trace (Chicago Road) to Chicago

WAGON TRAINS WESTWARD
ON THE OLD SAUK TRAIL

"Along the wagon road, along that slightly curving ridge of sand that seems once to have been washed by the waters of Lake Michigan, thousands of emigrants have passed, on their way to the westward. This was for many years the great thoroughfare for western travel. Coming from the eastward through La Porte and Valparaiso then on the line of the old Sac Trail, crossing Deep River at Wood's Mill, now Woodvale, and then passing Wiggins Point, now Merrillville and going out of Indiana at Dyer, the lines of white covered wagons passed on to Joliet. Only those along that road, which was four miles north of Crown Point, had much idea of the amount of travel that passed over it."

—Timothy Ball, 1900

MODERN ROADS THAT WERE
ORIGINALLY INDIAN TRAILS

Some sections deviate from the original routes.
In Cook County: Michigan City Road, Thornton-Lansing Road, Dixie Highway, Chicago-Thornton Road (Michigan Avenue), Vincennes Road, Chicago Road, Glenwood-Dyer Road, Sauk Trail

In Lake County: Ridge Road, Old Ridge Road (in Hobart), parts of Liverpool Road, Old Lincoln Highway (Route 30 from State Line to Joliet St., then Joliet Street/Seventy-third Avenue)

In Porter County: Dunes Highway (Route 12), Porter Road, Lincoln Highway (Route 30) west of Valparaiso, Indiana Highway 2

In LaPorte County: Indiana Highway 2, Route 20 east of Michigan City, Indiana Highway 35

Heights before heading west again.[1] At the same time, in eastern Porter County, the new Dunes Highway followed the course of the Potawatomi Trail along the ancient Calumet Shoreline.

Historian and politician A. F. Knotts noted that traces of the old Indian trails, especially where the new roads deviated from the old trails, could still be seen by the careful viewer as late as 1929.

As the Potawatomi left the area for reservations west of the Mississippi River, the fur trade ended. Joseph Bailly then turned his interests toward establishing the town of Bailly, which was to have a port on Lake Michigan. Undoubtedly, he hoped that this port at the mouth of the Calumet River (at what is today Miller Beach in Gary) would rival Chicago's port. Neither his port nor his city was ever built.

However, the rest of the Calumet Area was about to experience a great population growth. West of the state line, the Vincennes Trace (also called Hubbard's Trail, the State Road or, in Chicago, State Street) surveyed in 1833, connected Chicago with Vincennes, the historic capital of the Indiana Territory. At the east end of the Calumet Area, the Michigan Road was completed in 1833. This road connected Indianapolis and Michigan City, but because its designers did not think that they could cross the wide Kankakee marshes, the road was diverted into St. Joseph County. By means of these two roads, settlers from southern Indiana and Illinois could travel to and through the Calumet Area.

The first settlers who lived in the Calumet Area chose their locations based on several factors. Some, such as the Baillys

---

1. The original route of the highway roughly followed Indiana Highway 2 from LaPorte to Valparaiso. In Valparaiso it was on Lincolnway, in Merrillville Seventy-third Avenue, in Schererville, Joliet Street east of its intersection with U.S. Highway 30, and (aptly named) Old Lincoln Highway where it crossed U.S. Highway 41, Joliet Street (Route 30) in Dyer, and Sauk Trail in Cook County from close to the state line to the Chicago Road.

at Porter, the Earles in Liverpool and Hobart, the Hohmans at Hammond, and the Wells in south Cook County, chose to live on waterways. Others such as the Gibsons and Brasses in Gary and Munster chose locations along trails that were built upon the ancient shorelines. Still others chose the fertile lowlands between these ancient sandy shorelines or the rich soils of the Valparaiso or Tinley/Lake Border Moraines. Finally, after the railroads began to crisscross the county, potential entrepreneurs chose to live near the new train stations, just as businesses and subdivisions have recently located near interstate highway interchanges.

Several early pioneer settlements appeared in areas where the Potawatomi had their villages. These include Thornton, Hegewisch, Lake Station, Merrillville, Valparaiso, Hebron, and Westville. The natural features of the land that attracted the Indian also attracted the settlers.

Surprisingly, many settlers avoided the prairies of the Calumet Area, preferring to set up their homesteads in the wooded areas or near groves of trees. According to Indiana geologist W. S. Blatchley, "The settlers had come from well-timbered countries and had the erroneous belief that land that did not produce trees would not produce cereals [e.g., corn or wheat]." Several settlements were established on prairie grounds at the edge of wooded areas. Such towns include Crete, Thorn Grove (Chicago Heights), Crown Point, Merrillville, Valparaiso, Westville, and LaPorte.

Some of the early Calumet Area communities grew up around sources of waterpower, so essential for saw and gristmills. Examples include Thornton, Deep River, Hobart, Chesterton, and Valparaiso. Finally, a few industrial cities were planned by speculators who envisioned great ports on Lake Michigan and so platted cities on or near the lakefront. Called by John O. Bowers the Dream Cities of the Calumet, they are described later in this chapter.

The first Calumet Area lands in Indiana to go on sale to the public were those north of the Indian Boundary Line (north of the southernmost point of Lake Michigan). These lands were offered for sale at Crawfordsville in 1830. At that time Major Isaac Elston purchased the land at the mouth of Trail Creek.[2] Two years later, he platted Michigan City and offered lots for sale. His plans included a major port and shipping facilities as well as commercial and residential areas.

With the Indian treaties signed, surveyors came north to divide the Calumet Area into counties, townships, and square-mile sections. The creation of sections meant that land could be sold to

2. The Potawatomi called Trail Creek "Meehwaysebeway," meaning "a creek along which there was a trail." It was then named "Rivière du Chemin" (river by the trail) by early French explorers. Trail Creek is the only Calumet Area geographical name that is a direct translation of both the older Indian and French names.

We arrived at Michigan City in the evening. There was but a single house there at which we could stop. It was kept by General Orr. We there met with Major Elston, of Crawfordsville, who had become the purchaser of the section of land on which Michigan City was laid out, and he had just completed a survey and map of the town, which he exhibited to us, and offered to sell us lots. It was a great novelty to us, this map of Michigan City, and in the morning, when daylight came, and we could look out upon the land around us, the novelty was still more striking, for a more desolate tract of sand and barren land could hardly be conceived of. There was scarcely a tree or shrub to distinguish it, much less any houses; it was literally in a state of nature.

Major Elston had been attracted to it by the fact that it was the only place on Lake Michigan within the territory of the State of Indiana, where it might be possible at some future time to establish a commercial port. . . .

From Michigan City to Chicago, a distance of about sixty miles, the journey was performed by me on horseback. There was but one stopping place on the way, and that was the house of a Frenchman named Bayeux [Bailly], who had married an Indian woman.

—*Charles Butler, 1833*

private citizens. The creation of a county meant convenience to settlers because many government dealings and decisions could then be carried out locally.

Stagecoach Routes and Taverns

Because of its position at the southern edge of Lake Michigan, the Calumet Area was destined to become a center for transportation. Just as three east-west interstate highways today come into this region as they cross the Midwest, so did the railroads a century earlier. And before the railroads, the stage roads and Indian trails all had to pass through the region.

The earliest travelers used the lakeshore almost exclusively. One definite advantage of the lakeshore route was that it was impossible to get lost. Nevertheless, this route proved to be unsatisfactory. In winter, drivers, horses, and passengers were all hit by the blustery cold winds that blew off the lake. In summer, the four-horse teams had a difficult time pulling the coaches through the loose, dry sand. Only in cool damp weather was travel along the smooth sands of the present shoreline fairly easy. When the sand was packed and damp, one could travel the fifty miles from Michigan City to Chicago in just six hours; but when the conditions were bad, it took six days to make the same trip.

Nevertheless, in 1833 the first stagecoaches followed the lakeshore route between Baillytown and Chicago. To serve the new stage line, the Bennett Tavern, an inn and "house of entertainment," was built in 1833 on the Lake Michigan beach at the mouth of the Grand Calumet River, at today's Marquette Park. The following year, Hannah Berry opened a tavern some distance to the west of Bennett's, likely between Lake Michigan and Berry Lake in what is today Whiting. Until these inns were built, there were no "civilized" places to rest except for the Bailly Homestead in Indiana and the Mann trading post and ferry at the western mouth of the Calumet River (now South Chicago).

The new taverns served as places where the coach drivers would leave their exhausted horses and get fresh horses for the next step

Figure 27. This Calumet Area stagecoach ran between Valparaiso and LaPorte. LaPorte County Historical Society Museum.

of their travels. They also served as restaurants and inns where driver and passengers could get a warm meal and a bed for the night. The first inns were log cabins with one main floor and a loft accessible with a ladder. Guests usually slept in the loft. Solon Robinson noted that the innkeepers administered "to the necessities and not much to the comfort" of travelers who began to flock into the area. Historian Lance Trusty noted that some of the Calumet Area inns were probably among the worst in the nation.

Robinson wasn't alone in his opinions of these early inns. In 1836, Englishwoman Harriet Martineau wrote, "We had a good supper, except there was an absence of milk, and we concluded ourselves fortunate in our resting place. Never was there a greater mistake. We walked out, after supper, and when we returned, found that we could not have any portion of the lower rooms. There was a loft, which I will not describe, into which, having ascended a ladder, we were all to be stowed. I would fain have slept on the soft sand out of doors, beneath the wagon, but the rain came on."

Because travel on the Lake Michigan beach was so difficult, in 1837 inland routes along old Indian trails were adapted for the stagecoach. The northern route followed the high Tolleston Shoreline through what are now Tolleston, Hessville, Calumet City, and Roseland. The southern route followed the Calumet Shoreline through Liverpool, Glen Park, Highland, Munster, Lansing, and Thornton. Both of these routes have been called, at various times, the Chicago–Detroit Road. Innkeepers then built new establishments on these trails. These routes were preferable because they were sheltered from the lake's fierce weather, and while the roads were certainly not easy by today's standards, the ground never got as difficult as the loose, dry sand of summer on the beach. Being located on the ancient beaches, they were also high above the flood stage of the nearby rivers.

Many of the first northern Calumet Area settlers were innkeepers who hoped to cash in on the traffic going to and from Chicago.

Figure 28. Shabbona, an Ottawa and Potawatomi chief, was best known as the "Peace Chief." He was a frequent visitor of the Combs Inn in Hegewisch and the Gibson Inn in East Tolleston. A very strong man, he continued to dress in leggings and moccasins even after his daughters had adopted European dress. Timothy Ball said that his name meant "built like a bear." Shabbona Woods in Calumet City is named for him. Gary Public Library.

Eight innkeepers are listed in the 1850 census as living in Lake County's North Township alone. Roads from the east converged near Baillytown. From Bailly's inn, travelers would cross the Little Calumet River on the Long Pole Bridge, a frightening 1,000-foot rough-hewn bridge,[3] then follow one of the primitive roads to Chicago.

According to Frances Howe, Joseph Bailly's granddaughter, "A few bridges, strongly built of unhewn timbers, were thrown across some streams, a few hillsides were graded, and little else was done or needed." Packed dirt was a fine road surface when it was smooth, but ruts could be truly frustrating.

Various inland routes for these stagecoaches were tried, but all for some distance followed the routes of the ancient shorelines of Lake Michigan. From Baillytown, one could travel along the southern edge of the Tolleston dunes through Porter County, then along the high Tolleston Shoreline through Aetna and Hessville, then on to Hegewisch where travelers could cross the Grand Calumet River on a ferry. Others would cross the Grand Calumet at Hohman's toll bridge (in Hammond) and then north to Chicago. After the ferry at Liverpool was established in 1835, stagecoaches could go west from Baillytown, cross the Little Calumet on the Long Pole Bridge and Deep River at Liverpool, and follow the Calumet Shoreline (Ridge Road) through to Munster and Thornton, then north to Blue Island and on to Chicago.

Henrietta Combs Gibson, whose parents ran the inn at Hegewisch and whose in-laws ran the inn at what is now Gary, remembered, "Stages ran on a regular schedule like the railroads, so we knew when they would come and watched for them. The drivers would come from Michigan City to 'Mother' Gibson's inn [in Gary]. . . . They generally got their [noon] dinner there, then came to our place at Hegewisch for supper."

Members of the Gibson family established three inns in the 1830s, one each at what are now Munster, Gary, and Gibson Station north of Hessville. According to J. W. Lester, historical secretary of the Lake County Old Settler and Historical Association, in 1837, just as Lake County was being established, the Gibsons moved to

---

3. The "Ever-to-be-remembered-by-those-who-crossed-it" Bridge.

what is now Munster, built a log cabin along the old Calumet Shoreline, and established the first Gibson Inn. Lake County records show a license in 1837 being issued to David Gibson on the Sand Ridge Road for which he paid six dollars. The next year, Thomas and Anna Maria Gibson started an inn on the high Tolleston Shoreline at what is now Fourteenth Avenue and Madison in Gary.[4] The Gary inn was a large log building with two rooms on each floor. Lester wrote, "With a dooryard brightened by a variety of wild flowers . . . the Gibson place, shaded by stately oaks . . . [and] a natural grapevine swing, presented an inviting aspect to the worn traveler. Many tarried there and the Gibsons prospered."

Partly because of its location, and partly because of the hospitality of "Mother Gibson," the Gibson Inn was one of the most popular taverns in the Calumet Area. Solon Robinson, Timothy Ball, and members of the Bailly family were frequent guests.

Like many of the other Calumet Area inns, the Gibson Inn became a regular stop for stagecoaches traveling from Michigan City to Chicago. In later years, daughter-in-law Henrietta Gibson described the sounding of a horn that announced the coming of a stagecoach. At this signal, fresh horses for the stage would be brought out of the stable. Anna Maria Gibson kept the inn open for ten years after her husband died in 1850.[5]

In 1845, David and Elizabeth Gibson sold their inn on the Calumet Shoreline (Ridge Road) and established the third Gibson Inn between what is now Hessville and the Grand Calumet River.

Each of the many inns had its own menus based upon foods obtainable, both domestic and wild, and the skills of the local cooks. Al-

CALUMET AREA STAGECOACH INNS, 1832–1870

In Cook County: Calumet House, Eagle, and Mann's at South Chicago, Woodman's on Lake Calumet, Cassidy's/Combs and Reese's at Hegewisch, the Eleven Mile House in Roseland, Rexford's Blue Island House, Brown's Inn at South Chicago Heights, Dolton's Inn at Dolton, Levi Osterhout's Tavern in Riverdale, and Berry's Tavern in Thornton.

In Lake County: Bennett's Tavern at Miller, Berry's Tavern at Whiting, Gibson's Inn/Brass Tavern at Munster, Gibson's Inns at Gary and Hessville, Stillson's Tavern at Liverpool, Hohman's Tavern at Hammond, Scheidt's Inn at St. John, Lilley's Tavern in Cedar Lake, Wells' Tavern in Crown Point, and the State Line House in Dyer.

In Porter County: Ward's Tavern at Beverly Shores, the Green Tavern at New City West, Bailly's Inn at Baillytown, Butler's Tavern below the mouth of Salt Creek, Morgan's Stage House and Thomas' Hotel at Chesterton, the Old Maid's Tavern at Willow Creek, and Hall's Tavern in Valparaiso.

In LaPorte County: Perhaps a dozen hotels including Blake's and Lily's in LaPorte and Lofland and Taylor's and Olinger's in Michigan City.

Figure 29. Anna Maria "Mother" Gibson, ca. 1886. Indiana room, Gary Public Library.

4. Lester (1923) reported that the Gibsons sold the first inn [in 1838] to Allen Brass and then started the second inn. However, James Luther (in Ball, 1884) much earlier stated that Allen Brass told him that he didn't come to the area until 1845. Thus from 1838 to 1845 there probably were two Gibson Inns open at the same time: one in today's Munster, and one in Gary.

5. In 1923, the Potawatomi Chapter of the Daughters of the American Revolution placed a bronze marker near the corner of Fourteenth Avenue and Madison Street to mark the site of the Gibson Inn.

though menus of the Gibson and Brass Taverns have not been found, a menu from the nearby Oak Hill Tavern looked like the inset at left.

Pork	**Pheasant**
Quail	**Prairie Chicken**
Buckwheat Cakes with Maple Syrup	
Potatoes	
Bread and Butter	**Honey**
Tea **Coffee**	**Milk**

With the lack of fruits on the menu (berries were plentiful in the area), this must have been a winter menu. The cost for meals at the Oak Hill Tavern was 25¢ and for lodging 50¢. Lester, who reproduced this menu and rates in his manuscript about the Gibsons, noted that menus and rates were fairly standard at the several inns in the county.

The Munster establishment stood at the corner of today's Ridge Road and Columbia Avenue. In 1845 Allen and Julia Brass bought the inn and replaced the log cabin with a large two-story building. Business was brisk at the Brass Tavern with the six upstairs rooms housing ten to twelve visitors each night. The first floor contained two parlors (one used as a men's bar), a large dining room, kitchen, pantry, and bedroom. Wilhelmine Stallbohm Kaske, who grew up in the inn after it was sold to her parents in 1864, later described it as "a busy thriving place where life could not grow dull. Our nearest post office was Gibson, Indiana [north of Hessville], but news of the outside world was brought in by the transients." When a telegraph line was strung along Ridge Road to the Brass Tavern, news began arriving with unheard of speed. It was thus at the tavern (likely called Stallbohm's Inn by then) in 1865 that the local area first heard of the assassination of President Abraham Lincoln.[6]

Neighbors with some free time would stop at these inns to catch up on local and national news. As the social centers of the area, many of the inns were occasionally used for evening dance parties. Wilhelmine noted that such events in Munster attracted large crowds with folks coming from miles around. When the old inn burned to the ground in 1909, the *Lake County Times* described it as a famous landmark with huge fireplaces and good wine, both of which warmed travelers far from home. It continued: "The destruction of the old road house is like tearing a leaf from Lake County's most interesting history. . . . All the wagon traffic of the farmers to Chicago halted and passed there. There the farmers would unhitch their oxen and in later years their horses, to rest them and themselves. There they sat around the huge fireplaces, dividing the news that each had brought from his particular locality."

Figure 30. Julia Watkins Brass, who with her husband, Allen, ran the Brass Tavern from 1845 to 1864. National Society Daughters of the American Revolution, 1902.

6. In 1926, the Julia Watkins Brass Chapter of the Daughters of the American Revolution placed a bronze marker near the corner of Ridge Road and Columbia Avenue to mark the site of the old Brass Tavern.

Figure 31. The Brass Tavern. This drawing by Edward M. Verklan was based on early twentieth-century photographs of the building. Courtesy of the artist.

Squatters

Settlement of the Calumet Area began in earnest in 1833, even before the government was ready to sell plots of land. Expecting lands to be offered soon, hundreds of claim seekers or squatters began moving in without legal rights to the land.

Perhaps the first permanent settlers were LaPorte County residents Miriam Benedict, her children, including daughter Sarah, and Sarah's new husband, Indian trader Henly Clyburn. They arrived near what is now Westville in March 1829.

Jesse and Jane Morgan were among the earliest settlers (after the Baillys) to settle in Porter County. Arriving in 1833, the year that the Chicago–Detroit stagecoach line began operations, they established the Stage House Tavern on the Chicago–[LaPorte]–Detroit Road near where it crossed Sand and Coffee Creeks. Jesse started the area's first post office and served as postmaster for twenty years. Isaac and Sarah and William and Anna Morgan established farms farther south in Porter County. Morgan's Prairie and Morgan Township are named after this pioneer family. Within weeks, other settlers had arrived, staking their claims on the fertile prairie. Porter County's first school sessions were held that year at Jesse Morgan's home. According to George Garard, the teacher was a traveler who wanted a place to stay for the winter.

The first settlers in Lake County, other than the innkeepers along the Lake Michigan beach, were William Ross and his wife. In

SOLON ROBINSON'S FIRST APPROACH TO CROWN POINT

"It was the last day of October, 1834, when I first entered this 'arm of the Grand Prairie.' It was about noon, of a clear, delightful day, when we emerged from the woods, and, for miles around, stretched forth one broad expanse of clear, open land. . . . I stood alone, wrapt up in that peculiar sensation that man only feels when beholding a prairie for the first time—it is an indescribable, delightful feeling. Oh, what a rich mine of wealth lay outstretched before me. Some ten miles away to the southwest, the tops of a grove were visible. Toward that onward rolled the wagons with nothing to impede them. . . . Just before sundown, we reached the grove and pitched our tent by the side of a spring.

"What could exceed the beauty of this spot! Why should we seek farther? Here is everything to indicate a healthy location which should always influence the new settler. . . . After enjoying such a night of rest as can only be enjoyed after such a day, the morning helped confirm to us that here should be our resting-place. In a few hours, the grove resounded with the blows of the ax, and in four days we moved into our 'new house.'"

—*Solon Robinson, ca. 1840*

Figure 32. Solon Robinson, founder of Crown Point. Calumet Regional Archives.

1833 they staked out a claim, built a home, and established a farm on the banks of Deep River near where today it is crossed by Hobart's Sixteenth Street.[7] (This area was originally in Ross Township, which was named for this family.) The Rosses were soon joined by other squatters including Richard and Mariah Fancher, who chose land alongside Fancher Lake at the Lake County Fairgrounds, and Solon and Mariah Robinson, who built the first house in what is now Crown Point.

At that time, the nearest post office was in Michigan City, more than thirty miles to the east, so it was very difficult to get mail. In 1836, as a result of his efforts, a local post office was established and Robinson was named postmaster. Wanting to have his town designated as the proposed Lake County's seat, he first named the community and its new post office Lake Court House. Robinson then wrote letters to many East Coast newspapers extolling the virtues of the area. He even erected signposts pointing the way to his settlement. Within a few years, hundreds of squatters had moved into the Calumet Area. The day that the lands went on sale in LaPorte, they were first in line to secure legal rights to the lands upon which they had already settled. In fact, in 1836 they had formed a "Squatters' Union," pledged not to bid against each other, and managed (probably because they were numerous and armed) to discourage others from bidding at all.

Robinson and his brother Milo opened a store that catered to the needs of the new settlers and the large numbers of Indians who still lived in the area. Robinson stated that the Potawatomi were his best customers. Although they generally paid for their purchases with furs and berries, he preferred to deal with them than with the white settlers who thought themselves far superior to the Indians but then "gave us promises to pay, some which are promises to this day."

7. Howat (1915, p. 34) claimed that Ross settled on the west bank of Deep River. However, he later stated that Ross settled in Section 6 on the east bank of the river (p. 180).

Transportation

It is difficult in the present age to understand how difficult travel was in those early days. Sand dunes, marshes, creeks, and rivers all impeded travel. The present and ancient shorelines allowed easy transit but only parallel to the lake shore. In dry weather, even the beaches were troublesome as the dry sand made it difficult for horses to pull their wagons.

Bridges today are often so high that you can't even see the water below them. Storm sewers completely hide much of today's runoff. That wasn't the case in the 1830s. And until 1926, when Burns Ditch connected the Little Calumet River to Lake Michigan, flooding on that river was an enormous problem. The rivers and creeks of the Calumet Area were often so full of water that fording them was extremely dangerous. At times the Little Calumet River was more than a mile wide.

In 1836, Harriet Martineau noted that on a ride to Michigan City, the carriage "jolted and rocked from side to side, till, at last, the carriage leaned three parts over, and stuck. We all jumped out into the rain, and the gentlemen literally put their shoulders to the wheel, and lifted it out of its hole. The same little incident was repeated in half an hour."

Many farmers built their homes close to the high and dry former shorelines of Lake Michigan, growing their crops in the lowlands. They always expected high waters in the spring or after very heavy rains. Timothy Ball noted in 1900 that in flood stage, waters from the Little Calumet River practically reached from Ridge Road to the Tolleston Shoreline (about 169th Street in Hessville/Twenty-first Avenue in Gary).

Years later, conditions were not much better. William Gleason, superintendent during the construction of U.S. Steel's Gary Works, made his first visit to Gary in 1905. He later described the undeveloped and desolate area: "We came to a little swinging bridge over a 'run' [Gibson Run, no longer in existence]. On the four corners of this bridge there were ropes fastened to sticks driven in the ground. When the water was high, the rope fastenings prevented the bridge from floating away. When the water was low, the bridge settled into place."

In the early days, building a road meant removing trees and brush and leveling out the sand or clay surface. Horse-drawn wagons would soon leave huge ruts, making travel difficult, even on

Figure 33. Katie Koedyker, about 1880. Courtesy of Lester Schoon.

Figure 34. Skaters on the frozen Little Calumet River. South Holland Historical Society Museum.

the roads. One attempt to make travel easier was to cover the roadway with wood. If a sawmill was nearby, then planks of wood were laid down to make a pavement. The Michigan City–Valparaiso Road going through what is now Chesterton was partially a plank road. If no sawmill were handy, then logs would be laid down forming a very rough but passable surface. These roads were called corduroy roads, named after the fabric. Road builders must have been dismayed when these road surfaces began to rot within two years of being laid down. Gravel roads were much easier to traverse, but they were uncommon until the 1890s. To avoid crossing the Calumet marshes or the Little Calumet River, many travelers followed one of the ancient shorelines all the way to Blue Island and then north to Chicago. Capitalizing on the willingness of travelers to pay for assistance across the river, ferries across the Little Calumet were established at what are now South Chicago, Liverpool, Hammond, and Dolton.

Until the late 1830s, the only bridge in the Calumet Area was Long Pole Bridge across the Little Calumet River just west of the mouth of Salt Creek. Called the "ever-to-be-remembered-by-those-who-crossed-it" bridge, this 1,000-foot long bridge scared the living daylights out of travelers. In 1838, three bridges were built across Deep River and one each across West Creek and Center Creek. In 1839 the ferry across the Calumet River (in South Chicago) was replaced with a toll bridge. Others followed, including Hohman's toll bridge (in Hammond) built across the Grand Calumet in 1851.

Housing

The first homes built by the Calumet Area pioneers were primitive. Log cabins were built because sawed lumber was not available. Nevertheless, building a house was the first job the new settlers had. Many of the pioneers looked around for suitable land, built their houses where they liked, and then filed a claim for the property.

A few of the original log cabins can still be seen. Several have been restored by the National Park Service at the Bailly Homestead in Porter. Another at the Buckley Homestead near Lowell has been restored by the Lake County Department of Parks and Recreation. A third, the Heritage Cabin in Calumet City, has been restored by the Calumet City Historical Society. All of these cabins are open to the public at specific times.

For the early settlers, building materials were whatever was available nearby. Trees were cut down and shaped and notched at their ends with the broadax. Door frames were hewn out of logs as were the doors. Shingles for the roof were split along the grain using the tool called a froe. The floors were often simply dirt. If the owners could afford the time, logs were split and smoothed and placed on the ground to make a flooring surface. Before sawmills were established in the area, no lumber was available unless one traveled to Avery, Michigan, to purchase white pine boards. Cabins usually lacked windows. In an attempt to make these houses more livable, rags were saved and woven into rugs. Many Calumet Area log houses were built during a house-raising bee where neighbors would all gather and work together until the house was completed. Before disbanding and going back to their own homes, these pioneers would feast on wild game and dance to tunes such as "Old Dan Tucker" or the Scottish favorite, "Monymusk."

LIFE AND LIGHT IN 1851

"The majority of homes sixty years ago [1851] consisted of a single room, with a loft for the children above. The room below usually had a big fireplace in one end, generally five or six feet in length, and during the long, winter evenings the fire was kept brisk enough to furnish all the light needed about the room. When additional light was needed a saucer or small tin pan was partially filled with lard or some other kind of grease, then a strip of rag was inserted in the grease and lighted, and this rude lamp was carried to any place where additional light was needed. After this came candles, which were started by cutting strips of wick. . . . Dipping these wicks in melted tallow and taking them out to let them drip was continued until enough tallow had gathered around the wick to form a candle. . . . The making of candles by this process was an important duty in all well-managed households."

—John Ade, 1911

Bricks were nonexistent in the earliest days, and thus chimneys were built of wood, rocks, and clay. Wells had to be walled in with wood, which would rot and have to be replaced frequently. Fortunately, because of the abundance of glacial till in the moraines and the former lake bottomland, clay for brick making was readily available—once it was located. The first kiln for making brick opened in Cedar Lake in 1840. One in Crown Point began operation in 1841. By the late 1860s, Hobart had four brickyards in operation.

Others eventually opened in Blue Island, Dolton-Riverdale, Home-wood, Crete, Munster, Hobart, Porter, Chesterton, and Valparaiso. In the 1850s it was rare for a community in Indiana or Illinois not to have a brickyard nearby.

Gerrit and Janetje Eenigenburg, who settled in Oak Glen (now Lansing), were typical of many of the early settlers. Their son Harry remembered, "My father moved into his 160-acre farm in the fall of 1853 and built his little 16×24 foot house one story high with a small attic for the children's bedroom . . . on the old stage road—the only trail they had at that time, for there were no railroads or wagon roads. Our nearest neighbor was a man who lived alone a half mile away. Three miles to the east was the Stallbohm road house [then the Brass Tavern]. . . . Stagecoaches drove through our community every day each drawn by four horses with a lot of baggage piled on top."

Mills, Blacksmith Shops, and Cooperages

Figure 35. The John and Fenna Kickert family in front of their South Holland blacksmith shop. South Holland Historical Society Museum.

Not surprisingly, one of the earliest industries to be established in the frontier was the sawmill. LaPorte's first industry was probably a sawmill built in 1832 by the Andrew brothers. Timothy Ball noted that five sawmills had been built in Lake County by 1838.

As soon as settlers began farming, there was a need for gristmills, which ground wheat and corn into flour or meal for baking. Several millers, such as John Wood and George Earle, converted their sawmills into gristmills. The mills, powered by running water, had to be near streams with water flowing fast enough to turn the water wheel. In many cases, dams were built across creeks and rivers creating millponds. Water from the pond was then diverted to the mill where it would fall over the water wheel.

The earliest pioneers preferred oxen to horses because oxen could eat the grass found in the nearby prairies. Horses needed hay, which could only be produced on farms. However, once hay was available, the horse was the preferred work animal, and blacksmith shops then became required components of every village. In addition to providing much-needed horseshoes, blacksmiths made and repaired wagons, tools, and machinery.

As clothes were all homemade, carding mills where wool was prepared for spinning were also necessary. According to Porter County historian William Briggs, a carding mill was built on Salt Creek by Jacob Axe. Families would bring in raw wool sheared from their own sheep and then take home the carded wool to spin into yarn. Most families had a spinning wheel, but since few had a loom, the wool was spun into yarn at home and then taken to a weaver, who would make the cloth. The women in the family would then sew the new cloth into clothes.

Many communities also had a cooperage where tubs, barrels, and buckets were made. Local hickory was used for the hoops that held the barrels together. When hickory couldn't be found, white oak was used; however, white oak was brittle and broke more easily.

Cooking

In his history of Lake County, Sam B. Woods wrote, "Mother did her cooking [about 1850] over an open fireplace in which there was a crane. This crane, embedded in one side of the fireplace, would swing out so that she could put the pot or baking kettle on it and then would swing back over the flame. Mother had a record of baking up one barrel of flour a month. She was raised in Virginia and so she had to have her cornmeal. As soon as the early corn showed signs of ripening, we boys would have to go to the field, gather the ripest of it, and bring it to the house where it would be dried quickly before the fire. Then it would be shelled and taken to the mill to be ground into new cornmeal. Mother never seemed to tire of corn bread, but Father refused to eat it when he could get wheat bread."

Figure 36. Ann Sigler Woods, daughter of Hobart pioneers Samuel and Ann Sigler. Lake County Historical Society Museum.

Figure 37. Harvesting onion sets on the Jansen family farm north of Ridge Road in Munster. Onions were the big cash crop here on the sandy Calumet Shoreline and in the South Holland area. Munster Historical Society Museum.

Farming

Most of the pioneer families of the Calumet Area lived on farms. Life was rough, and several of the earliest settlers gave up and moved away. The families that remained formed a very stable nucleus; the descendents of many of these farm families may still be found in the region. Most farms ranged in size from 40 to 160 acres, and most families had plenty of children to help with the daily chores. For the first couple of decades, farmers raised the crops and animals necessary to meet their own needs. Crops not needed by the family would be hauled into Chicago or other cities to sell. With the arrival of good roads and railroads, it became much easier to transport excess crops to market.

The most fertile soils were along the southern edge of the Calumet Area—in the area of the Tinley and Valparaiso Moraines. The sand dunes and ridges along the ancient and current shorelines of Lake Michigan were thought to be rather worthless. The dunes' value was seen in its forests, which could be cut down, and its sand, which could be mined and sold.

Figure 38. John Santefort hauling cabbage to market. South Holland Historical Society Museum.

Because the Calumet Area is so diverse, some farms were on moraines, others along the sand ridges, floodplains, and former lakebottom. Some soils were suitable for root crops such as onions, carrots, or turnips. Other soils were best used for orchards; thus, fruit trees began to characterize the agriculture of some areas such as northern Porter County. Floodplains were often used for grazing or hay production. Farmers near rail lines with daily milk stops soon began raising dairy cows. If an area was close enough to a city so that fresh produce could be hauled (trucked) to markets there and sold, then "truck gardens" might be established. The name refers to the farmers trucking their vegetables to city homes or markets. South Cook and northern Lake Counties had many truck gardens that supplied Chicago and later the industrial Calumet Area cities along Lake Michigan.

The railroads had a profound effect on the farms of the area. The trains brought new farming equipment in, and they took fresh produce away. Farms, particularly in the Tinley and Valparaiso Moraine areas, began to grow larger with most of the produce being sold rather than eaten by the family.

Mineral Springs

In the 1890s, a deep well dug northwest of Porter (near Mineral Springs Road) produced an artesian well. This water had a high mineral content that proved to be economically useful.[8] An analysis determined that "the water from Porter is very free from injurious organic matters. It is very useful for drinking at the well in cases which need alternative or laxative treatment and it is also useful for baths and for sanitarium purposes."

Within a short time, the mineral water was being bottled and sold in nearby cities. The Carlsbad Mineral Springs Resort was opened in about 1900, and by 1912 a racetrack was opened nearby, but the state shut it down after only two seasons. Soon the Michigan Southern Railroad began bringing tourists from Chicago. Mineral Springs Road and the Spa Restaurant (now closed) are reminders of this once vibrant industry.

Other mineral springs were located in Porter County. One, with high iron content and some sulfur, was located between McCool and Crisman in Portage Township. It was believed by some to have "valuable medicinal qualities." Another, located in Pine Township, became for a few years the site of a sanitarium.

Dream Cities of the Calumet Area

The mid-1830s was an exciting time throughout the frontier. Beginning in 1832, when the Potawatomi Indians ceded their lands to the federal government, the Calumet Area was opened to wild

---

8. Cook and Jackson (1978) speculated that the well was dug by the Chicago Hydraulic Press Brick Company in the hopes of finding natural gas.

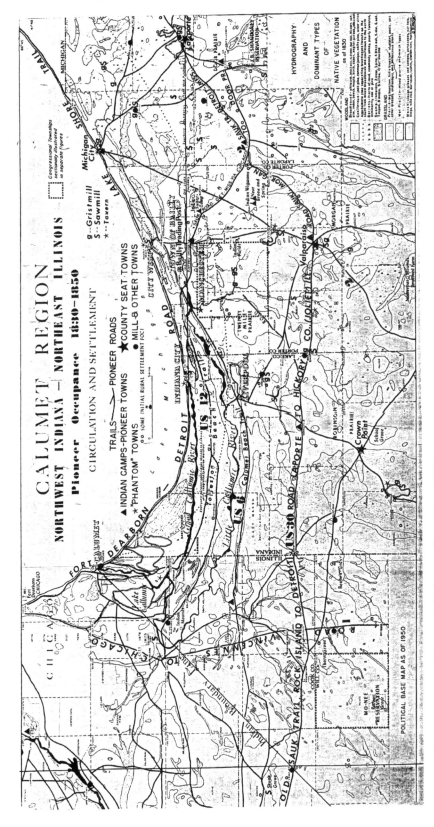

Map 9. Calumet Region Circulation and Settlement. From Meyer, 1956.

speculation and considerable settlement. Several great cities were planned for the southern Lake Michigan Shoreline. Historian John O. Bowers called these the "dream cities of the Calumet."

Each of these cities was on a land transportation route or was planned to have a port on Lake Michigan. Some were planned to rival the industrial might of cities on the East Coast or in England. (Three of them even were given names of English cities.)

The port cities were all on Lake Michigan at the mouths of rivers or streams. They were Calumet at the Calumet River, Indiana City at the Grand Calumet River, City West at Fort (Dunes) Creek, and Michigan City at Trail Creek. The others were Liverpool on Deep River, Bailly and Waverly on the Little Calumet River, New City West and Manchester on the Chicago–Detroit road, and (several years later) Sheffield east of Wolf Lake.

The economic panic of 1837 put an end to most of these dream cities. Of the lot, only Michigan City grew and flourished.

The "stagecoach and early pioneer period" came to an end with the arrival of the railroads. However, a few of the inns continued to operate for many years. Brown's Inn at South Chicago Heights was able to survive because it was near a railroad station. The Eleven Mile House in Roseland was moved twice and, being on busy State Street, remained open until the Dan Ryan Expressway was built. A few inns, such as the Brass Tavern in Munster (by then called the Stallbohm Inn), were eventually converted into private residences.

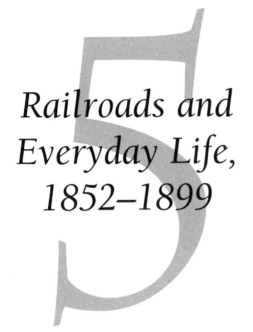

Railroads and Everyday Life, 1852–1899

The Coming of the Railroads

Much effort was spent in the 1830s and 1840s to improve methods of transportation in the new states of Indiana and Illinois. The Vincennes and Michigan Roads connected the Calumet Area to parts south. County governments designed and built primitive roads. However, the ideal transportation improvements were canals, a very old technology, and railroads, a very new one.

Illinois congressman Daniel Cook actively promoted the building of the Illinois and Michigan Canal in order to connect the Great Lakes at Chicago with the Illinois and Mississippi Rivers. Congress approved funds for the Illinois and Michigan Canal in 1827, and after much work it was completed in 1848. By connecting the new city of Chicago to the Mississippi River and thus to New Orleans, this canal made Chicago, rather than its rival, Michigan City, the great city on the lake. Chicago's population expanded by 600 percent in the ten years following the completion of the canal. Ironically, the first railroad shipment of cargo arrived in Chicago in 1848, the same year that the canal was completed. And although that railroad line was just a few miles long, it would soon be joined by scores of others coming from all parts of the country, making Chicago the rail capital of the Midwest.

Figure 39. Grand Trunk locomotive at the Oak Glen Station. Lansing Historical Society.

The first railroad in the Calumet Area was probably the Buffalo & Mississippi Railroad. The Indiana General Assembly granted a charter to this company in 1835, which was to run from Elkhart and South Bend through LaPorte and Michigan City, then follow the ancient Calumet Shoreline in Porter County past Baillytown, crossing the Little Calumet River near the Long Pole Bridge. This mysterious railroad is mentioned in government records in the 1850s, and it was shown on a Porter County map made in 1855, but it is not shown on any maps after 1875. Historian Powell Moore believed that it was never built. Researchers Sarah Cook and Robert Jackson proposed that it may have used wooden rails that have since decayed and that its trains were drawn by horses or mules. Morgan's side track, which stretched from Furnessville to Lake Michigan, was also an animal-powered railroad.

Beginning in the late 1840s, several eastern railroad companies decided to expand their lines in order to connect Chicago to eastern cities. To do so required them to cross the Calumet Area. These new lines were welcomed by local farmers and industrial leaders because they could easily bring in needed materials while serving as a conduit for getting produce and products to markets. City planners foresaw business and real estate booms.

Unlike the early Indian trails and stagecoach routes that followed the ancient shorelines of Lake Michigan, the railroad lines followed the maxim that "the shortest distance between two points is a straight line." Thus the new routes cut across the rivers and ridges of the Calumet Area. Bridges were built across the rivers and streams, trenches were cut through the high sand ridges, and elevated lines were built through the low-lying areas. The railroads became the first major change agents of the landscape.

THE FIRST "AIR LINES" THROUGH THE AREA WERE RAILROADS

In the 1860s, before human flight, the term air line *was used to describe a railroad with the shortest route between two points. The Cincinnati & Chicago Air Line Railroad was the name of the first railway (in 1865) to pass through Crown Point, Munster, and Lansing. In 1881 the Monon Railroad (then the Louisville, New Albany & Chicago Railway) merged with the Chicago & Indianapolis Air Line Railway (which at that time did not extend to either Chicago or Indianapolis). The Monon then extended that line into Chicago, passing through Munster and Hammond. These two "air lines" crossed near Maynard, in what is now west Munster. In the years since, both rail lines have undergone mergers and have changed their names. However the intersection where they cross is, 125 years later, still known as Air Line Junction.*

But in spite of all impediments, the great work went forward. Embankments were built, forests were cleared, hills were leveled, ravines were filled, rivers and streams were bridged, cross ties and rail were brought

up, and the toiling, sweating men had the satisfaction of seeing mile upon mile of railroad take form and put in readiness for the iron horse.

—Carlton J. Corliss, 1950

Although most of the early lines into Chicago came from the east, the first line into the city was the short Galena & Chicago line in 1848. And although much of the work was done by private enterprise, the federal government subsidized many lines through large land grants.

Four years after the Potawatomi gave up the last of their Calumet Area holdings, Illinois legislator Stephen A. Douglas proposed a central railroad for Illinois. When he ran for the Senate in 1846, he advocated an outright land grant for this rail line. Although elected, he couldn't muster enough support for the bill until agreements were made to extend the line into the southern states. It passed in 1850, making the Illinois Central the first land grant railroad in the country.

Figure 41. South Shore Railroad cut at Wilson's Siding, now Midwest Steel, ca. 1908. Ed Hedstrom collection.

In 1852, the first two railroads across northwest Indiana raced with the Illinois Central to be the first major line into Chicago. They were the Michigan Central from Detroit and the Michigan Southern from Toledo. The Michigan Southern reached Chicago first, on February 20th. The Michigan Central, using Illinois Central rails, entered the city three months later. The rivalry between the two lines ended in 1930 as they both became part of the New York Central system.

82   THE HUMAN TOUCH

Figure 42. Horse and manual labor used for excavating sand for the South Shore Railroad, ca. 1908. Ed Hedstrom collection.

The railroads had a profound effect in the Calumet Area. The first major sand mining of the dunes near Lake Michigan was to provide material for railroad embankments. Until the railroad lines went through, lumber was expensive and hard to get. Many folks still lived in log cabins. (It took two years, 1845–47, to build the Presbyterian Church in Crown Point because lumber had to be brought in by oxcart.) Just as milk, corn, wheat, and other crops could be sent out by rail, lumber was brought in and frame houses began replacing log cabins all across the area. Frugal farmers and townspeople dragged their old log homes to the back of lots and

Figure 43. Using dune sand to build an elevated line for the South Shore Railroad, ca. 1908. Ed Hedstrom collection.

Figure 44. The Dyer grain elevator. Dyer Historical Society Museum.

farms where they became stables, granaries, or cribs. The new frame houses soon had carpets, fine furniture, and even pianos.

To entice customers, railroads built nice (sometimes grand) freight and passenger stations. In addition, they erected grain elevators, hotels, parks, and even roads and bridges so that passengers could get to the stations.

The railroads also brought people into the Calumet Area. Several lines recruited laborers in Europe, and many of the workers, finding new jobs available in the area, decided to make their homes near the lines. Calumet (later Chesterton) became the center of an Irish settlement while Porter, Hobart, and Miller saw an influx of Swedes. Both groups found their way to South Chicago. Hundreds of German workers in Chicago settled in Indiana railroad towns such as Whiting, Hammond, Tolleston, Hessville, Schererville, and Chesterton.

By 1874, so many railroad lines had been built across the Calumet Area that geologist G. M. Levette said that "almost every acre is within easy distance of some depot where all the products of the soil, forest, or factory may be disposed of, for cash, at ruling market prices."

Between 1906 and 1908, just as U.S. Steel and the city of Gary were being developed at the southern tip of Lake Michigan, the Chicago, Lake Shore & South Bend Railway constructed an electric rail line across Cook, Lake, Porter, and LaPorte Counties. This road, which partially followed the ancient Tolleston and Calumet Shore-

Figure 45. The EJ&E. Southeast Historical Society.

**Michigan Southern & Northern
Indiana (later Lake Shore & Michigan
Southern)**   1852

Through LaPorte, Porter, Miller, and along the lakeshore to Ainsworth (South Chicago) and Chicago.

Michigan Central   1852

Through Michigan City, Lake Station, Tolleston, and Calumet Station (Kensington) to Chicago.

Illinois Central (IC)   1852

Through Thornton Station (Homewood) and Calumet Station (Kensington) to Chicago.

Chicago, Rock Island & Pacific   1852

From the southwest through Joliet and Blue Island to Chicago.

**Louisville, New Albany & Chicago
(Monon)**   1853/1882

From Louisville through Monon to Michigan City. In 1882, another line ran from Monon through Lowell and Hegewisch to Chicago.

**Joliet & Northern Indiana (Joliet Cut-
off) (part of the Michigan Central)**   1853–54

From Lake Station through Dyer and Bloom (Chicago Heights) to Joliet.

**Pittsburgh, Fort Wayne & Chicago
(Pennsylvania)**   1858

Through Valparaiso, Tolleston, and along the lakeshore to Ainsworth (South Chicago) and Chicago.

**Cincinnati & Chicago Air Line/
Chicago & Great Eastern
(Panhandle)**   1865

(later Pittsburgh, Cincinnati & St. Louis/Pennsylvania) Through Kouts, Crown Point, and Riverdale to Chicago.

**Chicago, Hammond & Western/
Indiana Harbor Belt**   1869

From Whiting, through Hammond (by the packing plant) to DuPage County, Illinois.

**Chicago & Eastern Illinois (C&EI,
earlier the Chicago, Danville &
Vincennes)**   1871

Through Crete, Bloom (Chicago Heights), and Riverdale/Dolton to Chicago.

**Baltimore, Pittsburgh & Chicago
(Baltimore & Ohio,/B&O)**   1874

Through McCool, Miller's Station, and along the lakeshore to Ainsworth (South Chicago) and Chicago.

Chicago & Grand Trunk   1880

Through Valparaiso, Maynard, South Lawn (Harvey), and Blue Island to Chicago. The first line to pick up milk every morning at stations.

**New York, Chicago & St. Louis
(Nickel Plate)[1]**   1882

Through Knox, Valparaiso, Hobart, Glen Park, Hessville, Hammond, and Hegewisch to Chicago.

**Chicago & Atlantic (Chicago & Erie/
Erie/Erie Lackawanna)**   1883

Through Kouts, Crown Point, Griffith, Highlands, Hammond, and Hegewisch to Chicago.

Elgin, Joliet & Eastern (EJ&E)   1888

A belt line circling Chicago and crossing every rail line going into the city. Also from Griffith to Chicago.

Wabash   1892

Through Westville, Willow Creek, Aetna, and Hammond to Chicago.

**East Chicago Belt /Hammond & Blue
Island (Indiana Harbor Belt)**   1896

After consolidation with other belt lines, from Indiana Harbor to Franklin Park and Chicago.

**Pere Marquette (Chesapeake and
Ohio)**   1903

From Michigan through Michigan City to Porter.

**Chicago, Cincinnati & Louisville
(Chesapeake and Ohio)**   1906

Through LaCrosse, Merrillville, and Hammond to Chicago.

**Chicago, Indiana and Southern (later
the New York Central)**   1906

From Indiana Harbor, through Gibson, Highlands, and Schneider to Danville, Illinois.

**Southern Indiana (Chicago, Terre
Haute & Southeastern/later the
"Milwaukee Road"),**   1907

Terre Haute to Chicago Heights.

**Chicago, Lake [South] Shore, and
South Bend (the South Shore)**   1908

An electric line from Chicago through Kensington, and the lakeshore communities to South Bend.

---

1. The name Nickel Plate evidently came from a statement by Cornelius Vanderbilt when he and owner Calvin Brice were negotiating the sale of the rail line. Responding to Brice's initial price for this railroad, he said, "Why, Brice, I wouldn't give that for your old road if it were nickel plated." Vanderbilt ended up paying the requested amount, and the term stuck.

Map 10. Major Calumet Area rail lines in 1910.

lines, made the dunes and lakeshore areas easily accessible. Residents of Chicago, Hammond, East Chicago, and Gary could now easily take a morning train to the Tremont station in the dunes and be back home in time for dinner. Although it has carried both freight and passengers, its passenger service has made this railroad, now known as the South Shore Line, the defining railroad of the Calumet Area.

By the early twentieth century, both Cook County and Lake County had more miles of railroad track than any other county in their respective states. The railroads changed forever the character of the Calumet Area. They accelerated growth and development of areas near their freight and passenger stations. They not only moved vast quantities of sand and glacial till in order to build their lines, but also hauled astronomical quantities of sand from lakeshore areas to Chicago and other communities in need of "cheap" fill.

Many Calumet Area communities owe their beginnings to the nearby stations on local railroads. Some even owe their names to the rail companies. For a while, Porter Station was the only rail station in Porter County and Lake Station was the only station in Lake County. Markham was named for a president of the Illinois Central Railroad. Whiting was named for a conductor on the Michigan Southern road. Griffith was named for Benjamin Griffith, an employee of the Grand Trunk. And Miller (originally Miller's Station) was likely named for a construction engineer on the Michigan Southern Railroad who lived near the station.

Railroads were used to promote various locations in the

Calumet Area. In the 1890s, both Harvey and Chicago Heights arranged excursions on the Illinois Central to bring potential landowners to their areas. And at least two railroad companies promoted the scenery of northwest Indiana to their Chicago customers in order to increase ridership. The first was the Lake Shore & Michigan Southern, which in an 1884 brochure touted its fourteen daily trains between Chicago and the "new summer resort" of LaPorte, Indiana, just "one and three-quarter hours ride from that city." The other was the South Shore Line, which placed great emphasis on advertising and public relations. In the 1920s, the South Shore Line ran an extensive poster advertising campaign extolling the attractions of northwestern Indiana, both industrial and natural. The Indiana Dunes recreation area was featured in twenty-three of the thirty-eight known posters made for this campaign. These posters were the subjects of a 1998 book, *Moonlight in Duneland,* edited by Ronald Cohen and Stephen McShane.

Figure 46. South Shore advertising poster: *Visit the Dunes Beaches by South Shore Line,* a 1926 lithograph by Otto Brennemann. Calumet Regional Archives.

The South Shore Line used some innovative means to create a market for its commuter trains. It developed recreation spots for Chicagoans as well as residential areas for Hoosiers near its stations. The railroad actively promoted and supported the creation of Indiana Dunes State Park, donated acreage for the park, loaned $200,000 for additional land purchase, and gave $25,000 toward

Figure 47. Nickel Plate Railroad Station in Hammond. Drawing by R. Ramsey Smith. Courtesy of the artist.

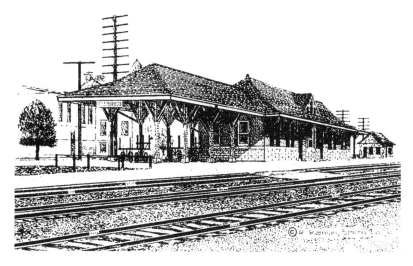

DEVELOPMENT AND THE CHANGING LANDSCAPE

AN 1884 PROGRESS REPORT BY TIMOTHY BALL

From Highland, a grand sand ridge extends westward to Lansing, and eastward for some miles toward Hobart. A road runs, a little north of the crest of this ridge.

There are three cuts now through this ridge,
- *one at Highlands made for the Chicago & Atlantic [Erie Lackawanna] Railroad;*
- *one a mile westward, where some thirty years ago a narrow ditch [Hart Ditch] was dug to let the water in the lowlands on the south pass through to the Calumet. The ditch has been so worn by the running water that the torrent of water that rushes through in springtime is now about 70 feet below the crest of the ridge. The opening at the top is now 125 feet wide;*
- *the third is near the State line, made for the [Monon] Railroad.*

Along this ridge was once an old stage road from old Liverpool westward.

the cost of building its resort hotel and bathhouse. In its attempts to become *the* commuter line for Calumet Area residents, the South Shore Line promoted the development of the Beverly Shores community. Indiana Dunes residents or visitors could easily catch the train at one of the South Shore Line's stations.

The distinctive architecture of the typical railroad station with its pitched roof and broad overhang seems to have endeared itself so much to Calumet Area citizens that many stations have been spared from the wrecking ball. In Griffith, the station has been turned into a museum and the three-story brick EJ&E tower was moved across the tracks so that it could also be saved. East Chicago turned its station into an office for its mayor. In the late 1990s, modern stations were still being built in that old-fashioned style (e.g., the new South Shore station in Hammond).

Eyewitnesses to History, 1850–1899

BERRY PICKING

Figure 48. Henry Schrage. Mike and Jill Schrage.

There were lots of berries, and we started the season with strawberries, then gathered raspberries and cranberries. We would take luncheon and a bag for the berries and be out all day. We went through the woods as far as Tolleston. We sold the berries at Ainsworth Station [South Chicago] or peddled them in Chicago, and got from ten to fifteen cents a quart for them. The railroad fare from Ainsworth to Chicago was fifty cents, and for that reason we generally walked.

—HENRY SCHRAGE, 1921, WHITING

CLEARING THE LAND

Trees had to be cleared to provide more farmland, and the trees served as a source of fuel. A typical winter day [about 1890] found Sam, Corneal, and myself grubbing trees and cutting and splitting wood. We would get up at or before sun-up and do the usual chores of milking and feeding the horses and cattle. After breakfast of bread and cheese, sometimes bacon, and always buttermilk, the three of us headed for the trees.

We had to dig to expose the tree roots first, and chop the roots off eighteen inches below ground level so that the plow wouldn't hit the roots when the land was developed for farming. Almost all the trees were oak. The black oak wasn't too bad, but the white oak had a tap root that went straight down and was hard to reach with an axe. . . . About 4:00 in the afternoon, we would start for home so we could get the evening chores done before dark.

Summertime was quite different! Between twelve and sixteen years of age, watching cows was the principal job. After milking in the morning, I would drive the cows east on Ridge Road about a mile or so, then head northeast, cross under the Nickel Plate Railroad through a large wooden culvert, and then down toward the river. We would go east about as far as Broadway is now. We had forty to fifty head of cattle and were usually joined by thirty-five head of Simon Koedyker and about twelve owned by Ben Johnson. We took our lunch but had to find our own drinking water. Such leisurely work was all too soon passed on to the younger boys in favor of learning the use of a hoe.

—Jacob J. Schoon Sr., 1966, Ridge Road,
west of Gary (Glen Park)

Figure 49. Jacob J. Schoon Sr.

FISHING ON LAKE MICHIGAN

I first came to Miller in March 1872, to my brother's at the fish house. It was near to where the [Marquette] Park is and close to the lagoon. . . . I was married in 1874 to Robert Carr. . . . We did all of our trading at Clark Station, west of here. Charley Kelley had a general store there. He was an engineer on the Michigan Central, and his wife run the store.

My husband was a fisherman and fished for whitefish and sturgeon. We could trade them for flour, buckwheat, pork, butter and so forth. I always helped do the fishing. When my oldest son was a baby, I took him with me and rolled him up in a blanket and laid him on the beach. As we moved our windlasses closer together, I moved the baby accordingly.

There were lots of white and blue cranes, and hundreds of bald eagles along the beach. When we went along the lake, we could see an eagle on every hill, but we don't see any more. . . . Once I was attacked by one and had a terrible time with it. . . . When I went down to the beach, it tried to get at my baby. The eagle was terribly hungry, and I fought with it for quite a while. My sunbonnet seemed to keep it away from my head and eyes, but I had to fight hard to keep it away; and it might have gotten the baby if it hadn't been for the bonnet. My husband was out in the lake in a boat looking after the nets, and when he heard me call, he came in and used his paddle on the bird and drove it off.

—Drusilla Carr, 1921, Miller Station

Figure 50. Drusilla Carr. Calumet Regional Archives.

CLOTHING

In those days men wore clothes made of buckskin and homespun. I remember going to the home of Benjamin Crisman, about two miles east of our place. In Mr. Crisman's family were several boys with whom I remained overnight. On the following morning after a very cold night, two of the boys who had buckskin breeches found they were frozen to such an extent that they had to take them downstairs to the fire and thaw them out. I wore homespun until I started to go out with girls. The girls in those days wore checked flannel homespun—skirts and petticoats all of the same material.

Wool [was] spun into yarn by Mother on her spinning wheel. It was then taken to a weaver who resided south of the place now called Wheeler and woven into cloth. Mother then cut and made suits and clothes for seven of us. We had no sewing machine, and everything was sewed by hand. Shoes for the family were not purchased at stores, but we had what is called "the neighborhood shoemaker," who went from family to family and took the measurements of the feet . . . and the shoes were made right in the homes.

—Darus Blake, 1929, Portage

SUNDAYS

Sunday began at 6:00 a.m. at our house. . . . The boys dressed and went out to do the chores; the older boys did the milking while the younger ones watered and fed the livestock. It was always my job to carry out the day-old milk after Mother skimmed off the cream to make butter. After the warm fresh milk was strained and set in pans to cool, we ate breakfast.

There was never any variation in our breakfast menu; each one was allowed two slices of bread—one could be eaten with cheese and one with syrup. Father and Mother enjoyed a cup of coffee, and the boys who milked were privileged to have one-half cup, but the rest of us were satisfied with a dipper of water or buttermilk. Three times a day, and seven days a week, Father prayed before and after each meal and read from the Bible.

When the snow was deep, we took the sleigh to the Sunday services at the First Reformed Church in Lansing, and the rest of the year we rode in the spring-board wagon. Neither vehicle could accommodate the entire family; so we were divided and went on alternate Sundays. . . . We stayed in Lansing all day and enjoyed eating dinner with friends or relatives and had lunch again before starting home. We usually arrived home about 5:00 p.m. and immediately began the milking and the other chores. After a simple supper, we just sat around for a while because Father never permitted us to play any games on Sunday. . . . By 8:30 or 9:00 p.m. everyone was in bed except Father. Every night he would smoke a pipe full of tobacco and drink a hot cup of milk before retiring.

—DELIA OOMS, 1966, RIDGE ROAD, WEST OF GARY (GLEN PARK)

Figure 51. Delia Ooms.

CUTTING TIMBER

The fine timber through the district [Hegewisch to Whiting] was a good source of income. We would cut the timber at some point as near as possible to Lake Michigan. We would then drag the logs to the lake and make them up into rafts. These rafts had to be made just right or they would go to pieces and [we would] lose the timber. We would then walk along the shore, towing the raft of logs behind us.

One man in this way could pull a couple of carloads. There were no piers in the way, and we could take them in this way as far [north] as the Calumet River. There was a tug at that place that we could engage to tow our logs to the Chicago market. There was good demand in the city for logs which were suitable for piling. . . .

I remember once [George W.] Clarke[2] had a great sign put up, on which he warned the public that he was the owner of 14,800 acres of land and that his timber rights were to be respected. The settlers were told that they could have all the timber they needed for building a house or barn, but should cut no logs to sell.

—HENRY REESE, 1911, WHITING

SCHOOL DAYS

The first public school [in Lansing] was a one-room structure, built on a half acre plot of land originally owned by my father. It was painted white, typical of the kind to be found on any four corners where population justified a school building. Henry Hildebrandt, a Civil War veteran, John Meyers, and my father were the school directors. Water was carried from our well to the school in open buckets, and a tin dipper was shared by all. I never had a woman teacher. We sang hymns before classes and then studied to "the tune of the hickory stick"

Figure 52. Hartsdale School. Schererville Historical Society.

2. In historical records, George W. Clarke's name is spelled both Clark and Clarke (often on the same page). Except in direct quotations, this book uses the Clarke spelling because it was most prevalently spelled that way in Lake County land transfer books of 1859–1864, the oldest records found (Held at the Calumet Regional Archives). Timothy Ball spelled it both ways. The 1911 *Whiting City Almanac,* the source of this quotation, used the Clarke spelling. John Bowers and Powell Moore spelled it without an e.

the rest of the day. A wood burning stove furnished heat to about forty children who were taught in ungraded classes.

—Mrs. George Pearson, 1954, Lansing

TEACHING SCHOOL IN 1865

Before I was sixteen, I dared to think I was armed [prepared] to teach, because I had an eighteen-months license to show. With the same in my hand, I walked to the little frame building on the east side of Cedar Lake, called the Binyon school.

The furnishing of that small room was very scant. The old box-stove had but three legs of its own, the other a brick caused it to rest on its side many times. Each patron [student] delivered a large load of wood sometime during the winter. The boys cut it into stove-lengths, and the girls would carry it into the schoolhouse.

The plank seats were without backs and so high that only the older pupils could rest their feet on the floor. They were made of hewn logs and held numerous slivers for the unshod feet. We had a small blackboard 3×4 made by the older boys. Our greatest handicap was lack of books to study the lessons. Some parents were too poor to buy the needed textbooks and thought the teacher would manage until times were better.

Our water supply the first years was carried from the outlet of the lake and contained real live specimens of nature. The children would laugh and say, "Oh, throw it out. We'll try again."

I had thirty-six pupils, aged from five years to twenty-three years. My salary was fourteen dollars per month.

How different sixty-three years ago! Now a bus calls at the door; a ride to a beautiful building; a teacher for every subject. I wonder if they are thankful. Who would like to be placed even for one day in such a school of sixty-three years ago?

Times are better. We don't want those old days back.

—Mrs. J. L. Hill, 1929, Cedar Lake

NURSING

Figure 53. Sam B. Woods. Lake County Historical Society Museum.

Mrs. Caroline Muzzall was the important person around our neighborhood when a new baby was expected. When it was time for the baby to come, we children would be told that we could go over to Mrs. Muzzall's and spend the night and she would come to our house and stay all night. When we would go back home the next day, we would find we had a new brother or sister.

If any family was too sick to wait on themselves, the neighbors would take turns sitting up with the sick ones and waiting on them. Several of these neighbors proved themselves to be really good nurses and were much in demand in several serious cases of sickness among us. They were friends indeed to friends in need.

—SAM B. WOODS, 1938, LOTTAVILLE (MERRILLVILLE)

SOCIAL LIFE AT THE STALLBOHM INN

Social life in the community was mostly of the visit-the-neighbor type, but we made a gay time of it. When I was a child, the tavern (today called an inn) was the social hall where infrequent but well-attended dances drew crowds from great distances. I can well remember my mother preparing large meals to be consumed after those dances. A Mr. Wettering, an old friend of the family, used to make the long trip out from Chicago to serve as an orchestra with his large and costly accordion. In later days we young people formed a dancing club which met every two weeks at some member's home. . . . We traveled miles for those dances.

—WILHELMINE STALLBOHM KASKE, 1934, MUNSTER

Figure 54. Wilhelmine Stallbohm Kaske. Munster Historical Society Museum.

FORSYTH HOMESTEAD BURNS

The year of 1871 was a year of drought and the whole country was burning up through lack of rain. . . . The marshes about us began to dry up, and filled as they were with a century's accumulation of vegetable matter, they became quite inflammable. I became very uneasy, especially as our house could not be protected against a fire in the woods and marshes. It was the house my father [Jacob Forsyth] had bought from Dominick Mutter, and its surroundings greatly endangered it. I urged my mother to bury our books, for our library contained about a thousand volumes—and this we did finally, wrapping them in sheets and covering them with sand. We buried some other valuables likewise. Meanwhile, the fires grew more frequent in the woods about us, although when my father returned from New York, he insisted that the danger was not serious. He had the books dug up and placed on the library shelves. Hardly was this done before the conflagration came. The fire swept up to our homestead so quickly that we had no time to save anything of value.

We all got into a big wagon and drove into a swamp, where we dug holes in the moist earth for greater protection and remained there until we felt we had a safe road out. . . . When the west-bound train stopped at the [Berry Lake] station, we learned of a greater calamity than ours—that fire had stricken Chicago also. . . .

After the Chicago Fire, there was an unusual call for wood from the farmers to the west and south. We sold as high as $3,000 worth of wood for fuel in a single month. The price was $1.00 per load.

—OLIVER O. FORSYTH, 1911, CASSELLA (INDIANA HARBOR)

THE DAY THE K. D. MARSH BURNED

Figure 55. Harry Eenigenburg. Courtesy of Helen Eenigenburg.

In 1871, it was the driest year on record. On Monday, October 9, 1871, the Chicago Fire started and burned a large part of Chicago down, but on Sunday, October 8, the K. D. Marsh was set on fire at the south end with the south wind fanning the flames over that marsh for the first time in history, as the marsh had just been drained the year before. . . . The two large hay dealers, Mr. Schultz and Mr. Baker, had just finished haying and had about fifty stacks of hay, which all went down with the flames.

The many herds of cattle were driven out to safety ahead of the flames. The farmers along the ridge road were plowing fire breaks all day Sunday and Monday and almost choked to death from the dense smoke that was rushing toward them, but they saved their homes. All the wild animals that were living in the marsh, such as wolves, foxes, woodchucks, and others, rushed across the ridge to the Little Calumet for safety. The fire burned in the marsh at least ten days, and the peat beds burned all winter until the spring rains. . . . The hay dealers lost all the summer's work of a hundred men and had no insurance.

—Harry Eenigenburg, 1935, Lansing

HOLIDAYS

There were only two holidays that were observed in our family: Christmas and the Fourth of July. As Easter was always on Sunday, that day was observed as we always observed Sundays.

On the Fourth of July, we always had a lot of firecrackers, large and small, and we were busy all day long exploding them. There were never any baseball games or picnics. On a couple of Fourth of July days, we had to work one-half pulling weeds out of the onions.

On Christmas we would go rabbit hunting—all through the woods and behind the house. All game was dressed and hung out to freeze, and we always enjoyed eating this meat. Our Christmas gifts consisted of an orange and some nuts. Mother always knitted a pair of mittens for all of us.

But let me tell you about one of my experiences on the Fourth of July [in 1899]. I was about eighteen years old, and the young folks around here were going to Chicago to visit Lincoln Park. I had heard about this park and was anxious to go. I asked a girl-friend if I could take her, and she said yes. So then I asked my father if I could get off work pulling weeds and go to this famous Lincoln Park. He said yes. . . . My father asked me if I had any money. I told him a little, so he reached into his wallet and gave me $3.50. We took the train from Highland, fifty cents round-trip for each of us, and then took the street car from the Loop to the

Figure 56. Dick J. Schoon.

Park and that cost 5¢ each. I recall that we ate dinner for 25¢. On arriving home, I still had money in my pocket.

—DICK J. SCHOON, 1966, RIDGE ROAD, WEST OF GARY (GLEN PARK)

Octave Chanute and Human Flight in the Dunes

By 1863, Octave Chanute (1832–1910) was the chief engineer of the Chicago & Alton Railroad. Respected in the rail business, he had designed many of the western rail lines, the first bridge across the Missouri River in 1869, and even the Chicago Stockyards. An aviation enthusiast, he was well read, and in 1894 he published a popular collection of articles entitled *Progress in Flying Machines*. His library in Chicago had one of the world's largest collections of aeronautics writings.

Figure 57. Octave Chanute's experiments with flight at the Indiana Dunes. Indiana Dunes National Lakeshore historical collection.

Chanute is best known for his experiments with gliders that took place at Miller Beach from June 22 to July 4, 1896. The dune area was suitable for him because it was near Chicago. The high lakeshore dunes provided a convenient "launching pad," and the sand allowed for somewhat soft landings. Unfortunately, the seventy-foot dunes that he used have since been removed. During his time at Miller, Chanute and Augustus Herring would launch his gliders, observe their stability, alter the wings and tail, and try again. He experimented with a multiwinged glider at Miller Beach which provided enough success that on his return to Chicago he redesigned it and returned to the dunes for more experiments six weeks later. Although Miller Beach was somewhat isolated, the curious did manage to find Chanute there. To avoid publicity, he conducted the second group of experiments at Dune Park east of today's Ogden Dunes. When Chanute completed his experiments in August, he and his group had made several hundred flights up to 350 feet in length.

Chanute advised the Wright Brothers during their years of flight experiments at Kitty Hawk. He was there just weeks before their first flight on December 17, 1903. The Wrights' success came when they added a motor and propellers to their version of the biplane design that Chanute and Herring had developed seven years earlier at the Indiana Dunes.

Figure 58. Octave Chanute. Indiana Dunes National Lakeshore historical collection.

Altering the Landscape

M ost parts of the Calumet Area look very different today than they did before settlement. The American Indians, French explorers, and the first travelers through the Calumet Area were fairly well bound by the characteristics of physical geography. Prehistoric Indians did construct some burial mounds, but human alteration of the region was minimal. By the 1850s, however, the landscape was changing as settlers and government agents—aided first by oxen and horses and later by diesel-fueled equipment—drained marshes, filled in wet lands, dammed rivers, lowered the tops of hills and dunes, and mined the earth for limestone, sand, and clay. While hardly offsetting the enormous quantities of sand removed from the Calumet Area, tons of black dirt were imported to provide the soils for new lawns in the new cities.

Railroad companies altered the shape of the Calumet Area as they built their lines and made it easier to ship out sand and timber. While much of this exporting was legal and a great deal was required for the industrialization and commercialization of the region, much illegal mining and lumbering occurred as well.

There have always been opposing viewpoints regarding the massive changes made to the landscape. For instance, in 1906 U.S. Steel made massive alterations to the Lake Michigan shoreline and the Grand Calumet River. Historian Powell Moore (1959, p. 275) described this as "an achievement of epic proportions." However, Bradley J. Beckham, referring to the same alterations, noted that "what took nature thousands of years to mold, man in the guise of progress subverted in a few months" (Lane, 1978, p. 28).

Logging

The first large-scale alteration made to the land was the removal of its trees. It is hard to believe now that large sections of Hammond were once forested or that Hobart, Whiting, and Michigan City were once important centers of the timber trade.

When first seen by both Indian and settler, many of the moraines and sand ridges were heavily forested. As early as 1847, Solon Robinson noted that the sand ridges in the northern part of Lake County originally were covered with "a valuable growth of pine and cedar, which has been nearly all stript off to build up Chicago." LaPorte County historian Jasper Packard wrote in 1876 that "the whole north side of the county is well timbered." He added, "Formerly the region bordering the lake was well covered with beautiful white pine; but this valuable tree has almost wholly disappeared, being cut off for lumber." The demand for lumber was high, as it was needed by local settlers, the railroads, as well as the developers of the new city of Chicago.

Figure 59. A wagonload of timber arrives by sled in Hebron. John Spinks collection.

Historians Timothy Ball, G. A. Garard, and Powell Moore all reported that timber thieves cut and removed a huge number of trees in Lake and Porter Counties. The demand for lumber was especially high after the Chicago Fire of 1871. The fact that large fires occurred in Indiana as well during that very dry year made timber even more necessary.

Moving and Removing Sand and Clay

SAND MINING

Quite early after settlement began, farmers who purchased land along the Calumet Shoreline (Ridge Road), in what was to become Munster and Highland, scraped sand from the tops of the ridge before building their houses there. The sand was then used to fill in nearby marshlands. In the same vicinity, when the Erie and the Monon railroads built their lines through these two towns, they first had to cut

Figure 60. Loading
dune sand into
waiting railroad cars.
Calumet Regional
Archives.

through the huge sand ridge. This sand was then used to raise the
railroad bed in the low wetlands both north and south of the ridge.

Although much of the Indiana dune sand was lost by a large
number of small alterations, wholesale sand mining resulted in the
greatest alteration of the landscape. After the Chicago Fire, as the city
began rebuilding its homes, department stores, and warehouses, it
was decided to expand the lakefront by building eastward into the
lake. To do so required vast amounts of material to dump into Lake
Michigan. Much of the fill obtained was Indiana lakeshore sand.

In the 1890s, the mining and exporting of sand was the principal
business at the railroad stations at Tolleston, Miller, and Dune Park.

Figure 61. The
Hoosier Slide, once
the Calumet Area's
tallest sand dune.
LaPorte County
Historical Society
Museum.

Figure 62. Leveling sand dunes to build Gary Works, 1906. Calumet Regional Archives.

Powell Moore noted that an estimated 50,000 railroad cars full were shipped out from Tolleston in 1897 alone. Two years later, the Sante Fe Railroad is said to have placed an order for 150,000 cars of sand to be obtained from Miller. In 1928, George Cressey reported that near Dunes State Park there was nearly a square mile of land from which the dunes had been removed and sent to Chicago. Large quantities of sand were also removed from the lake bottom by sand dredges. (No one owned the sandy near-shore lake bottom, so mining companies did not have to pay anyone for the sand.)

Illinois geologist J Harlen Bretz noted that whenever Chicago needed sand for fill, it got it from the "inexhaustible supplies heaped up in the dunes along the nearby Indiana lakeshore." As late as 1952, the Indiana Geological Survey reported that 5,000 tons of sand were still being removed daily from the Calumet Area. The report noted that large tracts "once comprising some of the most spectacular and picturesque dunes already have been cleared of sand." According to the authors, this was good: "After the sands have been removed, the property may be prepared for subdividing." They added, "Because of the many problems of building on sand dunes, the average house-holder probably will be better satisfied to live on the more level ground of the worked-out sand area." The report concluded that few large reserves of sand were still available to the sand industry, but that if the present conditions and demand continued, perhaps 50 to 100 years of sand operations were still possible.

The Hoosier Slide was once said to be Indiana's largest sand dune. It used to be at Michigan City where Trail Creek entered Lake

Michigan. This enormous dune (the name referred to its occasional avalanches of sand) was nearly 200 feet high. In 1900, Ball noted that "immense quantities" of sand had already been removed and taken by carloads to Chicago, but that it was "a huge mass yet."

Sand was also carted off to make glass at several Central Indiana factories. Some went to beautify sandless resort lakes, and some went to build up railroad rights of way. By 1920, it was all gone. The NIP-SCO power station now sits on the site of what was said to be the greatest sand dune in the country.

In Gary, the building of U.S. Steel's Gary Works (1906–1909) required vast amounts of sand to be moved (according to W. P. Gleason, 11 million cubic yards). Some of this was accomplished by leveling existing sand dunes. But as more sand was needed, it was pumped inland from the bed of Lake Michigan through huge suction pipes.

Downtown Gary's Broadway today is nearly flat (with a slight slope upward as one goes south). But before the city was developed, it contained a series of ridges and swales. One of the largest was a mile-long, seventy-five-foot wide, and six-foot deep swale at Sixth and Broadway. Henrietta Gibson described fishing for pickerel and black bass in that same swale—back in the 1880s.

With few exceptions, this dune and swale topography was smoothed off before city streets were constructed and lots sold. One exception was the swale (lagoon) in front of Gary's Horace Mann School, which was reshaped as a reflecting pool. Classes in the 1930s helped plant wetland plants along its edge. The lagoon, complete with swans, graced the school from 1926 until about 1959.

CLAY PITS, BORROW PITS, AND BRICKYARDS

There is an abundance of clay in the moraines and lake bottomlands of the Calumet Area. Many communities discovered this clay early on, and soon small clay pits and brickyards were established. Large brickyards were located in Blue Island, Pullman, Riverdale/Dolton, Lansing, Munster, Hobart, and Porter, most located alongside railroad lines so that they could ship brick to distant cities. By 1920, many of the brick factories had closed. In 1982, the American Brick Company in Riverdale, the last yard still operating in the Calumet Area, closed.

Although all of these brick plants are now closed, many of their clay pits remain. Several of them are now small lakes (such as those in Hobart, Lansing, and Munster), some have become landfills, and a few, such as at Yost School in Porter, are simply low-lying areas.

The Calumet Area has several borrow pits that were excavated to provide material for raising the level of the ground for major highways or for residential areas. Some of these pits have become landfills. Others have filled with water, forming small lakes that still dot the Calumet Area landscape. They can often be seen as one drives along local expressways. Some have become the focus of parks and campgrounds (such as Wampum Lake near Thornton and Minnehaha at Jellystone Park in Portage). Thorn Lake in South Holland was excavated in the 1960s by developer Marvin Jacobs to provide fill for the Elizabeth Seton Academy as well as for the residential area surrounding the lake.

Some things come full circle. Beginning about 1873, sand from what is now Gary was taken to Chicago for fill along the lakeshore (making Lincoln and Grant Parks). Then, beginning about 1907,

Figure 64. Using steam, horses, and manual labor to mine clay near a Calumet Area brickyard. Roger Wiers collection.

black dirt was shipped from the Munster brickyards (where it had covered the clay needed for bricks) to Gary, where it was used to create residential lawns. Finally, in the 1990s, clay was shipped from Chicago to Munster. It was removed when an underground parking lot was constructed at the Museum of Science and Industry. In Munster, it was used as cover for a sanitary landfill—at the same brickyard site where the soil had been removed eighty years earlier.

DESIGNED RESIDENTIAL LANDSCAPES

In one sense, nearly every Calumet Area residential neighborhood sits on a designed residential landscape. For about 100 years, most neighborhoods were small and were built only after the original uneven ground was leveled off and wetlands were eliminated. Since the 1960s, however, the scale of redesigning landscapes greatly increased. Instead of flattening the land and eliminating surface water, several of the larger developments have retained natural slopes and have incorporated water into their designs—even when no water existed there before. Many of these new "waterscapes" are located on the naturally undulating lands of the Valparaiso Moraine.

Lakes of the Four Seasons, which straddles the boundary of Lake and Porter Counties, was the first of the large-scale landscaped residential developments. Work on this project began in 1966.

Figure 65. Lake Holiday at the Lakes of the Four Seasons.

Eighteen hundred acres of farmland were reshaped to produce lakes and gently sloping grounds that were meant to appear natural and asymmetrical. The low areas were made lower, and dams were built to create a series of four lakes. This produced 288 acres of waterscape with twelve miles of shoreline.

Other large-scale residential water and landscape redevelopments have included Shorewood Forest and Aberdeen near Valparaiso and Pine Island Ridge in Schererville. In addition to the large developments, there are many smaller communities both in Indiana and Illinois built around quarry lakes or other artificial waterways.

Canals, Dams, Ditches, and Levees

Geologist Mark Reshkin noted in 1987 that alterations in the way water runs off the land have been the most dynamic of all the changes made to the Calumet Area environment. The draining of wetlands, the straightening and relocation of riverbeds, and the construction of canals have allowed for the transformation of a wild paradise or a seemingly uninhabitable wasteland (depending on one's views) into a major metropolitan area. Much of the Grand Calumet River, the Little Calumet River, and the Kankakee River now flow through straightened man-made channels.

Because the Calumet Area is on the Eastern Continental Divide, early explorers had to cross dry land in order to get from the St. Lawrence (Lake Michigan) River system to the Mississippi (Kankakee) River system. Three nearby canals, all in Illinois, have been excavated across this divide. The first was the Illinois and Michigan Canal, completed in 1848, which gave Chicago primacy on Lake Michigan. The largest is the Chicago Sanitary and Ship Canal, which reversed the flow of the Chicago River when completed in 1900 and thus prevented Chicago's sewage from emptying into Lake Michigan. The third is the Calumet Sag Channel, completed in 1922, which sends waters from the Little Calumet River westward to the Illinois River.[1] Thus both the Chicago River and part of the Little Calumet River now flow away from Lake Michigan rather than into it. These channels all follow the valley of the old Chicago Outlet, which was the natural exit of Lake Michigan waters during its Glenwood, Calumet, and early Tolleston phases.

In northwestern Indiana, there was a lot of talk but not much canal building. The primary transportation canal dredged was the 3.5-mile Indiana Harbor Ship Canal, which in 1888 connected the Grand Calumet River to Lake Michigan. In 1903, a canal was proposed to connect Lake Michigan at Michigan City to the Wabash River. Five years later, Congress considered building a canal to connect Lake Erie with the southern end of Lake Michigan. Supporters noted that such a canal would shorten the waterway from Toledo to Chicago by over 400 miles. However, neither was built.

Water-powered sawmills and gristmills require quickly moving water to turn their water wheels. Many of the mills were located along streams within the Valparaiso and Tinley/Lake Border Moraines because the ground there was steeper and the water moved faster than on the flatter lands closer to Lake Michigan. Unfortunately for the early millwrights, the water in these streams still moved too slowly to effectively power a mill. So, to increase the speed of the current, many of the early millwrights built dams across streams and rivers. Water flowing over the dams would then move quickly enough to power the mill and allow the millwright to make a small profit while fulfilling a community need. The dams also created mill ponds, some of which have become permanent features of the Calumet Area landscape.

1. According to geographer Alfred Meyer (1945), the name Sag comes from the Indian word *Saganashkee*.

Figure 66. Sagers Lake near Valparaiso, one of the Calumet Area's few remaining mill ponds. Historical Society of Porter County Old Jail Museum.

Sagers Lake south of Valparaiso was created in 1835 when a dam was built across a tributary of Salt Creek. Sager's mill closed in 1925, but the lake found another use. Lake Dalecarlia was created in 1853 when a Mr. Carsten dammed Cedar Creek. The dam was rebuilt in 1927 to create a summer resort. Both lakes are now year-round residential communities. The best-known mill pond in the Calumet Area is undoubtedly Lake George in Hobart, created in 1845–46 by Hobart's founder, George Earle.

Attempts to tame the rivers were not always supported by the new citizens of the Calumet Area. In some cases, what benefited one person would hinder another. About 1848, the Little Calumet River was dammed in the Blue Island area. This action raised its level by ten feet, provided water for the new Illinois and Michigan Canal, made it navigable by small vessels, and provided power to the Roll grist and flourmill. However, farmers along the river as far away as Indiana complained that this dam flooded large sections of their farms. For more than twenty years, their complaints fell on deaf ears. Finally, in 1872, the Illinois General Assembly passed a bill providing for removal of the dam, but three years later it was still there. So in 1875, some 30–50 Hoosier farmers, in the dark of night, took the matter into their own hands and blew up the dam. The water level dropped, mills shut down, and the farmers finally got their lands back.[2]

In 1850, Congress gave the states wetlands that it was unable to sell to settlers. Indiana and Illinois then decided on policies to sell these lands cheaply (about $1.25 an acre) to citizens or immigrants who would then drain them. The act provided that the pro-

2. The remains of the dam are still visible at Blue Island on the northern side of the river. They were for years part of the foundation of the Alwurn bridge—now abandoned.

THE HUMAN TOUCH

ceeds of the sale of these "swamp-lands" would also be used to pay for drainage. One hundred and eighty square miles of this land were located in Lake County alone, most of it either north or south of the well-drained Valparaiso and Tinley Moraines. The Little Calumet River floodplain, the Cady Marsh, and the Kankakee Marsh were all included in these swamplands.

Many of the first drainage ditches dug were in the marshy areas near the Kankakee River. In 1860, Indiana state geologist Richard Owen proudly noted "where formerly (not over three or four years since) a man would have mired, he now hauls tons of hay with wagon and team." Thousands of acres of land along the Kankakee River were drained in the late nineteenth century by means of these ditches. Then the Indiana portion of the Kankakee River itself was dredged and channeled.

An early drainage project north of the moraines began in 1862 when farmers in Highland and Munster collaborated to construct the Highland Big Ditch through the huge Calumet Shoreline's sand ridge. This effort successfully drained portions of the Cady Marsh. In 1880, Aaron Hart began draining the entire marshy former lakebottom by constructing a channel from Dyer to the Little Calumet River. The hardest part of the job was at the Calumet Shoreline itself (Ridge Road). Hart hired Eldert Munster, who did the job by filling a big wooden box with sand and dragging it out of the ditch with oxen.

Although Hart died during an inspection of the ditch in 1883, his wife and children had the job completed. Hart Ditch is now joined by two other ditches that have effectively drained most of the old

Figure 67. Hart Ditch and its new wagon bridge at Ridge Road. From Blatchley, 1897.

Figure 68. Burns Ditch in 1992.

Calumet Lagoon south of the ridge. The Cady Marsh Ditch drains the eastern portion, while Schoon Ditch drains the western part.

The Little Calumet River, and indeed much of the lowland areas between the various former Lake Michigan shorelines, have long been subjected to flooding. By 1900, some efforts were made to control the flooding and drain the untillable marshlands. With urban development and more intensive farming in this area, these floods were causing much damage. Burns Ditch in Porter County was designed to help solve the flooding problem by connecting the Little Calumet River in Porter County directly to the lake. Completed in 1926, it was named after Randall W. Burns, a local farmer and real estate developer. At the same time, several miles of the riverbed were straightened in an attempt to improve water flow. As noted earlier, with the construction of the ditch, river water from LaPorte and eastern Porter Counties no longer flows westward into Lake County; instead, it flows north through Burns Ditch into Lake Michigan. Also, rivers in western Porter County and eastern Lake County now flow east and then north into the lake. Thus the Little Calumet River now has the distinction of flowing in two directions. The western part of the river still flows westward into Illinois, while the eastern part flows toward Burns Ditch.

Since the 1920s, parts of the wide floodplain of the Little Calumet River have been developed into residential neighborhoods. Natural flooding of the river then resulted in natural indignation of land and homeowners. Thus in the late twentieth century the U.S. Army Corps of Engineers began a flood control project to build levees along the river from Gary to the Illinois state line. In a departure from some past efforts, many of the levees of this project have been built some distance from the river, allowing space for floodwaters to stand until the water level goes back down.

Expanding into the Lakes

Both Indiana and Illinois have expanded land areas by dumping sand, slag, and other materials into Lake Michigan and into several of the smaller lakes near Lake Michigan. In 1892, the state of Illinois planned to grant 1,000 acres of Lake Michigan to the Illinois Central Railroad so that the railroad could expand eastward. The U.S. Supreme Court, in a landmark case, determined that Illinois could not do this because it held the lake in trust for the benefit of the state's citizens. This principle, called the Public Trust Doctrine, still allowed Illinois to fill in portions of the lake, but only for public benefit.

For nearly 100 years, Indiana did not recognize this doctrine, which was not legally binding on the states. In that time, the state government allowed several private industries to expand northward into the lake. Between 1900 and the late 1970s, more than 3,775 acres of Lake Michigan in Indiana were filled in.

Several of the small lakes in the industrial sections southwest of Lake Michigan have also been partially or completely filled in. By 1927, Berry Lake, formerly in Whiting, and Hyde Lake, formerly in Hegewisch, no longer existed. Since the 1950s Lake Calumet in Chicago has been so filled in that there is little open water left beyond what is required for ships in its harbor.

An unexpected amount of sand has been accumulating in Lake Michigan near Michigan City pier since it was built in the 1870s. This pier has retarded the natural east-west movement of Lake Michigan waters. As a result, the water has deposited sand east of the pier, creating an extremely wide beach at Washington Park. As early as 1928, George Cressey noted that an "extensive accumulation of sand has taken place" on the east side of the pier. Unfortunately, the underloaded waters then naturally pick up sand from the beaches on the west side of the pier. This has resulted in costly beach erosion in the Beverly Shores area.

Ports on Lake Michigan

The first Calumet Area port on Lake Michigan was built at Michigan City. The harbor was first authorized by Congress in 1836, but it wasn't finished until 1870. Even then it could only handle pleasure and small commercial craft. Nevertheless, for many of the early years, it was through the Michigan City port that much of northern

Figure 69. Indiana's
International Port in
the 1970s. Port of
Indiana.

Indiana's harvest was shipped out. The next port was begun in 1870 at Calumet Harbor in South Chicago, when urban growth prevented industrial expansion at the Chicago Harbor.

During the early twentieth century, three private harbors were built in Indiana: the Indiana Harbor Ship Canal in 1901, U.S. Steel's Gary Works Harbor, 1906–1908, and Buffington Harbor in 1927, said then to be the deepest on the Great Lakes.

Plans to establish a public deep water port in Porter County were made in 1837 when City West was platted at the mouth of Fort Creek (where Dunes State Park is today). Efforts to build a port began anew in the 1930s, but nothing substantial was done until the opening of the St. Lawrence Seaway in 1959. The new port proposal was very controversial, with some recognizing the positive impact a port would have on jobs and others wanting to prevent any further industrialization of the dunes area. An agreement was reached in Congress whereby the port and the Indiana Dunes National Lakeshore would share Indiana's coastline. Indiana's International Port, now the Port of Indiana, was opened in 1969.

THE HUMAN TOUCH

PART THREE

Community Beginnings

7 Cook County Communities

Cook County, created in 1831, was named for Congressman Daniel Cook, who was instrumental in having Congress authorize the funding for the Illinois and Michigan Canal. This canal connected Lake Michigan to the Mississippi River and caused Chicago to become the economic capital of the Midwest.

Blue Island/Calumet Park

Blue Island is located just north and west of where the Little Calumet River makes its hairpin curve and begins to flow eastward. Calumet Park, adjacent to Blue Island, is located where the Little Calumet is connected to the Calumet Sag Channel. The city of Blue Island sits at the southern end of a high ridge, six miles long and one mile wide that is part of the Park Ridge (Lake Border) Moraine and was once an island in glacial Lake Michigan. Its east side, which faced the open lake, has a steep wave-cut cliff. Its west side, with the Chicago area's largest belt of sand hills, is now home to several golf courses and cemeteries. The *Chicago Democrat* in February 1834 stated, "The ridge, when viewed from a distance, appears standing in an azure mist of vapor, hence the appellation, 'Blue

Figure 70. The Blue Island House. Blue Island Historical Society Museum.

Island.'" It was years before anyone realized that it had indeed once been an island.

The low valley along the Calumet Sag Channel is the site of the ancient Chicago Outlet where the cold waters of glacial Lake Michigan, during its early phases, passed by as they headed from the lake to the Illinois River.

For years the abundant glacial clay beneath Blue Island helped make the city the "brick making capital of the world." In addition to clay, other quarries just outside the city mined sand and gravel from the ancient Glenwood Shoreline.

Blue Island, the site of several populous Indian villages, was one of the first communities established in Cook County. In 1834, Thomas Courtney and his wife, the first settlers, built a small cabin up on the ridge near the newly surveyed Vincennes Trail. Two years later, Norman and Julia Rexford arrived and built a fine hotel called the Blue Island House. To do so, they had to truck in lumber from Indiana more than 100 miles away as there was no sawmill in the area. The hotel, which was at the highest point of the southeastern portion of the ridge, welcomed thousands of Vincennes Trail travelers going to and from Chicago.

Peter Barton arrived in 1837, had a plat made for a village just south of the ridge he called Portland, and built a store on Wabash Road (Western Avenue). Also in 1837, John Britton established a blacksmith shop just below the Blue Island House. The following year, a post office was established at the Blue Island House with Rexford serving as postmaster. For several years, the area had two names: Portland was official, but most people preferred Blue Island. To make matters worse, in 1850 the federal government changed the name of the post office to "Worth," the name of the township.

One of the first religious organizations established in Blue Island was the Universalist Society, which started meeting in a schoolhouse in 1849. The German Methodist Society and the Catholic Church of St. Benedict were established five years later. First Congregational Church was started in 1860.

Blue Island experienced a burst of growth in 1848 when the Calumet "feeder" to the Illinois and Michigan Canal was built. Then in 1852, the first railroad, the Rock Island Line, was built through the village. In 1892 a branch of the Illinois Central arrived, just in time to take residents to the Columbian Exposition,

Figure 71. Norman and Julia Rexford. Blue Island Historical Society Museum.

Chicago's World's Fair. Two rail lines included Blue Island in their name: the Chicago, Blue Island & Indiana Railroad (Grand Trunk) and the Chicago & Blue Island Railway. The railroads provided faster service to Chicago than did the old Vincennes Road, and Blue Island lost some of its importance as a commercial center because rail passengers and freight could bypass the village on their way to and from the city. Beginning in 1848 dozens of German families arrived. Perhaps not surprisingly, within 10 years there were four breweries in operation. The high ridge and low water table was perfect for the location of enormous cooling cellars for the beer.

The village was incorporated in 1872, at which time it officially took the name Blue Island. For many years all village offices were divided equally between the Germans and the English-speaking Americans. By 1880, the population of the village had increased to 1542. Historian Alfred Andreas noted in 1884 that Blue Island was "among the prettiest little suburban towns in the West." In 1901, with a population over 6,000, Blue Island became a city.

Calumet Park, straddling the junction of the Little Calumet River and the Calumet Sag Channel, has within its boundaries the locks that control access to the channel. This small village was incorporated in 1912 with the name Caswell. Its name was changed in 1925 to Calumet Park.

Postscript: The Blue Island Historical Society Museum is located in the lower level of the Blue Island Public Library.

Calumet City/Burnham

The High Tolleston Shoreline passes through Calumet City along the Michigan City Road. Used by Indians long before European settlement, many Indian projectile points have been found along this road. (A small chipping station, where Indians once made arrowheads, was uncovered near the Sand Ridge Nature Center.) Northeast of this beach ridge are the low dunes and swales of the Lower Tolleston Shoreline. Green Lake, on this land just north of River Oaks Drive, is the site of an old clay quarry for a brick plant. For information about the Thornton Fractional High School Prairie and the Cook County Forest Preserve properties that have preserved some of the original landscape, see the epilogue.

Among the earliest settlers on the south side of what is today Calumet City were German immigrants Hans and Louise Schrum, who arrived in 1863. The Schrums' farm next to the state line was also the site of their Calumet Dairy and the Schrum (later Calumet) Pickle Works. (Their daughter, Magdelena, married C. S. Claussen, a member of a more famous pickle-making family.)

In 1868, a meat packing plant was established just east of the state line in a community that was soon known as Hammond. The

plant attracted many German immigrants, some of whom lived west
of the state line in what soon came to be called West Hammond,
Illinois.

In the 1880s, a third settlement was started when a large number of Polish immigrants arrived and bought property on the sandy
ground near the High Tolleston Shoreline. They named this area
around Pulaski Road Sobieski, after a seventeenth-century Polish
general. The first residential subdivision there was platted in 1891.

Reflecting the traditions of these two immigrant groups, the first
two churches were St. John Evangelical Lutheran, established by the
German settlers in 1888, and St. Andrew Roman Catholic, started
by the Polish settlers in 1891. By 1893, the three areas had more
than 500 residents. That year the residents voted to incorporate as
the village of West Hammond. The first postal substation in the
village opened in 1898. Two years later, its population was nearly
3,000. West Hammond continued to grow. When its population
surpassed 5,000 in 1911, it was incorporated as a city. The name
was changed in 1924 to Calumet City.

Burnham is located at the junction of the three rivers (Calumet,
Grand Calumet, and Little Calumet). The village was platted in
1883 by Telford Burnham in consultation with railroad magnate
George Pullman and other Chicago entrepreneurs. It was incorporated in 1907. In 1910, its population was 328. By 1920, its population had more than doubled to 795.

Postscript: The Heritage Cabin is composed of an older lower
section built in the 1830s and a newer upper section probably built
about thirty years later. In the 1860s it was the home of the Peter
Schrum family. In 1979, Evelyn Jackson, the Schrums' granddaugh-

ter, donated the building to the Calumet City Historical Society. It was then dismantled and carefully reassembled in Veterans Park west of Burnham Avenue, where it stands today.

The Sand Ridge Nature Center on Paxton Avenue has displays about the geography and natural history of the Calumet Area. The Center also includes several replicas of pioneer cabins. The Calumet City Historical Society Museum is located in the old public library building.

Chicago Heights/South Chicago Heights/ Ford Heights

Chicago Heights and Ford Heights are located on the Tinley Moraine and occupy some of the highest land in Cook County. South Chicago Heights is both on the Tinley Moraine (near State Street) and on a former glacial lake bottom (near Chicago Road). (See endsheets.) The northern edge of the moraine is easily seen in Ford Heights along Cottage Grove Avenue just north of Route 30. The low area north of the moraine was once a bay of Lake Michigan.

The area is bisected by two major historic roads: the old Sauk Trail and the Vincennes Trace (Chicago Road), the latter connecting Chicago with the former territorial capital of Vincennes. The area is also bisected by Thorn Creek, which flows northeastward to the Little Calumet River.

Two small limestone quarries were once located near Cottage Grove Avenue where it crosses U.S. Highway 30 in what is now Ford Heights. South of 26th Street and west of State Street is an area where for many years glacial clays were mined to make bricks.

In 1833, hunter and trapper Absalom Wells was the first settler in the area. He built a log cabin where the Vincennes Trace crossed Thorn Creek, but within a few years he headed farther west. (A historical marker west of Chicago Road now marks the site.) The first permanent settlers were Adam and Phoebe Brown, who also arrived in 1833 and built an inn at the intersection of the Sauk Trail and the Vincennes Trace—an intersection since known as Brown's Corners.

John and Sabra McCoy were the next to arrive, making their home on Thorn Creek west of the Browns. In 1835, a large group from Ireland's County Tyrone arrived, including John and Martha McEldowney, Robert and Jane Wallace, John and Rosanna Wallace, and Morris Murphy. Murphy became the area's first shopkeeper that year when he opened his store one and a half miles north of town. In the early years, the little community was known as Thorn Grove.

Thorn Grove's first school was built in 1836; its first teacher

Figure 73. The Thirty Mile House, looking north on Chicago Road from the Michigan Central Tracks. Chicago Heights Public Library.

was Miss Cooper, who earned $1.25 a week. In addition, she was given free housing with local residents. As was customary at the time, Miss Cooper had to resign when she got married.

The Reformed Presbyterian Church of Thorn Grove was formed in December 1843. Its first minister, John Morrison, unlike most of his congregation, was a Southerner who, even though he had once been a tutor to the family of Jefferson Davis, was an ardent abolitionist. Many Thorn Grove residents had similar convictions. The Batchelder and McCoy homes on Sauk Trail were "stations" on the Underground Railroad and held up to five fugitive slaves at a time. Upon darkness, the former slaves would be escorted northward to safe houses in South Holland or Roseland.

The Joliet and Northern Indiana (Michigan Central) Railroad arrived in 1853. Robert Wallace then platted the village where the new rail line crossed the Vincennes Road. The village was called Bloom. Some believe that the new name was to honor a German martyr, Robert Bluhm. Others maintain that it was to reflect the beauty of the nearby woods in spring. In any event, other railroads soon came, including the C&EI, the B&O, and the EJ&E. The post office at Strassburg was relocated to Bloom, and Robert Wallace became its first postmaster.

In 1866, the area's first German immigrants, Jacob and Wilhelmina Kirgis, opened the Kirgis Inn, also called the Thirty Mile House, on the east side of the Chicago Road. This inn, being on the primary north-south road of the county and near the depot, catered to both trail and rail travelers.

The Chicago Heights Land Association was formed in 1890. It purchased 4,000 acres of land near Bloom, planned factory sites, and built rail connections. New industries and residents were attracted to the area, and in 1892 Bloom was renamed Chicago Heights and incorporated as a village. That year the Association

Figure 74. The Victoria Hotel. Built in 1892, this modern facility boasted steam heat, hot and cold running water, electric lights, and first-class service. Chicago Heights Public Library.

organized special trains on the C&EI to bring prospective investors from Chicago, promoting Chicago Heights as an excellent manufacturing and industrial center. By 1897, the village had twenty factories including the new Inland Steel Company. It also could boast of having one of the finest hotels outside of Chicago—the Victoria, designed by Chicago architect Louis Sullivan. In 1901, with a population over 5,000, Chicago Heights became a city and elected John Thomas, the Inland Steel plant manager, as its first mayor. Its population nearly tripled in the next ten years.

South Chicago Heights, which because of the settlement at Brown's Corners can claim to be the oldest community in the south suburban area, was not within the corporate limits when Chicago Heights incorporated in 1892. Seeking to retain a separate identity, South Chicago Heights was incorporated as a village in 1907. In 1910, its population was 552.

Ford Heights was not incorporated as a village until 1949, when it took the name East Chicago Heights. The name was changed to Ford Heights in 1978.

Dolton/Riverdale

For many years, the villages of Dolton and Riverdale were thought of as one community along the Little Calumet River and in the area where today Thornton, and Hyde Park, and Calumet Townships meet (at 138th and Indiana). Riverdale is located at the westernmost point of the river where it turns and heads east toward Lake Michigan; Dolton is to the southeast. The flood plain at Riverdale is the site of the old Chicago Outlet, where the waters of glacial Lake Michigan flowed toward the Illinois River. The High Tolleston Shoreline along Michigan City Road (Lincoln Avenue) is an old Indian trail that passed through the northeast section of both villages. After 1885, local brickyards mined the rich clay soils near the river. Riverdale has the distinction of having the last operating brickyard in the Calumet Area.

The first settlers, the Clark Matthews family, arrived in 1836, settled south of the river (north of 138th Street), and operated a ferry across along the Little Calumet River where the Indiana Street bridge is now. Two years later, George and Catherine Dolton and seven children arrived. The Doltons had earlier settled in Chicago, but thought that Chicago was in an unfavorable location for growth. According to granddaughter Isabella Dolton, George and Catherine believed that Chicago was "too far north to be convenient for people on the way to the Far West." So they established an inn on the Michigan City Road (east of Indiana Avenue and north of 138th) About 1840, Levi Osterhout built and operated another inn (later the Girard House) along the Michigan City Road at what is now 134th Street. In addition to farming, George operated Matthews' old ferry until 1841 when he and Levi Osterhout built a toll bridge across the river. Many of the early settlers of the Dolton/Riverdale area were farmers who were natives of Holland, Sweden, or Germany.

Railroads have played a big part in the development of Dolton and Riverdale. The Illinois Central arrived in 1851. Within 30 years the Pennsylvania, C&EI, Chicago & Great Eastern, Chicago & Calumet Terminal, B&O, and several others all had lines. As the area was still rural, the trains hauled local produce to the growing city of Chicago. However the community was beginning to change: Conrad and Catharine Zimmer opened the first store, St. Paul's Lutheran Church was started in 1858, a post office was established in 1866 with Andrew Dolton serving as the first postmaster, and in 1868 both villages were platted.

Early industries included a distillery, a lumber company, brickyards, and a sauerkraut factory. The area got its second post office in 1873, when one was opened in F. A. Reich's general store. It and the village around it from that time on have been known as Riverdale. By 1884 three railroads and one highway crossed the Little Calumet River. All had bridges that could swing 90° so that the river remained navigable. And it is said that most families had a rowboat for pleasure riding on the clear Little Calumet River.

In 1889 Chicago annexed all of Hyde Park Township including what is now the Chicago community of Riverdale (north of 138th Street and the river). Three years later the villages of Dolton and Riverdale were incorporated.

Postscript: The Dolton Village Hall, built as a school in 1874, has been the village hall since 1916.

Glenwood

Most of the village of Glenwood is built on former lake bottomland northeast of the Tinley Moraine. Its most prominent geographical feature, however, is the old Glenwood Spit, a sand peninsula built up by the waves of Lake Michigan soon after the lake first formed. This spit was an extension of Glenwood Island (Glenwood-Dyer Road east of Highway 394). In 1897 Frank Leverett gave the name Glenwood to this, the oldest shoreline of Lake Michigan. The sand ridge is still the most visible evidence of the ancient Glenwood Shoreline.

Figure 75. The Dolton Village Hall.

The village was established where an eastern branch of the old Vincennes Trace crossed the former shoreline. Two of the first settlers were James Barton and Job Campbell, both of whom arrived in 1838. In 1846, Campbell and O. P. Axtell founded the town, which they called Hickory Bend. Four years later, a log cabin school was built east of the village.

In 1869, the C&EI Railroad built its tracks through the village and began service. The following year a post office was established and the village name was changed to Glenwood. So in 1871, when Campbell built a hotel, he named it the Glenwood House. Soon thereafter, a blacksmith and wagon shop, saloon, general store, numerous rail facilities, and the Glenwood Stockyards were established. The well-known Glenwood School for Boys was established in 1887. Originally called the Glenwood Manual Training School, it offered training in carpentry, plumbing, printing, and farming to boys from broken homes. Originally it had its own dairy herd.

Railroading, however, became Glenwood's biggest business. The village grew and was incorporated in 1903. Its population in 1910 was 581.

Postscript: The Mt. Glenwood Cemetery, a historic African Amer-

ican cemetery, was established in 1902 alongside the C&EI Railroad, which ran funeral cars out from Chicago. The cemetery contains the graves of Duke Slater, the first African American elected to the Football Hall of Fame, Marshall "Major" Taylor, in 1899 the world's fastest cyclist and history's second black world champion athlete, Charles Gavin, the first black member of the National College of Orthopedic Surgeons, and Elijah Muhammad, founder of the Nation of Islam.

Harvey/Dixmoor/Phoenix

Harvey, Dixmoor, and Phoenix sit on lake bottomland southwest of the Little Calumet River and northeast of the ancient Calumet Shoreline. In 1852, the Illinois Central Railroad crossed the river and built its line through the area.

The town of South Lawn was platted along the Illinois Central tracks in 1873. The first resident was John Gay, a local contractor. Harvey Hopkins established the Hopkins Mower Company in South Lawn in 1880 and soon employed over 100.

In 1890, Turlington W. Harvey purchased the factory and a large amount of nearby land, and organized the Harvey Land Association. His efforts were successful, and in the next three years much of the city was built, giving the village the nickname "The Magic City." In just two years the population reached 5,000. When South Lawn was incorporated in 1891, it was renamed for both Harvey Hopkins and Turlington Harvey. Four years later, Harvey became a city. Its population in 1900 was 5,395.

When the Shaffer AME Chapel was founded in 1896, it was the first black congregation in southern Cook County. Three years later,

Amanda Berry Smith founded Illinois' first orphanage for black children in Harvey.

Phoenix got its start in 1890 when the Harvey Land Association subdivided and began building homes in the area east of the Illinois Central tracks. Early residents were primarily of German, Dutch, Polish, or Irish descent. It was expected at that time that the new neighborhood would soon be incorporated by the city of Harvey. However, the citizens protested the annexation and organized their own village. Named after the Arizona capital, Phoenix was incorporated as a village in 1900. Its population in 1910 was 679, and this more than doubled in the next ten years.

Dixmoor, originally called Specialville, was named for Charles Special, the village board's first president. The village was incorporated in 1922. Seven years later, the name was changed to Dixmoor, the name of one of its neighborhoods.

Figure 78. Turlington W. Harvey, a bust on display at the Harvey Public Library.

Hazel Crest/East Hazel Crest

The ancient Glenwood Shoreline runs diagonally through the community of Hazel Crest. It can be found southeast of Interstate 294 and crosses Interstate 80 at Kedzie Avenue. The former beach can be seen from East Hazel Crest looking into Homewood, both south and west of 175th and Dixie Highway. The neighborhoods southwest of this are on the Tinley Moraine. The area to the northeast including all of East Hazel Crest was lake during the Glenwood phase. The Interstate 80/294 interchange is built on the ancient Calumet Shoreline.

In 1890, William and Carrie McClintock purchased eighty acres of land along where the Illinois Central Railroad crossed the old Glenwood Shoreline. The next year William platted the village, calling it South Harvey. During the real estate boom that preceded the Columbian Exposition in 1893, he managed to convince Illinois Central officials to establish a station at South Harvey and then arranged for excursions on the rail line for potential home buyers. Lots were sold, a post office was established, and McClintock became the first postmaster. Just as the new community was getting started, it was included in the village of Homewood, which was incorporated that year. However, after a two-year effort, the area was "dis-incorporated."

The first school was built in 1895 and the first church, the Hazel Crest Community Church (Methodist), was established two years later. By 1900, the community had a population of seventy-five. Seeking a separate identity from Harvey, the village and post office changed their names to Hazel Crest. It is said that the name came from nearby growths of hazelnut bushes, perhaps growing on

Figure 79. Hazel Crest's Community United Methodist Church before 1939. Hazel Crest Community United Methodist Church.

the sandy Glenwood and Calumet Shorelines. According to botanist D. C. Peatty, hazelnuts grow well on the sandy soils of the Calumet Area.

Hazel Crest was incorporated as a village in 1912. Its population in 1920 was 438. Following suit, the tiny village of East Hazel Crest, where the first PTA in southern Cook County was chartered, was incorporated in 1918. Its population in 1920 was 394.

Postscript: The original 1897 building of the Community United Methodist Church still stands on Lincoln Avenue.

Hegewisch

Until about 1100 years ago, what is now Hegewisch was part of Lake Michigan. The community is built on sands of the dune and swale topography of the lower Tolleston Shorelines. The dune ridges were dry, but the swales were often covered with water. Even today Hegewisch is nearly surrounded by water. Bordering it are the Calumet River, the Grand Calumet River, and Wolf and Powder Horn Lakes. One of the sand ridges was called Indian Ridge by the early settlers. Another was where Powder Horn Lake is today; the sand there was mined when the Indiana Toll Road and Chicago Skyway were built. Hegewisch was the site of an important Indian village.

Two inns were established near where the High Tolleston Shoreline was crossed by the Grand Calumet River. Reese's Inn was on Indian Ridge; Cassidy's was near a ferry crossing. A toll bridge was built across the Calumet River in 1836. George Bunt, the keeper, charged three cents for each team of horses driven across. In 1850, David Combs bought the Cassidy Inn.

Hegewisch was named for Adolph Hegewisch, who was president of the United States Rolling Stock Company in the early 1880s when it purchased 100 acres of primitive land and erected its plant. With the new company and good railroad facilities, the community grew, attracting many European immigrants. Within a few years, it could boast two railroad depots and a small business district. In 1889 Hegewisch was annexed to the growing city of Chicago. But being so surrounded by water, Hegewisch has remained somewhat isolated from the rest of the city.

Homewood/Flossmoor

Most of Homewood and Flossmoor are on the Tinley Moraine. Both villages are bisected by the Illinois Central Railroad, which was instrumental in their early development.

During the Glenwood stage, the eastern part of Homewood was covered by the waters of Lake Michigan. The diagonal ancient Glenwood Shoreline can be seen north of the intersection of Ridge and Halsted, at Maple and Ashland, and both south and west of the intersection of 175th and Dixie Highway. The cemeteries east of Halsted at Ridge Road are on a small sand spit that extended into Lake Michigan toward the Thornton coral reef.

Thirty-foot high sand dunes used to stand along Ridge Road near Halsted Street. They were removed in the 1920s when the sand was used to build the raised bed for the Illinois Central Railroad. The lowlands and ponds in that area, including the Izaak Walton grounds, are remnants of these sand quarries.

The southwestern part of Flossmoor (Crawford Avenue at Vollmer Road) was a small glacial lake at the end of the Ice Age.

One of the earliest families to arrive was the Benjamin Butterfield family which in 1834 settled where the Idlewild Country Club is now. Butterfield Creek is named after this family. Other early settlers, all farmers, were the Barton, Briggs, Clark, Campbell, Crary, Crandall, Gallener, and Hood families. James and Sally Hart arrived a few years later. In 1839, Samuel and Ottile Riegel emigrated from Germany and settled along a trail that became Riegel Road. They were joined by a number of other German settlers including the Gottschalks, Brinkmans, and Zimmers.

In 1853 James Hart platted a village which he called Hartford near the Thornton station of the new Illinois Central Railroad. The commercial area of Homewood began right away as Charles

Figure 80. Blacksmith shop, Mertens' General Store, and Brinkman's Saloon. From Adair and Sandberg, 1968.

Robinson built a general store and H. Brinkman opened the first hotel. When the post office was established George (or Samuel) Churchill, the first IC station manager, served as its first postmaster. In 1855, brothers Henry and Conrad Zimmer opened a general store.

In 1868, William Gottschalk established a large hay-pressing business employing up to 15 men. In later years his son Henry took advantage of the abundant glacial clays on the west side of the IC tracks and established the Homewood Brick Company

Hartford was the name of this new town, but the Illinois Central station was still called Thornton Station—for the town of Thornton two and a half miles to the east. Complicating matters, in 1856 George Morris platted a subdivision called Thornton Station next to Hart's village. Confusion over the name of the village and the nearby town of Thornton finally resulted in the name Homewood being chosen in 1869 for both Hartford and Thornton Station. At this time there were about 250 residents, most living east of the IC tracks. The first school was built by the German School Society of Thornton Station. German, as well as the "three R's," was taught in its small schoolhouse.

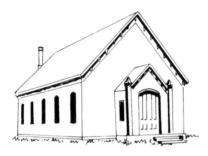

Figure 81. First Presbyterian Church of Thornton Station, drawn by Carol Cameron, 1983. Courtesy of her family.

The first church established in town was First Presbyterian in 1858. The German community started the St. Paul Evangelical Church (now St. Paul Community) in 1865. For more than forty-five years, these were the only churches in town. By 1880, the population had grown to 448. The village of Homewood was incorporated in 1893.

Flossmoor was originally settled by many farm families from Germany, including the Hechts, the Doepps, and the Vollmers. But it is the Illinois Central Railroad that can be credited for the founding of the village. It owned 160 acres of land which it had earlier purchased in order to provide fill for its line in Hyde Park, the site of the Columbian Exposition. When the soil on this land proved to be unsuitable for fill, the company decided to subdivide and sell the land. A depot was built, and in 1901 the village was platted and named Flossmoor. The IC even built the first six houses. Flossmoor was incorporated as a village in 1924.

Postscript: The Dorband-Howe House and Museum (1895) was one of several "working men's cottages" built by Henry Gottschalk for his employees. The houses were all built of red brick from Gottschalk's brick works. The museum is maintained by the Homewood Historical Society.

Downtown Homewood and its environs have a number of noteworthy buildings that are described on a "Walking Tour" brochure available from the Homewood Historical Society.

Lansing/Lynwood

The village of Lansing is bisected by the ancient Calumet Shoreline, which enters the town on the west at the Thornton-Lansing Road, roughly following Indiana Avenue on the west side of town and Ridge Road on the east side. North of the ridge, the land slopes down toward the Little Calumet River, which forms the village's northern boundary. Under Lansing is a thick layer of glacial clay that was mined for bricks from 1887 to 1949. The Calumet Shoreline was an Indian trail before settlement and was used as a stagecoach route from 1833 until 1853. The sand ridge used to be much higher than it is today. After the railroad was built, much of the high sand ridge was hauled by rail into Chicago.

Most of the early settlers who arrived in the Lansing area were either German or Dutch. The first permanent settlers were August Hildebrandt, his wife, and their son, who established a farm in 1843 near North Creek. Henry Krumm opened the Union Hotel on the Calumet Beach Trail (southwest of today's Ridge Road and Wentworth Avenue) in 1850. Three years later, John, Henry, and George Lansing arrived. (A fourth brother, Peter Lansing, arrived in 1865.)

Henry Lansing established the first general store in 1864. The next year, as John Lansing platted the village along the new Chicago & Great Eastern Railway (Panhandle) tracks, a post office was established and Henry was named the first postmaster. Not surprisingly, the new village was named Lansing.

The low areas north and south of the sand ridge of the ancient shoreline were meadows ideal for growing hay. Christian and Sophia Schultz farmed about 400 acres of these meadows. In 1872, Christian established a hay pressing business, shipping out 4,000 to 5,000 tons of hay each year.

Cummings Corners/Oak Glen developed near today's intersection of Torrence and Indiana Avenues and was first named after Kris Cummings, who arrived in 1851. Other early settlers were the Eenigenburgs, Zusts, Vierks, Bocks, Bisserts, and Tons. As in neighboring Lansing, most of the early residents were either Dutch or German immigrants. By the 1880s, after the Grand Trunk Railroad built its line, Oak Glen had a thriving business section with a post office, several stores, and four saloons. John C. Ton, who operated a clothing store and barbershop, also served as its postmaster and later Lansing's first village clerk. Indiana Avenue, on the old Calumet Shoreline, was the primary east-west route until Ridge Road was improved in 1915.

Figure 82. The Lansing/Busack Building, before Ridge Road was lowered to the level of the adjacent Pennsylvania Railroad tracks. The building, the oldest along the Calumet Shoreline, still stands; however, the basement now serves as the first floor. Courtesy of Harold and LaVerne Barkow.

The first of four brickyards, the Harlan Brickyard, opened in 1887. Five years later, the Labahn brickyards were located along the state line south of Ridge Road. The lakes at the Lansing Country Club are its old clay pits. The other brickyards were located in Bernice.

Bernice is the area along Bernice Road near Burnham and Chicago Avenues. Besides brickyards, Bernice had a depot, the Cross Boarding House, Bohemian Joe's Hotel, and three saloons. The brickyards stayed in operation until about 1930. Flanagin Lake, north of Bernice Drive, is the remnant of one of the clay pits. The Saxon Landfill on Bernice Road is at the site of another.

The earliest church in Lansing was the North Creek of Thornton Holland (now First) Reformed Church established in 1861. Services were in Dutch. Trinity Lutheran Church in Oak Glen began serving the German community in 1864. St. John Lutheran was then established in 1883 for the German families in Lansing. Both Lutheran churches had services in German. Not until the Methodist Church (still standing at Ridge Road and Chicago Avenue) was built in 1894 was there an area church with services conducted in English!

The village of Lansing was incorporated in 1893, uniting all three communities. Its population in 1900 was 830.

Lynwood, due south of Lansing, sits on lake bottomland except for the prominent Glenwood Spit (on the Glenwood-Dyer Road),

Figure 83. Ridge Road and the First Reformed Church, the oldest church on the Calumet Shoreline. Lansing Historical Society.

which extends southeastward almost to the state line. Evidence of that ancient spit can easily be seen as one drives south on Torrence Avenue and approaches the Glenwood-Dyer Road. The village was incorporated in 1961.

Postscript: The Lansing/Busack Building at 3353 Ridge Road was built by Henry Lansing in 1860. It was bought by Christian Busack about 1875 and is still owned by that family.

In the 1920s, Henry Ford purchased land in Lansing and Munster for an airport and airplane manufacturing complex. He built an airport, but the Great Depression ended his ambitious plans. However, the Lansing Airport and Ford's original hangar still serve the Calumet Area. The hangar is on the National Register of Historic Places.

Markham/Posen/Robbins

Both the ancient Glenwood and Calumet Shorelines pass diagonally through Markham. Southwest of the higher Glenwood Shoreline is the Tinley Moraine. (The shorelines were easier to recognize before I-57 and I-294 were built.) The villages of Posen and Robbins lie on Lake Michigan bottomland northeast of the Calumet Shoreline.

The Glenwood Shoreline runs between Hillcrest and Belleplaine Drives northwest to Midlothian Meadows. The Calumet Shoreline runs parallel and a little north of the Glenwood. From Midlothian Meadows it extends southeast through the I-57 interchange at 159th Street to the I-80/294 interchange. It crosses Kedzie Avenue at 165th Street.

Markham was incorporated as a village in 1925, taking its name from the Markham Yards, which are located along the Illinois Central tracks. The yards, designed in 1920 to be the largest in the country, were named for Charles Markham, former president of the Illinois Central Railroad. Markham became a city in 1967.

Within Markham is the Gensberg-Markham Prairie, a 100-acre nature preserve managed by the Nature Conservancy, Northeastern Illinois University, and the Natural Land Institute. Gensberg-Markham, named a National Natural Landmark, is one of the best high-quality grasslands in the Midwest. This and other nearby grasslands have become a source of pride for Markham, which calls itself the "Prairie Capital of the Prairie State."

Figure 84. Jennie Smith, the "Mother" of Robbins. Tyrone Haymore and the Robbins Historical Society Museum.

Posen, the oldest of these three communities, was first called Bremen (the name of the township). It was originally settled by a large number of German immigrants. Polish immigrants arrived in 1887, and when the village was incorporated in 1900, it was named after the town of Poznan in Poland.

Robbins got its start in 1892 when several African Americans moved into this area south of the Calumet Sag Channel. At that time, excitement surrounding the upcoming Chicago World's Fair resulted in land speculation southwest of that city. One of the new residents was a widow, Jennie Smith, later recognized as the "Mother of Robbins." This remarkable woman, the daughter of slaves, helped people build homes, helped organize the first two churches, Union Baptist in 1903 and Bethel AME in 1905, helped purchase the new village's first fire truck, and built a garage for it next to her home.

In 1910, Henry Robbins platted a subdivision and encouraged more African Americans to invest in the area—far away from the big city. By 1917 more than 300 lived in the district, many of them railroad employees. That year Robbins became a village, the first community in the northern half of the United States incorporated and administered by African Americans.

Early on, the village of Robbins played an important part in U.S. aviation history. African Americans Cornelius Coffey and John Robinson founded the Challenger Air Pilots Association, which in

Figure 85. The Historic Robbins Airport in 1931. Janet Bragg is behind the propeller, and John Robinson is at the far right. Tyrone Haymore and the Robbins Historical Society Museum.

1931 opened an aeronautics school and built an airport in Robbins where they could teach and fly without discrimination. Janet Harmon, who later became the first African American woman to earn a commercial pilot's license, provided the planes for the school. Unfortunately, a windstorm in 1933 destroyed the hangar and the three planes inside. Coffey then established the Coffey School of Aeronautics in unincorporated Worth Township (now Bridgeview), while Robinson helped to establish the teaching of aeronautics at Tuskegee Institute in Alabama. Many of the Coffey School graduates were among the first of the Tuskegee Airmen who achieved fame during World War II.

Morgan Park/Beverly/Washington Heights

Morgan Park and Beverly are located north of the city of Blue Island on the six-mile long Blue Island ridge that is part of the Park Ridge (Lake Border) Moraine and was once an island in glacial Lake Michigan. Washington Heights is located to their east on land that includes the Washington Heights spit, a sandy ridge that formed in the lake east of Blue Island. The spit is part of the ancient Calumet Shoreline.

In 1865 the Chicago & Great Eastern or Panhandle Railroad (later the Pennsylvania) crossed the tracks laid earlier by the Chicago, Rock Island & Pacific. The community that was soon built up near this intersection was known as Washington Heights. A post office opened in 1872, and Washington Heights (extending then from Halsted Street to Western Avenue) was incorporated as a village two years later. Washington Heights was annexed to the City of Chicago in 1890–91.

Morgan Park is named for Thomas Morgan who settled on the ridge in 1844 and established a cattle and sheep ranch. In 1869–70 the Blue Island Land and Building Company built the area's

Figure 86. Park Hall of the Morgan Park Military Academy in 1892. Built in 1873, this was the original building of the academy. It stood on 112th Street—where the academy gymnasium is now located—until it was destroyed by fire in 1893. Ridge Historical Society.

winding streets and upscale residential housing was advertised. By 1872 there were both Methodist and Baptist congregations in town. Morgan Park soon was also the home of the Morgan Park [Military] Academy (1873), the Chicago Female College (1875) and Baptist Theological Union (1877) and the American Institute of Hebrew (1881). In 1878, a post office was established and W. W. Washburne served as the first postmaster. In 1882 Morgan Park (then extending north to 99th Street) was incorporated as a village. Morgan Park, by a close vote of its citizens, became part of Chicago in 1914.

Beverly (Beverly Hills) is on that part of the Blue Island Ridge north of 107th Street. The neighborhood, which acquired its name when the Rock Island station at 91st Street was named Beverly Hills (after a town in Massachusetts), today contains sections that were once part of both the incorporated villages of Morgan Park and Washington Heights. Beverly became a distinct part of Chicago after it was incorporated into the city and the old village boundaries were erased.

Postscript: A National Historic District of architecturally significant houses in Morgan Park and Beverly is now composed of the blocks from 87th and 115th streets and between Prospect Avenue and Hoyne and Seeley avenues. Three non-contiguous Chicago landmark districts are contained within the national boundaries.

Roseland/Pullman/Kensington

Roseland, Pullman, and Kensington/West Pullman, today all neighborhoods of Chicago, are located west of Lake Calumet. Roseland sits prominently atop the ancient High Tolleston Shoreline while Pullman and Kensington are located on the lower elevations next to the lake. West Pullman is west of the Illinois Central Railroad and now extends south and westward to Stewart Ridge (around 123rd and Stewart Avenue) and the Little Calumet River. Stewart Ridge is a sand spit formed during Lake Michigan's Calumet phase. Historian Alfred Andreas noted in 1884 that from Roseland, "a magnificent view can be had of the palace-car city (Pullman) and the prairie settlements to the south-west of Chicago." The Chicago-Thornton Road (also called the Michigan City Road), followed the route of an old Indian trail which here is on the Tolleston beach ridge. Today this route is Michigan Avenue—and its interesting turns and jogs through Roseland still demonstrate how that old trail was not a straight line.

Roseland was settled in 1849 by fifteen Dutch families who purchased 200 acres of prairie land along the Chicago-Thornton Road. The settlers named their new home High Prairie in contrast to Low Prairie, the name for the also-Dutch South Holland community. (High Prairie, however, is lower in elevation than Low Prairie. Its name originated because the land was higher than the surrounding countryside.) Many of the new settlers were "Seceders" who had rebelled against the established church in Holland. Soon after their arrival, these Dutch pilgrims established a church of their own, the First Reformed Church. Their first church building was erected in 1849 on what is now 107th Street. The first school classes were held in that building as well.

Figure 87. Cornelius Kuyper, pioneer, shopkeeper, magistrate, and agent for the Underground Railroad. Pullman Research Group.

High Prairie's location on the Chicago-Thornton Road soon resulted in its becoming the leading village between Indiana and the city of Chicago. The first storekeeper was Cornelius Kuyper, who established a general store. The citizens of High Prairie were passionate abolitionists, and Kuyper and John Ton were instrumental in the operation of the Underground Railroad. They hid runaway slaves in their homes and barns and helped transport them to Chicago or to Indiana, where they would continue on to Michigan and then to Canada. In 1860, a post office, named Hope, was established in Goris Van der Sijde's general store. In 1874 Van der Sijde platted the village. The next year, both the name of the post office and the town were changed to Roseland, although many continued to call it High Prairie. With township offices established there, the village and its business community on Michigan Avenue grew, reaching a population of 800 in 1878.

Pullman got its start in 1880 when George Pullman, president of the Pullman Palace Car Company, purchased more than 3,000

Figure 88. The Pullman administration building and factory. For many years Lake Vista served as a cooling basin for exhaust waters from Pullman's mighty Corliss steam engines. The lake was filled in around 1900. Pullman Research Group.

acres of land on the western shore of Lake Calumet. There he built his rail car factories and adjacent town. Pullman was the world's first planned community of factories, homes, and stores designed by one architect (28 year-old Solon Beman), all of which were originally owned by the Pullman Company. The buildings were constructed of common bricks made from clay mined from the bottom of Lake Calumet and then fabricated in Pullman's own kilns. Face bricks were brought in from the Porter, Indiana, brickyards. The church, also owned by Pullman, was clad a rare metamorphic rock called greenstone, which he had brought in by train from Pennsylvania. Pullman planned to create a community that would eliminate "all that was ugly, discordant and demoralizing." Saloons were therefore banned, forcing thirsty workmen to walk a half-mile to Kensington for a beer. The elegant Hotel Florence, however, had a bar and those who were invited inside were welcome to imbibe. Four years after the infamous Pullman Strike of 1894 the company was forced to sell its non-industrial holdings. After surviving threats of demolition in the 1960s, Pullman was revitalized and in 1971 named a National Landmark District, then achieved Chicago landmark status in 1973.

Kensington was a railroad town that got its start in 1852 when the Michigan Central and Illinois Central Railroads built a depot near the shores of Lake Calumet which they called Calumet. The first store owner was Theodore Gohring, who kept his general store and saloon at the corner of Front Street and Kensington Avenue. In 1864, a post office was established. In the three years following the establishment of the Pullman factory in 1880, Kensington's population rose from 250 to nearly 1,300 persons—not including its non-resident laborers and visitors to its 23 saloons. In 1892, the West Pullman Land Association vigorously promoted the area west of Wentworth Avenue, much of which was the site of the old David Andrews farm established in 1837. The development resulted in many factories and more than 600 homes being built in just 4 years.

In 1889, Roseland, Pullman, and Kensington, and in 1895 most of West Pullman, were annexed to the city of Chicago.

Postscript: An annual tour of Roseland occurs every April. Walking tours of the Pullman Historic District are hosted on the first Sunday of every month, from May to October.

Sauk Village

The Glenwood Shoreline passes through the extreme northeast part of Sauk Village. Thus most of the village, southwest of the shoreline, sits on the Tinley Moraine. (See figure 12 in chapter 1.) The village is named for the old Sauk Trail, the oldest trail in the area. In the mid-twentieth century, much of the sand along the Glenwood Shoreline—from U.S. Highway 30 south past Sauk Trail—was mined. The many ponds near the state line are remnants of this mining.

The Samuel Sloan family, the first residents, arrived in 1835. The Frederick Reichert (Richards) family arrived in 1836, the same year that James Morrison established a store. In 1842, Christian Mueller became the area's first blacksmith. The community, originally named Strassburg (sometimes New Strassburg) after a city in Alsace-Lorraine, had the first post office in southeastern Bloom Township. Charles Sauter was the first postmaster. It was also at Strassburg that in 1839 Bloom Township's first religious services were held. The mission church formed here was called St. Jacob's (later St. James) Roman Catholic Church.[1] Its first building, erected in 1853, was rebuilt in 1875 after it was struck by lightning.

Figure 89. St. James Church before the building was lifted up and a basement was excavated. In 1975, the building became the Sauk Village Community Center. St. James Church.

Unfortunately for Strassburg, the post office was moved to Thorn Grove in 1853. The Strassburg area remained unorganized until 1957 when it was incorporated and named Sauk Village. (There was already a Strasburg in Illinois.) Sauk Village's Strassburg Elementary School maintains the historic name of this community.

Postscript: St. James Church, built in 1875, was the third building for this congregation, which was first established in 1839. The first two buildings were destroyed by lightning. The steeple of this building was also struck by lightning—proving that lightning may indeed strike the same place more than twice. In the late 1930s, the building was lifted up and a basement was dug beneath it. In November 1940, a tornado struck the church, damaging its steeple.

When the parish's fourth building was erected on Torrence Avenue in 1962, the old building was donated to the village of Sauk Village to become the village's "old" community center. (By the way, as of this writing, the new building has not been struck by lightning or a tornado.)

1. It is uncertain when the name was changed. However, Andreas referred to it in 1884 as St. James.

South Chicago (Calumet)/South Deering/
The East Side

South Chicago is situated near the mouth of the Calumet River on land composed of long sandy ridges, separated by marshy lowlands. Each of these north-south ridges marked the location of a former beach of Lake Michigan. To the west of the original settlement is Stony Island, today a hill along 92nd and 93rd Streets, but once an island in Lake Michigan (see chapter 1). South Deering is located on the west side of the Calumet River, and East Side is, of course, on the east side of the river.

In the early days, the rather deep Calumet River was an obstacle for those who used the lakeshore to travel from Detroit to Chicago, so in 1830 a ferry service was established. Johann "John" Mann was the ferry operator in 1835. Besides operating the ferry, he and his part-Potawatomi wife, Arkash Sambli, ran the Mann Tavern and traded goods with the Potawatomi Indians. In 1839, the ferry was replaced with a toll bridge located where Route 41 now crosses the river at 92nd Street. Travelers really appreciated the savings that the toll bridge offered.

CALUMET FERRY FARES		TOLL BRIDGE FARES	
2 passengers on foot	25¢	2 passengers on foot	12¢
1 rider and horse	25¢	1 rider and horse	18¢
1 horse and wagon	37¢	1 horse and wagon	25¢

In 1836, Lewis and Rachel Benton established a general store on the west bank of the river. Along with George Dole and Elijah and Elizabeth Hubbard, they also platted the village of Calumet with its streets all laid out in diagonal lines. At that time there were ten or twelve buildings in the village, including the Eagle Tavern and a hotel built by the Bentons called the Calumet House. Because the Calumet River was deeper than the Chicago River, this city was expected to have a larger harbor and eventually surpass Chicago in growth.

In 1851, the Michigan Southern & Northern Indiana Railroad was built nearby and a lighthouse was built at the mouth of the Calumet River, but no harbor was created. A post office was established in 1853. However, by 1855, with no harbor, the light at the lighthouse was extinguished and the lighthouse was sold. Most of the residents of Calumet left town.[2] Two years later, the post office abandoned the name Calumet and started using the name Ainsworth Station.

The history of the small limestone quarries at Stony Island is

---

2. See also the section "Dream Cities of the Calumet," in chapter 4.

not well known. They were in operation by 1868 but were closed by 1886, and it is unlikely that any rock was quarried after that date. Most of the quarry holes were filled in, and the area was developed as a residential neighborhood. One small depression served as the pool for the popular Dunes Motel (demolished in 1995).

Congress finally provided funds for a harbor at the mouth of the Calumet River, and construction began in 1870. The old lighthouse was repurchased by the federal government and put back into service. Mary Ryan was its keeper for the first seven years, in an era when that job was done primarily by men. The first boat, the schooner *Coral,* entered the harbor in 1871, the same year that the post office changed its name again—this time to South Chicago.

South Chicago was platted in 1874, and it grew up around the new harbor, which did indeed grow to be larger than Chicago's harbor. By then, three rail lines passed through the town: the Michigan Southern, the B&O, and the Pittsburgh, Fort Wayne & Chicago.

Figure 90. State Line Monument, about 1915. The oldest structure in the Calumet Area, it was placed near the Lake Michigan shoreline at the Illinois-Indiana state line in about 1830. Southeast Historical Society.

In 1880, the population of South Chicago was 1,962. Residents of the area established several churches. St. Patrick's Roman Catholic Church was the first serving the nearby Irish population. Immanuel Evangelical Lutheran served German immigrants, and First Congregational served much of the native-born population. Within the next six years, another ten churches joined them. Most of their congregations were composed of northern European immigrant groups such as Germans, Swedes, Danes, and Poles. The Calumet River was straightened and deepened, making the area attractive to industries that needed a deep-water port. Immediately west of South Chicago are Calumet Heights and Pill Hill. Both of these relatively newer neighborhoods' names reflect their being on the old Stony Island ridge.

South Deering is west of the Calumet River and northeast of Lake Calumet. Beginning in 1836, when a bridge was built over the Calumet River (at Hegewisch), Chittenden (Muskegon) Avenue served as the main route into Chicago. Travelers preferred it to the old route on the Lake Michigan beach because it was protected from the howling winds that often blew off Lake Michigan. Woodman's Tavern (built in 1844 just east of Lake Calumet) served many of the early travelers.

Figure 91. Immanuel Lutheran Church showing South Chicago's elevated sidewalks. Southeast Historical Society.

Before urban development changed this area, it was home to a vast array of wildlife. In 1873, Abe Kleinman built a hotel and hunting lodge at 112th Street and Chittenden Road. Residents made extra money by hunting and fishing and then selling their catch up north in Chicago.

Urban growth began around 106th Street in 1875 when the Brown Iron and Steel Company[3] established its plant on the Calumet River. Nicknamed Irondale, the community's first official name was Brown's Mill. In 1882, the name was changed to Cummings (for the president of the Nickel Plate Railroad). Finally, in 1903, the community was renamed South Deering for the Deering [International] Harvester Company, which had bought the Calumet Iron and Steel Works.

The East Side also got its start with the Brown Iron and Steel Company. Other industries soon followed, all attracted by the convenience of the new harbor and the nearby rail lines. The population grew, and all three of its rail lines soon had convenient passenger depots. For several years the area north of the rail lines was called Taylorville, while the area to the south was called Colehour. In 1874, the first school was established by members of the new Colehour German (Bethlehem) Lutheran Church. Matt Gallistel opened the first store in Colehour, and when the U.S. government opened a post office in the area in 1875, it was housed in Gallistel's store. The area's first newspaper, the *Daily Calumet,* got its start that year, too.

Drainage was a serious problem for these three communities, all on the low former bottom of Lake Michigan. Many of the houses were often flooded. Elevated sidewalks and streets were built so that people could get around without trudging through standing water. Driving through the area today, one can still see that the major streets are six to eight feet higher than the surrounding ground. They were raised in the 1880s to make them passable even during the frequent floods. In 1889, the *Chicago Tribune* noted that South Chicago's greatest need was drainage. It advised that the level of the whole town would have to be raised, noting, "There is plenty of material for filling . . . in the mountains of slag surrounding the roll-

3. Later the Calumet Iron and Steel Works, and later still, the Wisconsin Steel Company.

ing mills and in the sand dunes along the lake shore to the south of the city."

By 1889, the year that South Chicago, South Deering, and the East Side were annexed to the city of Chicago, there were mills, shipping facilities, several rail lines, a good-sized business district, and a population of about 20,000. The Chicago World's Fair four years later was a major event. Folks could easily get to the fair by any of the rail lines, and apparently most did. It was said that in 1893, the citizens of Southeastern Chicago really began to feel like they were part of the city.

Postscripts: The fifteen-foot high State Line Monument was first erected on the boundary of Indiana and Illinois about 1830. It has been restored and moved to the entrance of the State Line Generating Plant—still on the state line. The Southeast Historical Society Museum, housed in the historic Calumet Park Fieldhouse, has artifacts from the East Side, Hegewisch, South Chicago, and South Deering.

South Holland

The village of South Holland is a low-lying fertile area along the Little Calumet River. The extreme northeast part of the village is built upon sands of the High Tolleston Shoreline.

The first settler of what was to become South Holland was Don C. Berry, who arrived in 1838. But it was the group of settlers from the Netherlands who began arriving in 1847 that established the community and gave it its character. The first to arrive were Hendrik and Geertje DeJong and Cornelius and Marie Brut Arentze. In the next two years, dozens of Dutch families arrived and established farms in the area. The settlers called their new community Low Prairie.[4] Included in this group were the widow Antje Paarlberg[5] and Willem Coenrad Wust, a minister of the Dutch Reformed Church.

The settlers lost no time in establishing the Low Prairie (now First Reformed) Church and erecting a church building on South Park Avenue near the river.[6] In 1865 the "True" Dutch Reformed Church was established, and in 1886 the First Christian Reformed

Figure 92. Antje Paarlberg. South Holland Historical Society Museum.

---

4. Two years later, High Prairie, another Dutch settlement, was established at Roseland (Chicago). The names Low Prairie and High Prairie actually referred to their elevations compared with surrounding lands rather than in comparison with each other. Low Prairie—between two of the ancient shorelines—is actually higher in elevation than High Prairie, which sat atop the High Tolleston Shoreline.

5. Subject of Edna Ferber's 1924 bestseller, *So Big.*

6. This church can be seen in chapter 2 in a photo of the Little Calumet River in flood stage.

Cook County Communities   137

Figure 93. Putting in the main sewer down South Park Avenue, ca. 1910. All dug by hand. South Holland Historical Society Museum.

Church of South Holland was started. For its first several Sundays, this newest congregation met in an onion warehouse near the C&EI tracks. Services at all three churches were in Dutch. In fact, Dutch continued to be used Sunday mornings at some level until the 1940s.

The first public school, Gouwens School, was established in 1854, named after the family that donated the land. The next year, Johannes VanderBilt opened the first general store. Business was good enough that in 1862 Pieter DeJong opened a second store. Many of the families in South Holland were strong abolitionists; Jan and Aagje Ton's nearby house was used as a station on the Underground Railroad.

The first iron railroad to be built near South Holland was the Illinois Central in 1852. It was joined in 1865 by the Chicago & Great Eastern Railway (Panhandle). Four years later, the C&EI Railroad laid its tracks through the center of town and opened a freight and passenger station on 159th Street. The Grand Trunk Railroad arrived in 1880. The railroads brought increased economic growth to the village. In 1870, a post office was opened and Pieter DeJong served as its first postmaster. At his recommendation, the post office and village were named South Holland.

By 1900, South Holland's population reached 766, and although the village was incorporated in 1894, South Holland remained for many years a rural village. The farms were typically "truck gardens" that grew vegetables such as cabbage, carrots, po-

Figure 94. The Paarlberg Homestead.

tatoes, and onions. Farm families made regular trips to Chicago to sell their vegetables. The soils were so good for onions that South Holland soon became the "onion set capital of the world," growing more than half and marketing virtually all the onion sets in the country. By the 1950s, the South Holland area was producing more than 1.5 billion onion sets each year.

Postscript: The Van Oostenbrugge Home was built in 1858 by Jan and Evertje Van Oostenbrugge. The Paarlberg Homestead, built in 1870, was the home of Peter and Cornelia Paarlberg. Both homes have been restored by the South Holland Historical Society and are open to the public.

The True Dutch Reformed Church and Parsonage on 162nd Street were built in 1873–74. The South Holland Historical Society Museum is housed in the South Holland Public Library.

Steger

The village of Steger, which straddles the Cook/Will County line, lies partially on the Tinley Moraine (at State Street and along Cottage Grove Avenue) and partially on a former glacial lake (along the Chicago Road).

Two old highways are in Steger, although their intersection is in South Chicago Heights. They are the old Sauk Trail, the area's oldest east-west route, and the Vincennes Trace (Chicago Road), which once connected Fort Dearborn (Chicago) with the former Indiana territorial capital of Vincennes.

Steger was laid out in 1891. James Keeney, who platted the village, named it Dearborn Heights. Four weeks later, he changed the name to Columbia Heights in honor of the Columbian Exposition in Chicago. The town was best known, however, for the Steger piano factory established in 1893 by John Valentine Steger. Within twenty years, it became the largest piano factory in the world. As a result, Steger's name was given to the town when it was incorporated in 1897. Steger's population in 1900 was 712.

Thornton

The village of Thornton is best known for its hole in the ground, the huge Thornton Quarry. The ancient coral reef that underlies the area was underwater during the Glenwood phase of Lake Michigan. As the lake's surface lowered, the rock surfaced and a sandy beach developed around this circular island. The other prominent natural feature is Thorn Creek, which has eroded a rather deep valley through the village.

Thornton is located along the ancient Calumet Shoreline, but because of the natural erosion of Thorn Creek and the digging of the quarry, the shoreline is not very visible. The village is located at the intersection of a branch of the Vincennes Trace and the Indian trail/stagecoach route that followed the Shoreline. Alfred Meyer described Thornton as having had one of the largest Indian villages in the area. According to Andreas, the earliest settlers found arrowheads, pottery, and abandoned Indian fortifications.

Because of its strategic location on two major transportation routes, Thornton was one of the first communities in Cook County to attract permanent settlers. The first was William Woodbridge, who arrived in 1834 and established the first store in the village.

Figure 95. Workers at the Thornton Quarry. Thornton Historical Society Museum.

Figure 96. The Bielfeldt Brewery and the bridge over Thorn Creek. Thorn Creek was much larger before the Calumet Sag Channel was completed in 1922. Thornton Historical Society Museum.

In 1835, Gurdon Hubbard, John H. Kinzie, and John Blackstone built a sawmill on the banks of Thorn Creek (much deeper then than now) and Kinzie platted the village. The village and township were named for Colonel W. F. Thornton a commissioner for the Illinois and Michigan Canal.

The first schoolhouse was built in 1836 using lumber from the new sawmill. Don Carlos Berry established the first tavern (inn) in town and became the first postmaster. The economic prospects of the area were heightened in 1869 when the Chicago & Eastern Illinois Railroad was built through town and Thornton was connected by rail to Chicago. The first church in Thornton was built by the Society of Good Templars; it was purchased in 1876 by a new Methodist congregation. The St. Paul Lutheran congregation built its first church in 1873. (It was destroyed by a tornado in March 1904 and rebuilt on the same foundation the same year.)

The early settlers discovered that limestone (dolomite) was close to the surface of the earth, and the first quarry was opened by 1850. The rock was in great demand. It was easy to extract, and the railroad made it possible for limestone to be transported to distant locations. Today's quarry, operated by Material Service Corporation, is one of the ten largest limestone quarries in the world.

By 1880, Thornton, with a population of 400, had a brewery, five stores, two churches, two quarries, and two saloons. It was incorporated as a village in 1900.

Postscript: The Bielfeldt Brewery was established in 1858 by

John Bielfeldt. (During Prohibition, federal agents once poured 140,000 gallons of beer into Thorn Creek.) These buildings have survived a tornado and several fires. The St. Paul Lutheran Church building, rebuilt after the 1904 tornado, and raised up in 1922 (in order to build a basement below it) is now the home of the Thornton Historical Society Museum.

Lake County Communities

Lake County was created in 1837. From 1832 to 1836, the area that is now Lake County was the far western part of LaPorte County. For one year, 1836–37, it was part of Porter County.

Cedar Lake/Lake Dalecarlia

The town of Cedar Lake is located in the Valparaiso Moraine just south of the Eastern Continental Divide. At 2.5 miles in length, the lake, known earlier as the Lake of the Red Cedars, is the largest natural lake in the Calumet Area.

Peter and LaRose Surprenant (later Surprise) are said to have been the first settlers on the lake, arriving in 1833. Between 1834 and 1837, the families of Richard and Mariah Fancher, Hervey and Jane Ball, Charles Wilson, Robert and Elizabeth Wilkenson, Jacob and Thomas Brown, David Horner, James Knickerbocker, Adonijah and Horace Taylor, their father Obadiah Taylor,[1] Dr. Calvin and

---

1. Obadiah Taylor, who died three years after arriving at Cedar Lake, may be the only Revolutionary War veteran buried in Lake County. He was buried in the old pioneer West Point Cemetery at Cedar Lake.

Figure 97. Jane Ball. Lake County Historical Society Museum.

Dorothy Lilley,[2] and Horace and Betsey Edgerton all settled near the Lake of the Red Cedars. Dr. Lilley was a tavern/hotelkeeper there, built a sawmill at the outlet of the lake, and in a sense founded the community.[3] Lilley's hotel served as an important social center of the area. When Lilley died in 1839, Benjamin McCarty took over his efforts and platted the town on the east shore of the lake, calling it West Point. McCarty, who had helped locate the county seats for LaPorte and Porter Counties, actively promoted West Point and tried to have his town named the new Lake County seat. When West Point was not chosen, many of the pioneers moved southward and the West Point community nearly disappeared.

Cedar Lake had one of Lake County's first schools, a boarding school with students coming from as far away as Porter and LaPorte Counties. It was opened in 1839 in a log building with Jane Ball teaching all the children. Jane Ball Elementary School is named for her. It was Mrs. Ball's son, Timothy, who later wrote several histories of northwestern Indiana.

Cedar Lake also claims to have the county's first sawmill, library, kiln for brick making, and debate society. Near the lake grew up a number of separate small communities such as West Point, Armour Town (an ice harvesting center), Hanover Central, Tinkerville, Creston, Klaasville, Paisley, and Cook. The Monon Railroad in 1881 was built along the west shore of the lake. In 1906, the tracks of the Chicago, Indiana & Southern Railroad (New York Central) passed

Figure 98. Looking west across Cedar Lake, ca. 1895. Note the icehouses on the far shore. From Blatchley, 1897.

2. Robinson (1847) spelled the name Lilly; Ball (1884) spelled it Lilley.
3. Timothy Ball (1884) noted that Lilley obtained two licenses from the new county government in 1837. He paid five dollars for a license to sell groceries and dry goods and fifteen dollars for a license to open and keep a tavern. The fact that this license cost so much more than the other Lake County licenses issued that year (six dollars for taverns on both the lake front and the sand ridge and ten for the tavern at Liverpool) may indicate the relative importance placed on this site.

through Cook, on U.S. Highway 41. For many years there were post offices at Armour, Paisley, and Creston.

The Monon made it easy for Chicagoans to get to the lake, and by the 1880s Cedar Lake had become a resort community. Steamers and sailboats appeared on the lake, dozens of hotels were built, and excursions from Chicago were organized. Dance halls were built right up to the lake

Figure 99. The Lassen Hotel, a fine place to spend a weekend, now the Lake of the Red Cedars Museum. Cedar Lake Historical Association.

shore. Every summer there were thousands of visitors at the new resort community. Every winter the tourists left, and if it was cold enough, workers arrived and ice was harvested.

The "town" of Cedar Lake is relatively young. After several unsuccessful attempts to incorporate, the town was finally organized in 1965; however, lawsuits declared its incorporation invalid. Cedar Lake was incorporated (again) in 1967.

Lake Dalecarlia was originally a mill pond formed in 1853 by a man named Carsten who built a small dam across Cedar Creek. The mill was abandoned in 1885. The dam was rebuilt in 1927 to create the lake at the center of this residential community.

Postscript: In 1895 the Armour Company built a large rooming house for its ice workers at Armour Town, near the northwest shore of the lake—by the railroad lines. In the winter of 1919, Christopher Lassen, who owned a dance hall, pavilion, restaurant, and boat dock on the east side of the lake, purchased the rooming house and moved it across the frozen lake to his property. He remodeled the building and turned it into a fine resort, the Lassen Hotel. Lassen's excursion boats would pick up passengers at the Monon Station and ferry them to his resort. The building has been restored by the Cedar Lake Historical Association and is now the home of the Lake of the Red Cedars Museum.

The Monon Dining Hall and Dancing Pavilion (now Torrey Auditorium) were built in the 1890s as part of Monon Park, an entertainment complex built by the Monon Railroad for its passengers. In 1915, the Monon gave the park to the Moody Memorial Church of Chicago and the grounds were renamed the Cedar Lake Bible Conference Grounds.

Crown Point

Crown Point, the county seat of Lake County, sits on the border of the Valparaiso and Tinley Moraines. (The Tinley Moraine is north of the Main Beaver Dam Ditch, and the Valparaiso is south of it.) Its most famous kettle lake, Fancher Lake at the Lake County Fairgrounds, was named for the Fancher family, which settled on its

lakeshore in 1834. For more than 100 years (until 1945), ice from Fancher Lake was cut and stored for use in the summer months. Once the railroads came to town, Fancher Lake ice was transported to "far-off cities." Richard Fancher donated forty acres of his land including the lake to the county for use as its fairgrounds.

Four or five families, including Solon and Mariah Robinson and their two children, established a claim in what is now downtown Crown Point in 1834. Robinson founded the village, which he intended to be the county seat, and so he first named it Lake Court House. He encouraged dozens of others to settle in his town, and when a post office was located there in 1836 (the first in Lake County), it was placed in his store and he was named postmaster.

When a state committee named Liverpool the county seat in 1839, Robinson organized a protest that resulted in a new committee reversing the decision and giving the prize to Crown Point.[4] In 1842 Mr. Wells built a large tavern that contained a store at one end and a whiskey shop at the other.[5] It is interesting to note that in 1850, George Earle, the former promoter of Liverpool, was the architect for a new county courthouse on the square.

In 1835, Mrs. Harriet Holton established the first school in the county when she began teaching three students in a private home. A few years later, a log schoolhouse was built. This was replaced by a primitive frame building in 1841.

4. Timothy Ball (1873, p. 86) suggested that "Crown" was evidently in honor of Solon Robinson, the Squatter King, and "Point" was taken from the name of West Point, Crown Point's county seat rival.
5. Concerning the whiskey shop, Solon Robinson noted, "I cannot say that this improved the morals of the place. Certain it is, it has been the ruin of the owner."

Taking advantage of the abundance of glacial clay in the area, Mason's and Farrington's brick works opened in 1841. The first two churches, Methodist and Presbyterian, were built in the mid-1840s. Work was slow on both because good lumber for construction still had to be brought in by oxcart. The *Crown Point Register,* a weekly newspaper, began its operations in 1857. That year the community also got its first library as the McClure Library Association began lending books to area resident members.

Growth of the town was steady until 1865 when the Chicago & Great Eastern Railway (the Panhandle) started providing passenger and freight service to Chicago. The railroad caused the town to grow rapidly. With dozens of businesses and industries, and a population of about 1,300, Crown Point was incorporated as a town in 1868.

Construction on a new red brick and stone courthouse was begun in 1878. To build it, 500,000 bricks from the nearby Henry Wise brickyard were used. Within thirty years, the courthouse was found to be too small, and so in 1908 it was enlarged by adding two 2.5-story additions.[6] The courthouse was enlarged again in 1928 with two 1.5-story additions to make the structure the way it is today.

By 1910, with numerous businesses and nine churches, Crown Point's population had surpassed 2,500 people. Crown Point became a city in 1911.

Postscript: The old brick courthouse, now on the National Register of Historic Places, was saved from demolition by concerned citizens who formed the Lake Court House Foundation. The building now contains boutiques and the museum of the Lake County Historical Society.

The Old Homestead, at 227 South Court Street, was built in 1847 by Wellington and Mary Clark and is the oldest house in Crown Point. The Sheriff's Residence has been a part of Crown Point since 1882. The Lake County Jail was added to the back of the house in 1926.

Figure 101. Lake County Courthouse. Lake County Historical Society Museum.

The Historic Walking Tour brochure *First Walk,* published by the Chamber of Commerce and available at the old courthouse, describes many of the old homes along South Court Street.

6. When in the 1970s it was once again too small, the new Government Center was built on North Main Street.

Dyer

Figure 102. The State Line House, built about 1838. Dyer Historical Society Museum.

The town of Dyer sits along the ancient Glenwood Shoreline just east of where it crosses the Indiana-Illinois state line. South of the highway is a gently hilly region that is part of the Tinley Moraine. To the north is the lower, flatter, former Lake Michigan bottomland. The Glenwood Shoreline in Dyer was part of the Old Sauk Trail. In 1913 it became part of the Lincoln Highway—the country's first transcontinental highway. The "Ideal Section" of the Lincoln Highway was constructed on this route east of the old town in 1922. Three years later, this part of the Lincoln Highway was named U.S. Highway 30.

Although commercial development and road improvements have made the former shoreline difficult to recognize in a few places, sand dunes from that shoreline are still visible south of U.S. 30. One particularly tall dune still exists at Castlewood Drive.

The State Line House was perhaps the Dyer area's first building. It was an inn that served the hungry and tired traveling on the old Sauk Trail. Timothy Ball believed that it was in operation as early as 1838.

However, growth of the area didn't come until the "Joliet Cut-off" of the Michigan Central Railroad was built in 1854. The next year, a station was built and Aaron and Martha Dyer Hart, the area's largest landowners, settled nearby. The town would soon bear Martha's family name.

In 1856, John Streets built the first store. The Dyer post office opened the next year. Other businesses followed including a large grain elevator built by the Michigan Central. Within a few years Dyer became the primary shipping point in the county for agricultural products.

Figure 103. Aaron and Martha Dyer Hart, founders of Dyer. Munster Historical Society Museum.

The town was platted in 1858 by Barnard Nondorf. The following year, Hart's addition included Hart and Joliet Streets. Unlike the Harts, most Dyer inhabitants were German Catholics who in 1867 organized the St. Joseph Parish. Standing in front of that church today, one can still see (even after the reconstruction of U.S. 30 in the 1990s) the northward slope down into what had been Lake Michigan some 14,000 years ago.

By 1870, Dyer, with a flour mill, fifty families, and numerous businesses, was the largest community in St. John Township.

Three years later, Ball referred to Dyer as the best grain market in the county—and that was before the Monon and the EJ&E Railroads built their lines through the town. The railroads were a stimulus for more businesses including a creamery, Schaeffer's blacksmith, a pickle and sauerkraut factory, a flour mill, Batterman's Harness Shop, and Peschel's Tin Shop. The First National Bank of Dyer opened in 1903. (Its 1917 calendar featured a map which was the basis for the regional railroad map shown in chapter 5.)

Much of the former swampland north of the Sauk Trail was drained and made arable in the 1890s when Aaron Hart excavated the ditch that still bears his name. This ditch gave the meandering Plum Creek a direct route through the Calumet Shoreline ridge and down to the Little Calumet River.

Dyer was incorporated as a town in 1910. That year's census showed Dyer's population to be 545.

Postscript: The Dyer Union Protestant Church, the first nondenominational or "union" church in Lake County, was built in 1891 on North Hart Street. In 1962 the church became First United Presbyterian. The old building has been converted to commercial use.

St. Joseph's Church was built in 1903 after a fire destroyed the original white structure. The inscriptions on the windows are in German, the language of its first parishioners.

The Dyer Historical Society Museum is located on the ground floor of the town hall.

East Chicago

Before settlement, East Chicago was a wooded and sandy area characterized by wooded ridges and often wet swales, all parallel to the lakeshore, which made north-south travel nearly impossible. Historian Powell Moore (1959) described this wilderness as "more desolate and inaccessible than any other portion of the Calumet Region." Even when the Michigan Southern and the Fort Wayne Railroads were built through this area in the 1850s, they established no stations here.

Called the "Twin Cities," its two largest neighborhoods are separated by the Indiana Harbor Ship Canal, which connects the Grand Calumet River to Lake Michigan. The community to the east is called Indiana Harbor while that community on the west is simply known as East Chicago. Calumet is a third neighborhood not far from the Grand Calumet River near the city's southern edge.

Settlement of Indiana Harbor didn't begin until after the railroads were built. The Lake Shore and Michigan Southern line was first in 1852. The Pittsburgh, Fort Wayne & Chicago (Pennsylvania) came in 1858. The area's biggest investor at that time was George W. Clarke, who owned much of the lakeshore from the state line to Gary. His map shows a pier at the lakefront at Poplar Point, but it is doubtful that the pier was ever built. The first settlers were the families of Louis Ahlendorf and Dominick Mutter, who purchased 120 acres of land in 1857.

In 1867, Caroline and Jacob Forsyth[7] (sister and brother-in-law of Clarke) bought Mutter's and Ahlendorf's land, constructed a saw-mill near Lake Michigan, built cabins to house employees, convinced the Fort Wayne Railroad to build a siding, and established a business cutting and shipping the area's abundant timber. Forsyth named his community Cassella for his cousin, Ella Cass, who was married to the president of the railroad. Cassella was destroyed by one of the many great fires of 1871 and was not rebuilt. The name, however, persisted until 1901, when the area was renamed Indiana Harbor. That year the Lake Michigan Land Company offered fifty acres of free land to any company willing to spend one million dollars to build a steel mill on the site. Inland Steel Company, whose main plant was then in Chicago Heights, accepted the offer.

In 1887, the Standard Steel and Iron Company (a real estate, not an industrial company) platted a new city in the area that is now west of the canal. Many of the early north-south streets were named for the early investors: John Stewart Kennedy, Jacob and Caroline Forsyth, Joseph and Libby Torrence, and their daughter, Jessie Magoun. Investor Robert Tod was the namesake for Tod Park and the Tod Opera House. In an effort to show how close the area was to booming Chicago, the east-west streets used Chicago street numbers. Plans included a harbor, ship canal, and belt-line railroad. The first neighborhood was established between Forsyth (now Indianpolis Boulevard) and Railroad Avenues. The uneven ground was leveled and streets were built. The first industry was Graver Tank Works; the first resident was its superintendent, William Penman.

Growth was rapid. Four churches were established in just three years: First Methodist in 1888, First Congregational in 1889, and St. Mary's Roman Catholic and St. Paul's Lutheran in 1890. East Chicago was incorporated as a town in 1889, the same year its post office opened. At the first town election, Penman was elected treasurer and Fred Fife was elected clerk. Four years later East Chicago became a city with Penman as mayor. By 1900, East Chicago had a population of 3,411.

In 1901, work began on the harbor. The ship canal was begun two years later. With its new harbor and canal, new industry, and the Indiana Harbor Belt and other railways, East Chicago proudly advertised itself as the area "where rail and water meet." Soon the

Figure 104. William H. Penman, first settler and mayor of East Chicago. East Chicago Public Library.

---

7. Jacob Forsyth's name was, as was George W. Clarke's, sometimes spelled without, and sometimes with an e at the end. This book uses the former spelling, which was found to be most prevalent in the Lake County land transfer books of 1859–1864 held at the Calumet Regional Archives.

Figure 105. The Indiana Harbor Ship Canal, ca. 1903. East Chicago Public Library.

harbor was Indiana's largest and busiest. A post office opened in Indiana Harbor in 1902.

East Chicago got its second steel mill in 1914, when the Mark Manufacturing Company established a plant just northwest of the ship canal. Clayton Mark was the first East Chicago industrialist to build housing for his employees. In a development similar to George Pullman's, he built 103 white stucco homes, stores, playgrounds, and baseball and football fields and named it Marktown.

The city grew quickly. The population quintupled between 1900 and 1910. More than half the population at that time was foreign-born, with men outnumbering women more than two to

Figure 106. Marktown on a 1920s postcard. East Chicago Public Library.

one. Boarding houses, a dozen churches, and 110 saloons catered to the needs of the new arrivals. East Chicago had become a major industrial community.

Postscript: Marktown is still a quiet residential island surrounded by heavy industry. The community may be unique in that every one of the original buildings still stands. In 1975, Marktown was placed on the National Register of Historic Places.

Gary

(See separate sections on Miller and Tolleston.)

Gary, the largest city in the Calumet Area, extends from the shores of Lake Michigan to the Lake Border Moraine. In addition to the present shoreline, all three former shorelines and the Grand and Little Calumet Rivers are located within the city—all crossing in an east-west direction. From north to south they are the Grand Calumet River, the high Tolleston Shoreline—named for the Tolleston neighborhood on the west side of the city, the Little Calumet River, the former Calumet Shoreline (Ridge Road), the Griffith Spit (Glenwood Shoreline) between Forty-third and Forty-fifth Avenues, and in southernmost Glen Park, the northern edge of Hobart Island, part of the Lake Border Moraine.

Before development, the ground in northern Gary alternated between long sand ridges and swales that must have resembled corduroy. The Lake Michigan beach and the High Tolleston and Calumet Shorelines were all used as Indian trails and for stagecoach routes.

EARLY SETTLEMENTS

The first permanent settlement in what is now central Gary was the Gibson Inn, established by Thomas and Anna Maria Gibson in 1838. It was located on the Tolleston Shoreline near the present corner of Madison Street and Fourteenth Avenue across from where Froebel School was later built.[8] The inn was a two-story building with sitting and dining rooms on the ground floor and two large bedrooms above. Thomas Gibson died in 1850, but Anna Maria kept the inn going for several years afterward. She sold the building in the 1890s.

In 1881, the large Aetna Powder Plant was built on the desolate Tolleston Shoreline about one mile west of Miller. This rather empty and forsaken-looking location was chosen because of the constant danger of explosions. The ridges and sand dunes of the ancient

---

8. In 1923, a granite monument marking the site of the Gibson Inn was placed on the grounds of the Bailey branch of the Gary Public Library at Fifteenth and Madison.

shoreline were used to good advantage as they could contain explosions and shelter employees. In 1894 a post office was opened and the next year the Wabash Railroad was built through Aetna, eliminating the need to transport products to Miller's Station for shipping. Aetna was incorporated as a town in 1907. By then, this tiny town (about one-half square mile) had its post office and store, a few homes, and several boarding houses. There was no church, but ministers from Hobart and Miller would come and preach in the boarding houses. Explosions did occur. One, which in 1912 killed six employees, occurred just minutes before a crowded South Shore passenger train was to pass by. A mammoth explosion in 1914 shattered windows in downtown Gary two miles west. During World War I, the plant had 1,200 employees, but after the war the plant closed as the expanding city of Gary brought civilization too close to its doorstep. Aetna was annexed by Gary in 1924.

Clarke and Pine Station were built on undulating former lake bottomland several miles north of the high Tolleston Shoreline. Clarke, also called Clarke Station (later Clark), was located on the Grand Calumet River where it was crossed in 1858 by the Pittsburgh, Fort Wayne & Chicago Railroad. It was named for George W. Clarke, one of the earliest investors in northern Lake County. The main business at Clarke Station was cutting and shipping 60,000 tons of ice each year. Many of the laborers lived in Tolleston, where they mined sand during the warm months. In 1860, the Clarke Station post office was established. By 1870 the little community contained about sixteen families and Kelley's general store. Clark Road today, north of Fifth Avenue, passes through what had once been this isolated village and goes north to the site of the old settlement of Pine Station.

The tiny hamlet of Pine Station centered about a small station on the Michigan Southern Railroad not far from the Lake Michigan shoreline. Although it was listed as one of the three most important stations in the early 1850s, it was soon eclipsed by newer stations, closer to the population center of the county. In 1906, with a combined population of little more than 100, Clarke and Pine Station were annexed by the first act of the new town of Gary.

Figure 107. Glen Park School, still standing on Broadway. Calumet Regional Archives.

Glen Park was established between the old Glenwood Shoreline at Forty-third Avenue and the crossing of the Joliet Cut-off and the Nickel Plate Railroads. In 1894, William Reissig and Charles Williams, a real estate salesman, platted the town and paid half fare for Chicagoans to come out on the Nickel

Plate and view the new little community. The community was named Kelly in honor of a Nickel Plate Railroad official. When a post office was established in 1898, Reissig served as the first postmaster.

By 1900 the little community was better known as Glen Park. Who named it that is now unknown, but that year Timothy Ball noted that it must have been a Chicagoan, for "Lake County people are not inclined to the name of Park."

After Gary was founded in 1906, Timothy Englehart removed sand from his property on Ridge Road in order to build an elevated road extending through the marshlands north of the village to the Little Calumet River. (This raised roadway can still be seen between the Indiana University Northwest campus and the river.) Englehart then coaxed the county into building a bridge across the river, and Broadway was extended south from Gary to Glen Park. Not surprisingly, the city then annexed the Glen Park area (south to Forty-fifth Avenue). Streetcar service to the mills was started and mill workers could indeed buy houses in Glen Park and commute to their jobs up north.

Glen Park's first church, the Glen Park Christian Church, was organized in 1910 and met at the new Glen Park School; its first building was completed on Washington Street in just one day, March 18, 1911. In 1926, the city annexed the southern part of Glen Park.

EAST TOLLESTON/BRADFORD/JERUSALEM/CALUMET

The area around Seventeenth and Broadway had a lot of inauspicious beginnings. Fred and Henry Bradford platted a town there in 1890 that was known as both Bradford and East Tolleston. The main east-west road was the old Chicago-Detroit Road on the ancient High Tolleston Shoreline (about Fourteenth Avenue) past the site of Mrs. Gibson's old inn. A furniture factory and a varnish factory brought some source of employment and a school was built. But the panic of 1893 resulted in the near death of this little village.

In 1894, Louis and Evva Bryan bought out the Bradfords and planned a new city called Calumet that was to extend from the Wabash tracks to the Little Calumet River. Bryan established a piano stool factory and a newspaper, the *Calumet Advance,* and served as justice of the peace and part-time postmaster. For eight years he also ran a sand-mining business, sending out two trainloads of sand *every day.*

When the United States Steel Company decided to build a steel mill north of his community, Louis Bryan was the first to sign the incorporation petition for Gary. He then served as the city's first treasurer. William Howat called Bryan Gary's first citizen.

Figure 108. The distinctive 150-foot concrete water tower and filtration plant in Jefferson Park, ca. 1911. The uncompleted First Presbyterian Church is in the background. Calumet Regional Archives.

U.S. STEEL AND THE BEGINNINGS OF THE CITY

In 1906, the Indiana Steel Company, a subsidiary of U.S. Steel, began building its new mill at the southern tip of Lake Michigan. In order to accomplish this, 9,000 acres of land were purchased, the Grand Calumet River was re-channeled, a harbor was dredged, new rail lines were laid, three existing rail lines were relocated, and 11 million cubic yards of sand were excavated.[9] (In 1925, Gary's second harbor was constructed at the Buffington site on Gary's far west side.)

A. F. Knotts, a former mayor of Hammond, handled the purchasing of land in 1905. The next year, a post office was established and Gary was incorporated as a town, named for Elbert H. Gary, chairman of the board of U.S. Steel. Knotts's brother Thomas became the first town board president, and by its first vote, the new

9. A photograph of a team of horses leveling the Gary sand dunes can be seen in chapter 6. A popular story in the area is that the building of U.S. Steel resulted in the moving of more earth than was moved while building the entire Panama Canal. Although a good story, it is not true. According to U.S. Steel executive W. P. Gleason (1922), 11 million cubic yards of earth were moved in the construction of Gary Works while 268 million cubic yards were moved during the construction of the Panama Canal.

Figure 109. Gary town board members inspecting the new sewers, 1906. Calumet Regional Archives.

town board annexed the Clarke and Buffington areas west of the town.

With a huge demand for workers, Gary became one of the fastest growing areas in the country. Within a year its population reached about 10,000. After two years of heavy construction, the first shipment of Minnesota iron ore was unloaded at Gary Works on July 23, 1908. Powell Moore noted that U.S. Steel's Gary Works was then described as the "greatest steel plant in the world."

Gary was reincorporated as a city in 1909, the same year that Emerson School opened and Glen Park was annexed. In spite of already being incorporated as independent towns, Tolleston was annexed in 1910, Miller in 1918, and Aetna in 1924.

Trains were the lifeblood of the early city. They brought in new workers, building and raw materials, machinery, and produce for makeshift businesses such as the Colosimo Fruit Stand.

GARY SCHOOLS: "SPLENDID CIVIC MONUMENTS"

Each Gary high school built between 1909 and 1932 was designed by nationally known architect William Ittner as "a splendid civic monument . . . a potent factor in the aesthetic development of the community." The main entrance of each school faced south, and nearly all of the classrooms faced east, south, or west so that, as much as possible, each classroom would be filled with natural sunlight.

The growth of the steel industry reversed the relative value of areas in the city. From 1838 to 1906, the high Tolleston Shoreline was the center of hope and development. The Gibson Inn and the towns of Aetna, Calumet, and Tolleston were all established on this former shoreline and stage route. However, beginning in 1906, development was related to the lake. The mills and company-designed neighborhoods were built on these formerly worthless lands, while the higher previously settled lands south of the Wabash Railroad were relegated to the poorest of the new city's new residents, both black and white. As black professionals moved to Gary, they too could only find housing in the area south of the tracks.

By 1910 Gary had a population of 16,802 with more than two men for every woman, perhaps twenty churches, and 217 saloons (most of them south of the tracks). Twenty years later, the population was over 100,000.

Figure 110. Historic Emerson High School. Calumet Regional Archives.

Postscript: Emerson and Glen Park Schools were built in 1909. Emerson is now a magnet school for visual and performing arts. Glen Park School was built as a Calumet Township school—just as

Gary was considering annexing the Glen Park area. It is now privately owned.

The Gary Land Company Building was the first permanent structure built for the new city. It housed Gary's first post office and served as Gary's first town hall and high school. It was moved to Jefferson Street, where it stood for several years before being moved to Gateway Park on Fourth Avenue. The building was restored in 1982 and became the home of the Gary Historical and Cultural Society.

Figure 111. Gary Land Company Building. Calumet Regional Archives.

Griffith

Within the town of Griffith are the ancient Glenwood and Calumet Shorelines and the floodplain of the Little Calumet River. Ridge Road, formerly U.S. 6 and Griffith's oldest transportation route, is built on the sandy Calumet Shoreline. North of the ridge, the land slopes down toward the Little Calumet River. South of Ridge Road, along Cady Marsh Ditch, is a long flat area that was once part of the extensive Cady Marsh. This land was lake bottom during the Glenwood phase. The sandy higher central and southern part of town (generally south of Pine Street) is built upon the west end of the Griffith Spit, a series of long sandy peninsulas or off-shore ridges that were deposited by moving waters during the Glenwood phase of Lake Michigan. Perhaps the best remaining example of these spits is located south of the Grand Trunk Railroad just east of Broad Street. Most of the others have been leveled off as the town was developed.

Settlers began arriving in the 1850s. Among the first were the families of Mathias and Anna Miller, Jacob and Augusta Helfen, Nicholas and Susanna Hillbrich, and Peter and Emma Redar. With no town nearby, these farmers traveled to Dyer or Schererville for supplies or to attend church services.

Although called a "Ridge Community" today, Griffith's beginnings were not on the Calumet Beach ridge but south of it, where in 1880 the Michigan Central Railroad's Joliet Cut-off was crossed by the Chicago & Grand Trunk Railroad. The Grand Trunk was welcomed by local farmers because it was the first rail line that would pick up milk every morning and take it into Chicago. The junction was named for Benjamin Griffith, said to be either a civil engineer or a surveyor for the Grand Trunk.

In 1883 the Chicago & Atlantic (later Erie Lackawanna) and five years after that the EJ&E Railroads built their tracks—with all four lines crossing at the same site. Historian Timothy Ball called

Figure 112. The Grand Trunk Depot, now Griffith's Depot Museum.

this junction in Griffith the "grandest railroad crossing in Lake County"—and that was before 1906 when the Chicago, Cincinnati & Louisville (Chesapeake & Ohio) Railroad extended its line through Griffith and crossed at this same junction.

Griffith's excellent rail connections promised much for a new town. However, in 1890 the only nearby resident was the station manager. All that changed in 1891 when the town was laid out by Jay Dwiggins. An ambitious developer, he encouraged both industries and potential employees to move to his new town, which he widely advertised as "Chicago's Best Factory Suburb." The original part of town was northeast of the junction with streets named for the founders: Jay, Dwiggins, Elmer (Jay's brother), and Arbogast (Dwiggins's notary public). Broad Street was originally known as Junction Avenue.

Griffith's post office opened in 1891, and the town enjoyed spectacular growth for a couple of years. It suffered a temporary business and population decline beginning with the Panic of 1893 before growing again. In 1904 with a population of 359, Griffith was incorporated as a town. The Ridge Road area was annexed in 1914.

In 1915, after more than twenty years of worship services in homes, stores, and the town hall, Griffith's First Methodist Church erected its first building. First Christian Church was started after a series of revival services in 1920, and St. Mary's Church was established in 1921. By 1920, Griffith had a population of 630.

Postscript: Griffith Historical Park at Griffith's "grand" railroad crossing features several railroad cars, the 1914 Grand Trunk Depot, which now serves as the Depot Museum, and the two-story EJ&E Tower, moved across the tracks to the park in July 2000.

Hammond

The city of Hammond extends from the present Lake Michigan shoreline south to the Little Calumet River. The city is bisected by the Grand Calumet River just north of the downtown area and the High Tolleston Shoreline. This ancient shoreline runs from Hohman Avenue and 165th Street southeast to 169th and Kennedy Avenue. It then follows 169th Street through Hessville. Just south of Lake Michigan are Wolf Lake and Lake George. In 1884, historian Alfred Andreas referred to the Hammond area as originally an "unbroken forest of heavy timber, but which has long since mainly disappeared, under the aggressive civilization of the white man's ax."

The first settlers in what would eventually become Hammond were German immigrants Francis and Margaraitha Humpfer. They arrived in 1847 and began farming north of the Little Calumet River in what is today southwestern Hammond—an area that for many years was known as Saxony. In 1851 Ernst and Caroline Hohman settled on the north side of the Grand Calumet River near the state line, just north of today's downtown area. They established an inn (Hohman's Tavern) and built and operated a toll bridge across the river. Caroline's sister Louisa and her husband William Sohl soon built a home on the south side of the river. After the Michigan Central Railroad was completed in 1852, William Sohl opened the area's first store near the new Michigan Central station.

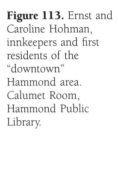

Figure 113. Ernst and Caroline Hohman, innkeepers and first residents of the "downtown" Hammond area. Calumet Room, Hammond Public Library.

In 1868, George Hammond, for whom the city is named, established a meat packing plant nearby on the same river. Hammond, who needed the railroad to transport beef and the river to harvest ice for shipping the beef, revolutionized the meat packing business with his refrigerated rail cars. Because of its stench, the slaughterhouse was intended to be distant from the large residential areas of Chicago, yet the eighteen workers at the plant had to live nearby. The community that grew up around the toll bridge, packing plant, and railroad station was variously called Hohman, Hohman's Bridge, and State Line Slaughterhouse. When a post office was finally established in 1873, it was given the less descriptive name of Hammond.

Marcus and Irene Towle arrived in 1869. Marcus, who served as the first postmaster, platted the town of Hammond in 1875. He opened a lumberyard, a sawmill, a planing mill, the First National Bank, and numerous other businesses. The meat packing plant, the other businesses, and the population grew rapidly. In 1883 Hammond was incorporated as a town; less than four months later, it became a city with Towle serving as its first mayor.

Figure 114. A lumber schooner docked at the Hammond Lumber Company on the Grand Calumet River. Calumet Room, Hammond Public Library.

In 1897, the new city annexed the Roby/Robertsdale section with its Lake Michigan frontage. This area had also been devoid of much settlement until the railroads built their lines, the Michigan Southern & Northern Indiana in 1851–52, the Pittsburgh, Fort Wayne & Chicago in 1858, and the B&O in 1874. All three lines were built parallel to each other and very close to the lakeshore (then not considered at all valuable). George

Figure 115. Marcus Towle, founder of several local businesses as well as first mayor of Hammond. Calumet Room, Hammond Public Library.

M. Roberts donated land to the Fort Wayne railroad, which then named the station Robertsdale. In 1874 a large hotel was built at the intersection of what are now Sheffield Avenue and Indianapolis Boulevard. This hotel was to be the anchor of a great new industrial city named Sheffield, the last of the never-built "dream cities of the Calumet" described in chapter 4. The only remaining evidence of this dream city is the name of the avenue.

The area called Roby, named for landowner Edward Roby, borders the city of Chicago at the lakefront. A post office opened there in 1891, and for several years it was billed as the smallest in the world. In the late 1890s, Roby was well known for its racetracks, casino, and boxing arena. However, the gambling at Roby was quite illegal and no tax monies were paid to support local communities, so eventually it was shut down. In later years Roby was the site of dance halls, amusement parks, and restaurants.

Wolf Lake proved to be a valuable asset to the area when the Knickerbocker Ice Company started harvesting ice every winter. The 1911 superintendent, Phil Smidt, later established a restaurant nearby. The company didn't last long; the restaurant is still in operation.

By 1890 Hammond was Lake County's largest community with a population of 5,428. St. Margaret's Hospital, the first hospital in the northern Calumet Area, was opened in 1898. That same year W. B. Conkey built the world's largest printing and bookbinding plant. By 1900 with numerous industries, two banks, fourteen churches, one synagogue, and a water works providing Lake Michigan water, the population topped 12,000.

In 1911, Hammond began a twelve-year effort to annex the area south to the Little Calumet River including Saxony, Gibson Station,

Figure 116. Ice harvesting on Wolf Lake. Calumet Room, Hammond Public Library.

and Hessville. The effort was finally successful in 1923, and with that action Hammond's final boundaries were set.

Postscript: Mueller's Hardware Store, in business since 1887, has been at its location at 416 Sibley Street since 1902. The original tin ceiling was made within the building. A Nickel Plate locomotive, Milwaukee Road boxcar, and a South Shore Line caboose are located on the grounds across Sohl Avenue from the Hammond Area Career Center.

Hessville/Gibson Station

Hessville's major east-west street, 169th Street, runs along the High Tolleston Shoreline between the Grand and Little Calumet Rivers. At Gibson Woods, north of 163rd Street at Parrish Avenue, there are still some of the once-numerous small ridges that were formed as the lake level dropped from the High Tolleston to the present shoreline. Gibson Station was located about one mile north of Hessville—where the Gibson rail yards are today.

In 1850, Gibson Station was a thriving passenger station for the Michigan Central Railroad. At first the station was called West Point because it was at the west end of the line. For about one year, all passengers disembarked here and took stagecoaches the rest of the way into Chicago. Although information is scarce, it appears that the first settlement here was that of brother and sister David and Elizabeth Gibson who built their home (and likely an inn) about 1845 at the site of today's Gibson Railroad Yards. Gibson hired a Scottish woodchopper to teach the children at the small settlement and in doing so is given credit for starting the first school in North Township. In 1850, Joseph and Mary Hess established a bakery and restaurant near the station. The Gibson post office was established in 1857, and until Hammond's post office was opened in 1873, the residents of that city had to retrieve their mail from Gibson.

The Chicago, Indiana & Southern Railroad (later New York Central) and its roundhouse and turntable were built in 1906. The Gibson rail yards soon became a major switching location for the New York Central and its affiliate, the Indiana Harbor Belt Railroad, which then established its headquarters there.

Figure 117. Joseph and Elizabeth Hess, founders of Hessville. Hessville Historical Society, Little Red Schoolhouse.

Hessville was founded in 1852 when the Michigan Central line was completed to Chicago and Gibson Station's passenger business declined. Joseph and Mary Hess moved about one mile south, established a general store, and platted the town on the High Tolleston

Figure 118. The
Joseph Hess School,
now the Little Red
Schoolhouse.

Shoreline. Joseph and his second wife, Elizabeth, made friends with
many of the Potawatomi who still lived in or traveled through the
area. Joseph served as postmaster for nearly forty years. He was also
elected the first trustee of North Township and served in that ca-
pacity for twenty-two years. As trustee he was able to have two
bridges built across the yet untamed Little Calumet River.

Hessville, which owed its existence to the railroads, didn't get
its own line until 1882 when the Nickel Plate line was built. The
north-south Chicago, Indiana & Southern Railroad was built in
1906. In 1911, the much larger city of Hammond began an effort
to annex Hessville, which was then still unincorporated. In an attempt to resist the big city, Hessville residents held an election at
the Joseph Hess School in 1918 to determine whether they should
incorporate as an independent town. With seventy-eight votes in
favor and two against, the community was incorporated. Hessville's
influence lessened, however, as Hammond's increased. The town of
Hessville was short-lived; it became a part of Hammond in 1923.

Postscript: The Joseph Hess School, Hessville's Little Red Schoolhouse, was built in 1869. Stone from the Thornton Quarry was
used in its construction, but its high price resulted in cheaper brick
being used for the upper portion. This school was moved to Hessville Park on Kennedy Avenue in 1971, where it now houses the
Hessville Historical Society Museum.

Highland

The name Highland is a short form of Highlands, a name that appeared on railroad maps of the area to mark the high sand ridge of
the ancient Calumet Shoreline at Ridge Road. Before settlement, the

shoreline served as an Indian trail and stagecoach route. North of the ridge, the land slopes down toward the Little Calumet River, which forms the town's northern boundary. In Wicker Park and between Franklin and LaPorte Streets (from west of Kennedy to Fifth Street) is a steep slope that was either the north side of an offshore sand bar or a slope eroded during the Algonquin phase of Lake Michigan. South of the ridge was an extensive wetland that was originally a lagoon. Later, part of the great Cady Marsh, it was drained by Hart and Cady Marsh Ditches.

Figure 119. Michael and Judith Johnston. Highland Historical Society Museum.

The earliest settlers were Michael and Judith Johnston, who built a house in 1848 near today's intersection of Ridge Road and Grace Street. (A granite marker on Ridge Road marks the location.) Michael Johnston built the first bridge in the area over the Little Calumet River. Judith became the town's first schoolteacher, and Johnston Elementary School is named for her. Other settlers arrived and established farms on the rich soils north and south of the ridge. The first railroad was the Grand Trunk, which built a line through the south part of town in 1880. However, as there was no station there, it did not affect the growth of the area.

The C&A line was different. In 1883 the Chicago & Atlantic (Erie) Railroad cut through the high sand ridge to lay its tracks and gave local farmers access to the Chicago market. The name Highlands soon appeared on railroad maps.

Also in 1883, and at the intersection of the railroad with the great sand ridge, John Clough[10] laid out a town for which he plotted First through Fifth Streets and Highway, Jewett, Wicker, Clough, and Lincoln Streets. When the post office was established that year, it was named Clough Postal Station. The name was changed to Highland five years later.

By 1900, Highland sported several homes, a blacksmith shop, a kraut factory, two general stores (one with a post office), a Dutch Reformed Church, and a People's Church.

Early in the twentieth century, two additional railroads built their lines through Highlands: the Chesapeake & Ohio with tracks alongside the Erie's, and the north-south Chicago, Indiana & Southern west of downtown. Soon companies dependent upon rail transportation were established in town. One such company was Libby, McNeil, and Libby (Libby's) which processed Highland-area vegetables. Another, the Gary Granite and Stone Company, made sand

10. Clough rhymed with rough.

Figure 120. New York Central Depot. Note the name Highlands on the building. Drawing courtesy of the artist, R. Ramsey Smith.

bricks out of the abundant ridge sand—and, unfortunately, in the process removed the distinctive sand ridge from Kennedy Avenue all the way east to Cottage Grove Avenue.

In 1910, with a population of 412, the town of Highland was incorporated.[11] In spite of the fact that the official name of the town was now Highland (not Highlands), for many years thereafter the *Lake County Times* continued to use the names Highland and Highlands interchangeably. And the railroads, which had originated the Highlands name, continued to use that name until the station was torn down in the 1950s.

Postscript: The Highland Historical Society Museum is located at the Lincoln Community Center.

Hobart/Ainsworth

Hobart's primary geographical features are Hobart Island, the Griffith Spit, Deep River, and Lake George. Turkey Creek from the west and Duck Creek from the east add their waters to Lake George and Deep River. The largest mill pond in the Calumet Area, Lake George, was formed in 1845 or 1846 when a dam was built across Deep River.

Hobart Island is the name of the long hill, a part of the Lake Border Moraine, that was once an island in glacial Lake Michigan.

11. The 1910 U.S. Census gave new the town 304 citizens, but a special census taken for incorporation purposes indicated that it had 412.

The long ridge called the Griffith Spit, north of Hobart Island, is easily seen on Liverpool Road just south of Thirty-seventh Avenue. Lake George and Turkey Creek lie in the low area that was once Hobart Bay, a quiet inlet of glacial Lake Michigan south of Hobart Island. The southern part of the city around U.S. Highway 30 is atop the Tinley Moraine and contains the route of the old Sauk Trail (Seventy-third Avenue/Old Lincoln Highway). In the earliest days, Old Ridge Road was directly connected with the Ridge Road that today extends from Gary westward to Lansing, Illinois. It was then one of several roads called the Chicago–Detroit Road.[12]

Hobart was one of the first areas in Lake County to attract settlers. William Ross and his wife, the county's first settlers, established their home in the wilderness along Deep River near where it is crossed by Sixteenth Street today.

Samuel and Ann Sigler, their daughter Elmira and her husband, William Hurst, and another daughter, Melvina, and her husband, Joseph Mundell, all arrived in 1837. The Siglers opened a general store at the intersection of Ridge Road and Liverpool Road in 1846. The Mundells established a dairy farm that continued to be maintained in their family for three generations.[13] Joseph Mundell also worked as a wheelwright. Among other things, he made spinning wheels that were in great demand as more settlers moved into this new frontier area. The first school was constructed in 1845 on Center Street (where the Masonic Temple is today). Early teachers included Edward Morse, Mrs. Joy, and Henry Kern.

By 1847 George Earle (who earlier founded the town of Liverpool) established a flour mill and a sawmill, and for these he dammed Deep River, creating a lake that he named for himself. Demand for wood was high, so the sawmill was busy as the heavily timbered area around Hobart was cleared, providing lumber for local and distant use. In 1848 Earle platted the town, which was originally known as Earle's Mills but soon became Hobart (named for George's brother).

The Pittsburgh, Fort Wayne & Chicago Railroad, which was built through the area in 1858, allowed Hobart to grow into a prosperous manufacturing town. It was joined in 1882 by the Nickel Plate and in 1888 by the EJ&E line. Many of Hobart's early churches were established in this period, including Augustana (Swedish) Lutheran in 1862, First Methodist in 1869, Trinity Lutheran and St. Bridget's Roman Catholic (both German) in 1873, and First Uni-

Figure 121. George Earle. Hobart Historical Society Museum.

12. Pleak (1947) refers to an advertisement dated 1854 from the "possessions of Earle." It read, "For Sale, Flour and Saw-mill located at Hobart . . . on the Chicago–Detroit Road."

13. Mundell Field (the site of old Mundell School) is located on land that was once the Mundell family farm.

Figure 122. The old mill, ca. 1912. Destroyed by fire in 1953. Hobart Historical Society Museum.

tarian in 1874. In 1876, First Unitarian Church erected the very first Unitarian church building in Indiana—a structure that the congregation still uses.

Brick making was established at Hobart because of the forty-foot thick deposit of glacial clay beneath the city. By the late 1860s Hobart had four brickyards in operation. The clay pits were conveniently located near the Pennsylvania tracks near Lake Park Avenue and by 1897, sixty carloads of brick a month were being shipped by rail to all parts of the country. The two largest yards from the late 1880s through the 1910s were the Kulage Brickyard south of the Pennsylvania tracks and the Owen Terra Cotta Works (later National Fireproofing, later still NATCO), north of the tracks. Today's Amber Lake is NATCO's former clay pit.

Local historian George Garard wrote in 1882, "Hobart owes its prosperity more to its brick yards than to anything else." In 1897, Indiana state geologist W. S. Blatchley noted that Hobart had "one of the largest, best-known and most valuable deposits of silty clay in northwestern Indiana." The Brickie Bowl, Hobart High School's football stadium, is named in honor of Hobart's once-extensive brick industry. It is a natural amphitheater formed when it was the valley of nearby Duck Creek. (Duck Creek was moved when the stadium was built.)

By 1870, with 500 residents, the mill, and many businesses, Hobart was the largest community in the northern part of Lake County. Hobart was incorporated as a town in January 1889 with a population of about 1,300. In 1921 Hobart became a city.

The Grand Trunk built its line through Lake County in 1880. As it did not go through the city of Hobart, it established a competing station south of the town at Ainsworth. The station was busy every day as it picked up milk from the area farmers and took it into Chicago. By 1900, Ainsworth had a fine two-story brick school

Figure 123. Hobart Brickyard, ca. 1895. From Blatchley, 1897.

building and a population of about fifty. A post office was established there in 1882; it remained open until 1934. Ainsworth was annexed to Hobart in 1993.

Postscript: The picturesque Pennsy Arches were built in 1858 to carry the Pittsburgh, Fort Wayne & Chicago Railroad over Deep River. The Pennsy Depot at Lillian and Illinois Streets was built in 1911–12. It was restored in 1987 and is now used as a retail store.

Five of Hobart's nineteenth-century church buildings are still in use. They are the ones built by the Augustana Lutheran (1869), the German Methodist (1872), Trinity Lutheran (1876), First Unitarian (1876), and the Swedish Methodist, now called Michigan Avenue United Methodist Church (1889). The last two are still used by the congregations that built them.

Downtown Hobart has a number of buildings built as long ago as the 1870s. A walking tour brochure is available from the Hobart Historical Society, which has its museum in the old Hobart Public Library, built in 1914–15 with a Carnegie Foundation grant. Ainsworth School, built in 1912, is now privately owned.

Lake Station/Liverpool/New Chicago

The city of Lake Station sits atop all three of the ancient shorelines of Lake Michigan. At its northernmost edge and north of the wide floodplain of the Little Calumet River are the sand dunes of the High Tolleston Shoreline. The floodplain is lake bottomland that was part of the old Calumet Lagoon during Lake Michigan's Tolleston phase. Central Avenue rises up and over the Calumet beach ridge a few blocks east of Ripley Street. West of Ripley, this ridge

is best seen along Riverside Drive. From this road there is a spectacular view of the Glenwood dunes on the south side of Deep River. North and east of River Forest High School, Deep River flows along the Glenwood Shoreline—separating the Calumet dunes on the north side from the Glenwood dunes on the south side. The town of New Chicago, nestled between Hobart and Lake Station and mostly south of Deep River, is primarily situated on the sands of the Glenwood Shoreline.

Before settlement, American Indians passed through this area using a trail atop the ancient Calumet Shoreline. The site of Riverview Park, protected on three sides by the river, is said to be an old ceremonial ground for several Indian tribes. Liverpool Road from Ridge Road north to Clay Street generally follows the old Potawatomi Trail (Calumet Beach Trail), which in 1833 became the Chicago-Detroit stage road. Its bridge over Deep River is at the site of an old ferry over the river.

Liverpool is located where Deep River cuts across the Potawatomi Trail on the old Calumet Shoreline and joins the Little Calumet River. It is one of the oldest communities in Lake County and was its county seat from 1839 to 1840. Being on the old stage road, and at the Little Calumet River (which provided access to Lake Michigan), Liverpool attracted land speculators early on. Abner Stillson built a tavern in 1835. The next year, John Davis and Henry Frederickson platted the town with the river flowing through its center. A ferry was established across Deep River. That same year, George and Mary Earle arrived from England and purchased most of the town site. Earle then began his quest to have the town named the county seat. His rival, Solon Robinson, was promoting Crown Point for that honor. In 1839, when county commissioners named Liverpool as the new county's seat, residents in the central and southern parts of the county complained. The next year, even though Earle had already begun construction of a log courthouse, a new committee decided on Crown Point.

As Crown Point grew, Liverpool declined and the Earles eventually moved south and established the town of Hobart. At about 1846, Liverpool's tavern was moved to the riverbanks and floated downriver to Blue Island, where it housed workers on the Illinois and Michigan Canal. The building (now cut in half) still stands at 2336 West Collins Street. An 1870 fire destroyed much of the remaining part of the town. What was left of Liverpool then became a ghost town, not to be reinvigorated until the twentieth century. In 1913, members of Local 133 of a theatrical employees' union

established a camp along the banks of Deep
River. In doing so, they gave the name
Camp 133 to this area.

Solon Robinson and many other authors (who probably based their story on
Robinson's text) all stated that the Liverpool
courthouse was floated down the river to
Blue Island and transformed into a tavern.
However, in 1929, Arthur Patterson insisted that the "old tavern" was what was

Figure 125. The Old
Audubon Hotel. Lake
Station Historical
Society Museum.

sent down the river. Trying to clear up the misconception, he em-
phatically stated that the old courthouse was left standing and that
it simply rotted away. He recalled chasing rabbits out from under
its old timbers.

Lake Station was platted in 1852 by George Earle alongside the
new Michigan Central Railroad, the first railroad to enter Lake
County. As the only station in the county for several years, this was
literally *the Lake station*. The Michigan Central Railroad built its
repair yards there and also built a large, two-story depot, telegraph
office, and "eating-house." Next to the depot, the railroad placed a
beautiful park with large swings. Timothy Ball described the station
grounds as "the largest and most tastefully laid out of any in the
county." It was the site of many a picnic. As soon as Edward Saunders built the large Audubon Hotel, the Michigan Central built a
plank walk to connect it with the depot. Saunders also became the
first postmaster. For many years, Lake Station was the primary shipping center of the county and as such the town prospered. Most of
its citizens were employed by the railroads.

By 1870 Lake Station had about forty families, a hotel, five
boarding houses, numerous stores, and five saloons. As other railroads built their lines through the area and the number of train
stations multiplied, the town lost its early importance. By 1900,
Lake Station had been reduced to one store and a population of
only 100.

Then in 1906 Gary was founded. Less than a year later, John
Earle, grandson of George, announced plans for a new suburb to
be called East Gary. Thus on June 1, 1908, in trying to capitalize
on the spectacular growth of the new city, while at the same time
attempting to prevent being absorbed, East Gary, composed of the
older communities of Lake Station and part of Liverpool, was incorporated as a town. Its population in 1910 was 484. East Gary
became a city in 1964. In 1972 East Gary annexed the rest of the
Liverpool area. Then in 1977, with Gary's boom long past, the city
took back its original name of Lake Station.

Just about the same time that Lake Station took the name of
East Gary in hopes of latching on to the real estate boom of that

city, the name New Chicago was chosen for the same reason (as East Chicago had done about twenty years earlier.) New Chicago was incorporated as a town in 1906. The next year a post office was established, but it only remained open for about ten years. In 1910 its population stood at 105. With an area of less than one square mile, the town is still geographically one of Indiana's smallest.

Postscript: The Lake Station Historical Society Museum is located at 4700 Central Avenue.

Leroy

The small rural community of Leroy is located in the Valparaiso Moraine about six miles southeast of Crown Point. It was on a farm near Leroy that the mastodon bones at Gibson Woods were found.

Leroy got its start with the building of the Chicago & Great Eastern Railway (later the Panhandle) as a shipping terminal for agricultural products. Shortly thereafter (1869), Amos Edgerton built a store near the rail line and the U.S. government opened a post office. In 1875 Thomas McLaren laid out the town of Leroy (first named Cassville for landowner Dr. Levi Cass). As happened many times in the Calumet Area, the first storekeeper, Edgerton, also became the town's first postmaster. Brothers Samuel, James, and Peter Love built the elevator. Samuel and his wife, Ellen, ran a general store. The town became a busy shipping point where local farmers would bring in grain and hay for transport to Chicago and other markets. In 1881, the Love family alone shipped out 25,000 tons of hay. By 1900 Leroy (sometimes then spelled LeRoy) had three stores, two churches (one Presbyterian and one Methodist), a brick schoolhouse, and about 100 citizens.

Lowell

Lowell sits on the gently sloping southern flank of the Valparaiso Moraine, according to historian Timothy Ball, the best agricultural land in the county. The low area in the center of town, where Cedar Creek flows today, is the remains of a channel where glacial meltwaters once rushed southward to the Kankakee.

In 1835 Samuel Halstead claimed land for a mill on Cedar Creek and probably built a log cabin, the first home in what was to become Lowell. Other early settlers included Horatio Nichols and physician and justice of the peace Jabez Clark and his wife, Marietta.

Two churches got their start even before the town was established, both starting with settlers gathering in various homes for services. Lowell Methodists trace their beginnings back to a class organized in 1837. The Lowell Christian Church (today Church of Christ) began with the gathering of seven "disciples" on a Sunday morning in 1842. In the early days, Lowell Christian Church was referred to as the Lone Star Church because it was the only "Christian" Church in the county.

Figure 126. Martha and Melvin Halsted. From Ball, 1904.

The first post office in the area was established in 1843 in the home of James and Martha Sanger (where Lowell High School is today). It was originally called the Outlet Post Office—Cedar Creek is, after all, the outlet from Cedar Lake.

In 1848, Melvin and Martha Halsted and Melvin's mother, Patty Halsted, moved to what is now Lowell and bought the old mill site on Cedar Creek. A man of many talents, Melvin built a sawmill and a flouring mill and in 1852 laid out the town (named after the industrial city of Lowell, Massachusetts). Jonas Thorn soon established the town's first general store and inn.

Halsted discovered that the clay soil in the area was suitable for making bricks, and so he built a brick works, which in 1849 made over 400,000 red bricks. Perry Clark, the son of Jabez and Marietta Clark, also opened a brickyard. With no railroad to easily ship their products to other locations, brick became the building material of choice for the new town. Lowell got its first church building in 1856 when Melvin Halsted built and deeded to the Baptists a brick building at the corner of Main and Mill Streets.

In 1868 Melvin Halsted built a 3-story brick woolen mill (later a gristmill), which was at the time the largest building in Lake County. That same year Lowell was incorporated as a town. Even without a railroad connection, the town grew quickly. In 1869–70, three churches, First Methodist, Lowell Christian, and St. Edward Roman Catholic, all built their first buildings, all of them brick. By 1872, Lowell boasted a population of 550 and, according to Timothy Ball, the largest and finest school building in the county. Lowell was finally joined to the modern world when the Monon line was built through town in 1882.

In 1900, the town of Lowell had a population of 1,275. That year Ball called it the "principal agricultural business town of Lake County."

Postscript: The Halsted House, at Main and Halsted Streets, built in 1850, was one of the first brick homes built in south Lake County. It was purchased by the Three Creeks Historical Association

about 1976, then restored 1999–2002 for use as a town historical museum. The Buckley Homestead, near Lowell, is a living-history farm operated by the Lake County Parks and Recreation Department. It has several historic buildings including a restored 1840 log house, a replica of a 1900 schoolhouse, and the 1910 Buckley home.

Figure 127. The Halsted House.

Merrillville

The town of Merrillville is located on three moraines. The Lake Border Moraine (Hobart Island) is at the far northern part of town near Fifty-sixth and Broadway. Turkey Creek now occupies the low area that was once a quiet bay that existed south of this former island. The Tinley Moraine is in the center of the town (along U.S. Highway 30). The northern edge of this moraine, part of the ancient Glenwood Shoreline, crosses the town in an east-west direction but in many places is difficult to recognize because Hobart Island to the north prevented the development of a sand beach. Seventy-third Avenue, which generally runs a little south of this shoreline, was part of the Old Sauk Trail. The Valparaiso Moraine is at the far southeast section of town. Main Beaver Dam Ditch and Deep River divide these two moraines.

In 1835, Jeremiah Wiggins established a land claim along the old Sauk Trail near the location of McGwinn's Village, a once-populous Indian village and dancing ground. For a number of years the area, about a block east of Broadway, was known as Wiggins Point.[14] The Saxon, Merrill, and other families soon arrived and established farms and businesses. William Merrill was a blacksmith; Dudley and Julie Merrill operated a country store. After Wiggins died in 1838, the name Centerville was adopted, but when a post office was established in 1847, it was named Merrillville. (There was already a Centerville in Indiana.) By 1870 the community had twenty-three families, several businesses including the California Exchange Hotel, and a two-story brick school building. Methodist circuit riders and local citizens organized the first church services in this little town as early as 1845. A Methodist church organization was formed in 1862, and its first church building was erected in 1879.

Merrillville's early growth was slow due to the lack of a railroad.

14. A flagpole and bronze plaque at Seventy-third and Broadway commemorates McGwinn's Village and the establishment of Wiggins Point.

When the Grand Trunk Railroad was built in 1876, it passed by north of the village and established stations at nearby Lottaville and Ainsworth. Soon after the turn of the century, the C&O built its line right through the center of town and put a station at what is now Seventy-third and Broadway.

Figure 128. Ross Township School and its horse-drawn school buses. From Howat, 1915.

The village of Turkey Creek was established by a Mr. Winchell in 1834 near the present corner of Sixty-third Avenue and Harrison Street. The area attracted many German settlers who established the Merrillville area's first Roman Catholic church, St. John the Baptist. The first mass was celebrated in a log cabin in 1841. When a new building was erected in 1863 on what is now Harrison Street, the name of the parish was changed to Sts. Peter and Paul.

The village of Deep River (or Woodvale) was located where the Sauk Trail is cut by Deep River. Deep River's first permanent residents, John and Hannah Wood, arrived in 1835. In 1837 John built a sawmill, and then in 1840 he built Lake County's first gristmill—later converted to a flour mill—the first continuing industry in the Lake/Porter County area. Wood built a dam on Deep River and created a sluiceway to power the mills.

Wood also built a general store, shoe shop, cheese factory, and several houses, but refused to sell any lots, preferring instead to keep control over "his" town. (A temperance man, he wanted to prevent saloons from being built.) Wood called the community Woodvale, but the post office, which opened in 1838, used the name Deep River. By 1900 Deep River had a population of about fifty, many of them members of the Wood family.

Lottaville and Independence Hill are both on the west side of Merrillville along Highway 55. Lottaville was a station on the Grand Trunk Railroad and had its own post office from 1881 through 1905.[15] Independence Hill, south of the old Lottaville station, was platted in 1926.

The town of Merrillville was incorporated in 1971, including the old areas of Centerville, Turkey Creek, Lottaville, and Independence Hill. Deep River was added to the town in 1994.

Postscript: Two of the oldest mills in the Calumet Area are located in Merrillville. The older of the two is at Seventy-third and Madison Street on a branch of Turkey Creek. It was built in 1851 by John and Elizabeth Law as a distillery. (Merrillville was evidently

Figure 129. John Wood Sr. From Goodspeed and Blanchard, 1882.

---

15. According to Bruce Woods, 1975, Lottaville was named for Charlotte Woods, daughter-in-law of William Merrill and daughter of Bartlett and Ann Sigler Woods.

Figure 130. Wood's Mill photographed in 1985 by James Fisher. Calumet Regional Archives.

well known at that time for its spirits.) During its long history, "The Old Mill" has served as a steam-powered gristmill, the area's first gas-powered mill, a tavern, restaurant, dance hall, school, candy store, and pizzeria.

Wood's Mill is a three-story red brick gristmill, now the main attraction at Deep River County Park. It was built in 1876 by John and Hannah Wood's son, Nathan. Called one of the finest mills in the county, it could grind twelve bushels of grain in an hour. Nathan Wood sold the mill in 1908, and by 1930 it was abandoned. The dilapidated building was purchased and restored by the Lake County Park Department and opened to the public in 1977. The gift shop/visitor center, built in 1904, was the Woodvale church.

The Ross Township School, on Seventy-third Avenue, was built in 1896. It is now the home of the Ross Township Historical Museum.

Miller

Miller (now part of Gary) lies on sands of the Tolleston Shoreline. The Grand Calumet River used to empty into the lake at Marquette Park. After a new channel from the river to Lake Michigan was opened in Illinois, drifting sand closed the mouth of the river and caused the nearly flat Calumet River to change direction of flow. The lagoon at Marquette Park is at the head of the old river that now flows west instead of east. Marquette Park got its name because it is believed that it was here that in 1675 Father Jacques Marquette camped near the beach.

At Miller, before settlement, the lower Tolleston Shoreline was

Figure 131. The Lake Street Bridge over the Grand Calumet River. This well-used bridge connected Miller with the Lake Michigan beaches. Calumet Regional Archives.

a series of some fifty parallel east-west sand ridges separated by low, often wet swales. The Miller Woods portion of the Indiana Dunes National Lakeshore preserves many of these ridges and swales. Indian Boundary Avenue marks the old territorial boundary line. The land north of that street was made part of the Michigan Territory when it was created in 1805. It was returned to Indiana in 1816 when Indiana became a state.

The Bennett Tavern, built in 1833, stood for a few years on the beach along the first stagecoach route from Detroit to Chicago. In 1837, the town of Indiana City was platted at the mouth of the Grand Calumet River. However, it never was much more than a plan on paper. It is doubtful that any lots were ever sold.

However, also in 1837, much of what was to become the Miller business district was purchased by William and George Ewing and George Walker. Called Ewing's Subdivision, it was located one and a half miles south of Lake Michigan. It was fairly isolated because the dune and swale topography made travel difficult. That changed in 1851 with the building of the Michigan Southern & Northern Indiana Railroad. Yet Miller remained a small community for many years. In 1870 it was still a small town of about twelve families.

According to station agent George William Cook, John Miller was a construction engineer for the Michigan Southern Railroad in 1851. "At that time trains had to stop every thirty miles for water and wood for the engine boilers. Mr. Miller lived . . . thirty miles from Chicago and from LaPorte. The stop was made near his home. It then became customary for members of the railroad crew to say, 'Our next stop is Miller.' " For several years, a sturgeon and white-

Figure 132. Miller School. Indiana room, Gary Public Library.

fish industry was centered around Miller. (See Drusilla Carr's description of the fishing industry in chapter 5.)

In 1874, the B&O became the second rail line through town, and in 1908 the South Shore was built. The railroads have played an important part in Miller's economy. Two of Miller's biggest businesses in the 1880s and 1890s were the shipping of sand and ice. The Santa Fe Railroad is said to have placed an order in 1899 for 150,000 cars of sand to be obtained from the Miller area. Ice was harvested from nearby Long Lake.

Beginning about 1868, Miller began to attract a large number of Swedish immigrants and in a short time Miller became known as a Swedish village. Not surprisingly, the first church was the Swedish (now Bethel) Lutheran Church started in 1874. For its first twenty years, its services were conducted (in Swedish) in nearby school buildings. The congregation's original building on Lake Street, built in 1894, still stands. In 1901, the English-speaking members of the community established the Chapel of the Dunes. Its original 1901 building, also on Lake Street, is still in use. In 1915 the church was lifted up and a basement was excavated. At the same time it was enlarged—but only by expanding eastward so that the original west face of the building was not altered.

The Miller's Station post office opened in 1879. (It changed its name to Miller in 1882.) In 1907, Miller was incorporated as a town, and three years later its first census listed 638 residents. However, only eleven years later it was annexed by the city of Gary. In 1930, a bronze statue of Father Jacques Marquette was placed at the entrance to the park, which was then renamed in his honor.

Postscript: Miller is fortunate in that its two earliest church buildings, Old Bethel Lutheran Church and Chapel of the Dunes, are still standing and still in use. Miller School, prominently standing at the south end of Lake Street, was built in 1910. It was closed for a few years, but reopened in 1996. Miller Town Hall was built in 1911. For many years it served as a fire station.

Munster

Driving down Ridge Road today, you can't miss the sand ridge of the ancient Calumet Shoreline on the south side of the road. A beach 11,500 years ago, and an Indian trail before settlement, what is now Ridge Road became a stagecoach route in 1837. North of the ridge, the land gently slopes down toward the Little Calumet River except along Ridgeway and Alta Vista Avenues where there is a striking view of a scarp—a steep slope eroded during Lake Michigan's Algonquin phase. South of Ridge Road was an extensive wet area that was once a lagoon. This land was then part of the Cady Marsh before it was drained by Hart and Schoon Ditches. Lakewood Park on the town's south side is the site of the National Brick Company plant, which for more than sixty years took advantage of the area's twenty-two–foot thick deposit of glacial clay. Two of its quarry holes are now lakes.

Figure 133. Cornelius P. Schoon, a man out standing in his field. Onions grew well on the sandy soil of the ancient Calumet Shoreline. Munster Historical Society Museum.

The earliest structure in Munster was a log inn, built on the Calumet Beach Trail by brother and sister David and Elizabeth Gibson in 1837. In 1845, Allen and Julia Watkins Brass bought the site, built a large two-story frame building, and named it the Brass Tavern. When Allen Brass left Lake County to join the gold rush in California, Julia and her family ran the inn (see photo and drawing of the Brass Tavern in chapter 3). In 1864, they sold the inn to Johann and Wilhelmina Stallbohm. Besides serving as a way station for travelers, the inn was a gathering spot for neighbors, including the many Dutch farmers who after 1853 began establishing truck gardens along this stretch of land. In the 1920s the DAR placed a tablet at the site of the old tavern.

Active settlement in the area that was to become Munster began in 1855 with the arrival of immigrant families from the Netherlands. The first to arrive were Peter and Aartje Jabaay. They were soon joined by the families of Dingeman and Gurtje Jabaay, Arie and Sarah Jabaay, Antonie and Jannigje Bouman, Eldert and Nieltje Monster, Cornelius and Lena Klootwyk, Peter and Gertrude Kooy, and Giel Swets. Their non-Dutch neighbors included Ira Dibble and Chauncey and Julia Wilson. Farmhouses were built on the sand ridge, and the low fertile areas between the ridge and the Little Calumet River became their fields. As truck gardens, the common crops grown were cabbage, potatoes, and onions. Travelers through town often noted the smell of fresh onion in the air.

For many years the only railroad in town was the Monon. There was no station, but trains would stop at the Jansen home on Ridge Road for passengers. The Grand Trunk and the Chicago & Great Eastern Railway crossed south of town in an area then called Maynard.[16]

In 1900 Munster was a small village with two schools (one

16. Maynard is the area around Forty-fifth Street and Calumet Avenue. Once part of the vast Hart estate, it was named after Maynard Hart.

Figure 134. Munster's Ridge Road, ca. 1910. This photo shows the Munster Christian Reformed Church, school, and parsonage. Munster Historical Society Museum.

public, one private), one church, and two stores—one of them with a post office (established in 1892) named for its postmaster, Jacob Munster. It was an agricultural village. Timothy Ball was so impressed by the settlement that he called it "a Happy Valley," a rather interesting name for a community located along a ridge! In 1906, Munster got its first industry when the National Brick Company began operations at Maynard.[17] With a population of about 500, Munster, including the Maynard area, was incorporated in 1907.

Postscript: Klootwyk General Store, Munster's oldest commercial building, still stands at 619 Ridge Road. Heritage Park is the site of the old Brass Tavern. The Kaske House at Heritage Park, containing the Munster Historical Society Museum, is on the National Register of Historic Places.

Ross

The small village of Ross is about one mile south of the ancient Calumet Shoreline (Ridge Road) between Glen Park and Griffith. Much of the area was built on sands of the Griffith Spit, that long series of sandbars that developed in ancestral Lake Michigan northwest of Hobart Island. Ross was built next to the station on the Joliet Cut-off of the Michigan Central Railroad.

A plat for the village of Ross was filed by William Ross in 1855. The first house was built by Cornelius and Dianna Vanness and was

17. Munster's brickyard was the last one in Indiana to use glacial clays. All other brickyards today use shale.

used as a hotel and store. Other early settlers included the Horner and Woodbridge families. The post office opened in 1857 with John Wheeler serving as postmaster. That same year a grain elevator was built next to the railroad. The elevator was different from the norm—it had a large bridge that ran up over the building so that horses or oxen would have to pull farm wagons up to the top where the grain would be dropped into the building. According to Sam Woods, farmers from all over Lake County would come to Ross to unload their grain.

Originally Ross was in Ross Township, but the village found itself part of the new Calumet Township when that township was created in 1883. The village's population in 1900 was about seventy-five.

St. John

St. John lies in the southern part of the Tinley Moraine in the center of a large area formerly called Prairie West. Although not the highest ground of the moraine, St. John does sit astride the Eastern Continental Divide. West Creek, which once carried meltwaters from the glacier, flows south into the Kankakee River, then southward to the Gulf of Mexico. Turkey Creek and Main Beaver Dam Ditch flow north toward Lake Michigan, eventually reaching the North Atlantic.

John and Johanna Hack, the first settlers in west Lake County, arrived in 1837. Their farm was south of Joliet Street and west of what was later the Monon Railroad (around the Hack Cemetery). Other German families including Mathias and Maria Redar and Joseph and Anna Schmal arrived the next year. In 1842, John Hack built a small distillery where he made whiskey and peach brandy.

In 1843, Hack established the first Roman Catholic congregation in Lake County and also built its first chapel (about a half mile southeast of the present church building).[18] Three years later, the community instituted the first Catholic school in the township. When a post office was established in 1846, the residents decided to name it St. John's, not after the saint but tongue-in-cheek after

Figure 135. John and Johanna Hack, first settlers of St. John. St. John Historical Society, Inc.

18. John Hack built the first chapel. Dissenting neighbors soon built another. According to William Tuley, it is uncertain as to whether the log chapel along Route 41 is the first or the second chapel. He surmised that because church records state that Hack's church was a frame building, the log church is thus the one built by his neighbors.

Figure 136. Old Settlers' Church, built about 1843. Returned to St. John in 1974. St. John Historical Society, Inc.

the postmaster and founder of the community, John Hack. The "St." was added merely because it sounded better. Hack served as postmaster for eight years, giving up the position two years before he died.

In 1847 John and Mary Scherer arrived from Prussia and established what may have been St. John Township's first saloon.[19] Nearby Bernard Scheidt built an inn serving Crown Point–Chicago travelers. In 1856 the St. John the Evangelist Church, with the largest congregation in Lake County, had a new brick building and an impressive twenty-five-foot steeple. By 1870, the St. John's area had twenty-seven families and several businesses.

The Monon Railroad arrived in 1881, and local farmers started taking milk to the new St. John's train station and sending it off to Chicago. That year Peter Thielen platted the town of St. John's, keeping the name that honored his father-in-law, John Hack. The town was located along the new Monon tracks; the original streets were Thielen, Hack, Orth (now Joliet), and Schmal (now Ninety-third). The little town grew and soon had a small commercial district. Early businesses included Thiel's blacksmith shop, the St. John elevator, Gerlach's sawmill, a creamery, and a slaughterhouse. St. John's got its second railroad when the Chicago, Indiana & Southern (New York Central) rail line was laid in 1906. In 1911, the town was incorporated and its name shortened to St. John.

Postscript: In 1974, the 1843 log chapel, which long ago had been moved to the Crown Point fairgrounds, was returned to St. John, renovated, and was again dedicated for use as a place of worship.

Schererville/Hartsdale

The town of Schererville sits along the old Glenwood Shoreline. However, much of the shoreline is hard to see today because a great deal of the dune sand was removed long ago. The shoreline roughly follows Joliet Street through the eastern part of town (nicely visible near Schafer Drive), and then follows Highway 30 west of its intersection with Joliet Street. This section of the shoreline was part of the old Sauk Trail. The original trail at its intersection with Highway 41 was about 500 feet south of the current highway. The road was moved northward in 1928 when the underpass at the New York Central Railroad was built.

---

19. The Scherer's son Nicholas was later the founder of Schererville.

The Glenwood Shoreline is still quite easy to see looking north from the intersection of Indianapolis Boulevard and Highway 30. South of the intersection is a gently hilly region that is part of the Tinley Moraine. To the north is the old lake bottom. The newer eastern part of U.S. Highway 30, from the junction with Joliet Street eastward, built in 1935, goes through the moraine.

Joliet Street itself has been changed over the years. It was first paved in 1911 using the gravel and tar "macadam" process. Then in 1926, when the road was paved with concrete, parts of the road in the downtown section were raised up to the level of the Panhandle Railroad crossing.

Schererville is named for Nicholas Scherer, a native of Germany, who worked at various times as a ditch digger, a railroad bed builder, sand miner, real estate developer, and farmer. Scherer and his wife, Frances, had seventy acres of land along the Glenwood Shoreline (now Joliet Street). In 1866, Scherer and N. D. Wright

Figure 137. Frances and Nicholas Scherer, founders of Schererville. Schererville Historical Society.

established the town along the trail, where it was crossed by the new Chicago & Great Eastern Railway. Their little town grew. By December it had a new post office with Nicholas Scherer as postmaster. Within a few years John and Frances Thiel arrived, and soon Thiel's blacksmith shop opened on Joliet Street. Peter and Lena Redar and Michael and Helena Grimmer ran a general store nearby. The Grimmers also served as Schererville postmasters—Michael for four years and Helena for eight years. The middle school in Schererville is named for Michael Grimmer, who was also a teacher, township trustee, county auditor, state legislator, and church organist/choir director.

Like most of St. John Township's population, Schererville's earliest residents were German Catholics. In 1873 they organized the parish of St. Michael the Archangel and built their church prominently along the old Glenwood Shoreline, on land donated by the Scherers.

Aaron Hart was one of the earliest residents of the Schererville-Dyer area. He amassed some 20,000 acres of land, much of it useless marshland in the low areas between Lake Michigan's old Glenwood and Calumet Shorelines. In 1880 Hart began draining the

Figure 138. St. Michael's Church atop the Glenwood Shoreline. Dyer Historical Society Museum.

marsy former lake bottom by constructing a ditch north to the Little Calumet River. He established the village of Hartsdale one mile north of Schererville. Hart's Ditch did make the marshland farmable and profitable, but although two rail lines, the Joliet Cut-off and the Panhandle, both passed through Hartsdale, his town never grew. His farm at Hartsdale, however, was quite successful. He had about forty employees who helped him grow grain and vegetables and raise dairy and beef cattle. The big cash crop was hay. The Hartsdale site is today along the tracks under the Indianapolis Boulevard bridge including the eastern section of Briar Ridge.

By 1900 Schererville had its church, two stores, a large brick school, and a population of about 250. Schererville, including Hartsdale, was incorporated as a town in 1911, the same year as nearby St. John. Two years later, Joliet Street became part of the Lincoln Highway, the nation's first transcontinental highway.

Postscript: The Stumer/Gard Building, built about 1880 by John Stumer, served for many years as Schererville's post office and general store. George and Elizabeth Gard ran the store from 1908 until 1959. In 1918 the building was enlarged. Then in 1966 the building was rotated so that it faced Junction instead of Joliet Street. It still serves Schererville as a retail store.

St. John Township School No. 2 was built in 1853 on the northwest corner of St. John Road (Patterson) and Seventy-seventh Avenue. It was closed in 1907, moved, and used for many years as a private garage. In 1993–94, it was disassembled, moved again, and rebuilt behind the St. John Township building on U.S. 30. The school was nearly identical to the Hartsdale School pictured in chapter 5.

Figure 139. The Gard Store about 1900. In those days it faced Joliet Street. Schererville Historical Society.

Tolleston

The village of Tolleston, which gave its name to the ancient shoreline of Lake Michigan that runs through it, was a railroad town. In 1857, George Tolle, a German Chicagoan, platted the village alongside the Michigan Central Railroad near where it would soon be crossed by the Pittsburgh, Fort Wayne & Chicago line. Tolle sold most of his lots to German immigrants who made their living by farming or by working for the railroads. A post office was opened in 1860. Tolle set aside four lots for a church, and in 1868 St. John's Lutheran Church was founded. It is today the oldest church in Lake County north of the Little Calumet River. The settlement grew, and by 1870 Tolleston had about eighty families.

Frank Borman, grandfather of the Apollo 8 astronaut, described the Tolleston of his youth as a "wonderful wilderness for small game. . . . There was no limit to the wild ducks in the marshes and swamps. . . . There were a great many deer . . . that would run with the cattle in the surrounding woods during the summer." He also noted, "My father told me that there were a great [number of] timber wolves here at that time."

One of Tolleston's biggest businesses in the 1890s was the shipping of sand. According to the *Lake County Star*, an estimated 50,000 railroad cars full were shipped out in 1897. Many residents of Tolleston worked in the summer mining sand and then spent the winter cutting ice at the tiny community of Clarke Station to the north.[20]

By 1900, the population of the community had grown to about 500. By this time the small town had a growing commercial district that included the Gibson Hotel run by Charles and Henrietta Gibson (son and daughter-in-law of Thomas and Marie Gibson, who had established the much earlier Gibson Inn in 1838). It was at this hotel that U.S. Steel officials stayed as they planned the building of the Gary and the world's largest steel mill.

The Tolleston Gun Club: A Clash of Cultures

Before the founding of the city of Gary, game was plentiful along the floodplain and marshes of the Little Calumet River. The Tolleston Gun Club was established along these wetlands south of the village of Tolleston in 1873 as a recreation spot for wealthy Chicagoans who enjoyed coming out to the country for weekend shoots. Frederick How, president of the club from 1873 to 1896, noted, "We didn't have time to take a week away from our businesses, but we could easily run out to Tolleston to stay over Saturday and Sunday."

The exclusive club owned up to 2,240 acres of land and fenced much of the open river-bottom areas long used in common by local

---

20. Sand mining at Tolleston continued throughout most of the twentieth century. At first, sand dunes were excavated. Later, sand was dug out of the ground, creating large open pits that were then used as dumps or landfills.

Figure 140. Tolleston fire station, new truck, and crew. Calumet Regional Archives.

farmers. Whereas farmers trapped animals for food or to supplement their incomes, wealthy club members hunted for sport. (It was common to shoot ducks before breakfast—the club record stood at 139 ducks bagged all in one morning.) Local boys who wandered onto club property were shot at by the club's game wardens. Peter J. Schoon recalled that the club members would come from Chicago "to spend money and have a wild time," and that the members "weren't interested in running trap lines because that's hard work; you have to get up early to do that." The hard-working pioneers resented the wealthy sportsmen who permitted killing of game for sport but "denied the poor man a brace of ducks for his table." After a fatality in 1894 and another during an 1897 fight that involved more than twenty men, public opinion turned against the club, and it soon disbanded.

Tolleston was incorporated as a town on September 4, 1906 (less than two months after the incorporation of Gary) primarily to avoid its being swallowed up by Gary, which had already annexed Clarke Station, Pine Station, and Buffington. Soon, however, Mayor Knotts of Gary and Tolleston's board president, W. S. Gallagher, began consolidation talks. In March 1910, rumors flew that East Chicago was going to annex all of the northwestern part of the county including Tolleston. Gary was urged to annex Tolleston first.[21] So, in May, when East Chicago decided to annex Hammond, Gary

A CALUMET AREA IRONY: THE BORMAN NAME RETURNS

In 1910, when Gary annexed Tolleston, all the Tolleston streets lost their original names and were given Gary names. Main Street became Grant, and Borman Boulevard (named for a prominent Tolleston family) became Eleventh Avenue. Then in 1969, Gary honored its native son, astronaut Frank Borman, by naming Interstate 94 the Borman Expressway.

21. The *Daily Tribune* advised, "It's up to Gary to annex first."

annexed East Chicago, Hammond, Whiting, Miller, and Tolleston. Eventually reason prevailed and all the supposedly annexed territories regained their independence except for Tolleston. The Tolleston town trustees could not convince two-thirds of its citizens to sign a petition against annexation, and it became part of the city of Gary.

Whiting

The tiny industrial city of Whiting, nestled on the Lake Michigan shoreline, is very flat today. However, like much of northern Lake County, it was originally composed of a series of long parallel sand ridges separated by shallow wet swales created as the Lake Michigan shoreline gradually receded over the last 1,500 years. Powell Moore described the pre-settlement Whiting area as "one of the most uninviting areas of the region." It was easy to walk or ride along a ridge, but to cross to another ridge could be very difficult. The largest swale, large enough that it was often called a lake (Berry Lake) was on the east side of town. As the community and its industry were developed, the ridges and wetlands disappeared. Berry Lake was eventually drained by Standard Oil Company. The first building was likely Hanna Berry's tavern, built about 1833 between or near Berry Lake and Lake Michigan.

In 1852, the Michigan Southern and Northern Indiana Railroad built the first rail line. It was joined seven years later by the Pittsburgh, Fort Wayne & Chicago Railroad. Neither built a station.

Heinrich and Augusta Eggers, who arrived from Germany in 1848, are believed to have been the first permanent settlers. In the years following, the Reeses, Schrages, and several other German families arrived. Heinrich Eggers and John Vater built an icehouse on Berry Lake and began shipping ice to Chicago. Many of the others made their living working for the railroads.

The little community got its name from Herbert "Pop" Whiting, an engineer on the Michigan Southern, who ditched a freight train on a siding to allow a passenger train to safely pass by. Apparently, afterwards people called the area Whiting's Turn-off. There was no regular passenger service, but trains had to stop to get wood for fuel and water. For many years the trains hauled sand, gravel, and ice from the Whiting area into Chicago.

Starting in 1866, a Lutheran minister from Chicago made periodic trips to conduct services for the German-speaking families in the South Chicago/Whiting area. But it would be several years before Whiting had a church of its own. In 1871 Whiting got a post office, but that didn't change the character of this little community. Until 1889, Whiting was (as described by Powell Moore) a "sleepy hamlet clustering around Henry Schrage's [general] store." Jennie

Figure 141. Pop Whiting. Whiting Public Library.

Figure 142. The new Whiting Public Library in 1906. Whiting Public Library.

Putnam remembered that when she and friends would go out on 119th Street they would step on garter snakes. She said that there were no sidewalks anywhere in the town.

In 1889, things changed. That year the Standard Oil Company established its refinery at Whiting and became the first major heavy industry to build in northwest Indiana. The place hasn't been the same since. The rapid growth of Whiting can be seen in the following voting statistics: in 1890, about 75 votes were cast in an election; in 1900, nearly 1,500 votes were cast. The "wide-open" part of town was called Oklahoma. Near the refinery's west entrance, it consisted of "rows of saloons, gambling dens, and houses of ill repute." It was a particularly wild place on payday.

The first church in Whiting was Plymouth Congregational, which was started in 1890. The next year, three churches were established: Sacred Heart Roman Catholic, First Methodist, and St. John Evangelical Lutheran. In 1899, St. Mary Assumption Byzantine Catholic Church became the first Byzantine Rite Catholic church in the Midwest. A few years later, St. Paul's Evangelical Lutheran Church became the first Slovak Lutheran church in Indiana.

By 1900 Whiting had a population of about 6,000. It was incorporated as a town in 1895 and then as a city in 1903.

Postscript: The Whiting Public Library was built in 1905–1906 on land donated by the Standard Oil Company and with funds provided by Andrew Carnegie. Its additions have allowed this historic building to retain much of its original appearance. Whiting High School, one of the oldest high school buildings in the Calumet Area, has served the students of this city since 1910. The Whiting/Robertsdale Historical Museum is located in an old barbershop on 119th Street.

Winfield/Palmer

The town of Winfield, on the hills of the Valparaiso Moraine, sits on the Eastern Continental Divide. Deer Creek and Deep River flow northward toward Lake Michigan; Stoney Run flows southward and joins the Kankakee River.

Jeremy and Susan Hixon arrived in 1835 and laid claim to property at the edge of the prairie. Like other settlers, they wanted to be near trees which would shelter and provide them with fuel and building materials. But they also wanted to be near the prairie, which was easier to turn into a farm. At that time there were no houses within five miles. In 1849 Hixon, who earlier had built Michigan City's first lighthouse, got the contract for building the first frame courthouse at Crown Point. When Winfield Township was separated from Center Township in 1843, Hixon named it after the popular general Winfield Scott.

The first brick home in the township was built by Jacob Wise, whose son Henry operated a brickyard in Crown Point. The Chicago & Atlantic built its line through the township in 1881, and the tiny community called Winfield was located where 117th Avenue met the tracks.

Palmer was named for its founder, Dennis Palmer. In 1854 Dennis and Mary Palmer established a farm in southern Winfield Township. In 1882, Dennis platted the town alongside the Chicago & Atlantic tracks (today at 125th and Randolph). The Palmers donated the land for the train depot and milk shed. They also owned the first store and ran the first post office. The first blacksmith shop was built by James Wilkinson. By 1900, Palmer was a busy station where farmers would drop off cans of milk every day. The settlement had a population of about eighty-five, a couple of stores, and a brick school building.

For 150 years, Winfield has been primarily an agricultural area. By mutual agreement it was part of the Crown Point school and library systems. However, to avoid being annexed by neighboring Merrillville, the town was speedily incorporated in 1994. The new town included the original settlement of Winfield and part of Palmer.

Porter and LaPorte County Communities

Porter County was created in 1836 and named for David Porter, an admiral during the War of 1812. From 1832 to 1836, this area was part of LaPorte County.

Boone Grove

Boone Grove is near the southeast edge of the Valparaiso Moraine just north of the Boone/Porter Township line. As its name implies, the town was established in a wooded area, and many of the original trees were kept standing as the little town grew.

The Boone Grove post office was established in 1843 with Aaron Little serving as its first postmaster. The Boone Grove Christian Church was established in 1852. In 1881, the Chicago and Atlantic (Erie Lackawanna) Railroad was extended through the area and a station was established. Timothy Ball described the town as a very pleasant village. He added, "The entire Boone Grove community is intelligent and prosperous."

Chesterton/Crocker

The town of Chesterton extends from the sands of the ancient Glenwood Shoreline, southward across the Lake Border Moraine to the flat-lying lands of the former Chesterton Bay, During the Glenwood phase of Lake Michigan, Chesterton Bay was a good-sized inlet separated by the moraine from the open waters of Lake Michigan.

Chesterton also straddles the old Indiana-Michigan territorial boundary, ten miles south of the present Indiana-Michigan state line. Indian Boundary Road and Woodlawn Avenue are located on this old line. Indian Boundary got its name because this line was also the boundary of lands ceded by the Potawatomi to the state of Indiana in an 1826 treaty.

Coffee and Sand Creeks, which originate in the Valparaiso Moraine, flow north through the town and empty into the Little Calumet River. Legend has it that in about 1833 when Coffee Creek was in flood stage, a mail carrier dropped a sack full of coffee into this swollen stream and thereby gave it its name.

Chesterton can trace its beginnings to the establishment of the area's first post office. Jesse and Jane, Isaac and Sarah, and William and Anna Morgan, along with William and Ann Thomas, were among the earliest settlers (after Joseph and Marie Bailly) to arrive in Porter County.[1] Jesse, Isaac, and William were brothers; Sarah and Anna were sisters. Jesse and Jane, who arrived in 1833, staked out a farm and established the log Stage House Tavern on the Chicago–[LaPorte]–Detroit Road near where Morgan Lake is today.[2] A post office at Morgan's home was established in 1835. Originally called the Coffee Creek Post Office, its name was changed to Calumet in 1849. Morgan served as the postmaster for twenty years.

In 1852, the Lake Shore and Michigan Southern Railroad laid tracks across Porter County. William Thomas then platted the town, which he called Calumet. Many of the town's new citizens were Irish railroad laborers. Not surprisingly, the first church in town (in 1858) was called St. Patrick's.

In 1850, Porter County authorized the building of a plank toll road from Valparaiso through Calumet to Michigan City. The road was built, but not as planned. Only about two or three miles of it ever had wooden planks. Part of this road became old Route 49 (today Calumet Road). William and Ann Thomas established the

---

1. Morgan Avenue, School, Lake, Prairie, and Township are all named after this pioneer family. The Thomas Library is named after the William and Ann Thomas family.
2. The other two Morgan families established farms in Washington Township on "Morgan Prairie."

Thomas Inn aside the road (at Lincoln Avenue).[3] Earlier, their son Enos (who was also the son-in-law of Jesse and Jane Morgan) constructed a dam across Coffee Creek and built a sawmill, so lumber was available for building houses and barns.

By 1862 the town of Calumet had one church, two saloons, a hotel, two stores, four carpenters, and a blacksmith. In 1865 Calumet residents formed the First Methodist Episcopal Church. Three years later, J. B. Lundberg established a profitable furniture and undertaking business (related businesses, of course). Lundberg became the first licensed embalmer in Indiana. In 1869, the community was incorporated as a town and took the name Chesterton. Unfortunately, growth did not occur, the town went into debt, and within nine years Chesterton was "dis-incorporated."

The Chesterton area attracted a large number of Swedes who, in 1879, opened two new churches, Bethlehem Lutheran and the Swedish Methodist Church, both with services in Swedish. In the 1880s, German immigrants, many of whom worked at the brickyards in nearby Porter, established St. John's Evangelical (now St. John's United) and St. Paul Lutheran, both with services in German. Yet, in spite of the number of churches, Chesterton was known as a "tough" town with over nineteen saloons for a population of about 300.

In 1881, Swedish immigrant C. O. Hillstrom moved his organ factory from Chicago to Chesterton and set up shop on Broadway. With about 30 employees, the Hillstrom Organ Factory made fine pump organs that were shipped to all parts of the country. After making more than 35,000 organs, the organ factory closed when

Figure 143. *Chesterton Tribune* and livery stable. The *Tribune* still uses the building. The livery stable is gone. Westchester Public Library Archives and Dan Bruhn Photography.

3. A sketch map in a book owned by Jesse Morgan shows a tollbooth not far from the Thomas Hotel. The book is owned by the Westchester Historical Museum located just north of the old hotel site.

American tastes changed and pianos rather than organs became the fashionable instrument to have in one's living or drawing room.

A weekly newspaper, the *Chesterton Tribune,* was established in 1882 but went out of business after only 35 issues. It was reestablished in 1884 by Arthur Bowser and became one of Chesterton's real successes.[4] The *Tribune* moved into its new building on Valparaiso Street (Calumet Road) in 1904 and has been there ever since.

The Chesterton area had several early industries, a few brickyards, a glass factory, and even a china factory, which made use of the abundant sand and clay in the area. Chesterton was reincorporated in 1899. At that time, this small town of 788 was the second-largest community in Porter County. Its population was up to 1,400 by 1910.

Crocker, originally called LaHayn, was established in 1892 around a railroad station near the crossing of the Wabash and the EJ&E Railroads. Soon after the station opened, Charles LaHayn, Jr., opened the area's first saloon. To keep his beer cold, LaHayn built an icehouse to store blocks of ice that he would cut from nearby Crocker Pond. The saloon was soon joined by a grocery and post office, a blacksmith shop, a shoe repair, and a butcher shop. Crocker was annexed by Chesterton in 1969. LaHayn Road and Crocker Street preserve the community's early names.

Postscripts: The Westchester Historical Museum is located on the ground floor of the Westchester Public Library Service Center at the corner of Calumet and Indiana Avenue.

Historical Tour of Chesterton, a pamphlet available at the Thomas Library, describes many of the very old homes and other buildings in the oldest part of Chesterton. Of particular interest are the Brown Mansion, built in 1885, St. John's United Church, built in 1880, and the Bethlehem Lutheran Church, built in 1882.

Hebron

The town of Hebron is located at the southern edge of the Valparaiso Moraine. When first settled in 1835, most of Boone Township, north of the Kankakee Marsh, was prairie land with a few groves of trees spaced like islands in a lake. Hebron was located by one of these groves. Half a mile south of town is the site of "Indian Town," an old Indian village where Potawatomi people lived until about 1842.

Hebron is the only Calumet Area town with a biblical name,

---

4. Bowser was later elected to the Indiana Senate, where he wrote the Reclamation Law that allowed U.S. Steel to expand northward by filling in Lake Michigan.

Figure 144. An unidentified pair in front of the McCune (later Stagecoach) Inn. Note the dirt road. John Spinks collection.

and as might be expected, local churches played a part in its establishment. Two congregations were established in the very early days of settlement: the Methodists, who trace their history back to 1835, and the Reformed Presbyterians, who were organized two years later. The Presbyterians built their church at the intersection of two rural roads, a place that soon became known as "The Corners." The Methodists' log building, built in 1844, was half a mile to the south. That same year, John Alyea subdivided his land and created three one-acre lots at the intersection adjacent to the Presbyterian church. He sold two lots and built a blacksmith shop on the third. The next year, when a Mr. Bagley built the first house in town, the Presbyterian minister, Wilson Blaine, arranged for a post office to be established. He gave the name Hebron to the post office and was appointed its first postmaster. In 1846 two stores were opened, and the town slowly began to grow. The first hotel (today's Stagecoach Inn) was opened in 1849 by James McCune.

The Chicago and Great Eastern Railway (Panhandle), built through town in 1864, spurred more growth. Almost immediately Burrell Pratt built a second hotel. The Folsom Brick Company, the first brickyard in southern Porter County, then started providing bricks for a number of commercial and residential buildings in the Hebron area. By 1880, Hebron could boast five churches, four blacksmith shops, four general stores, three barbershops, two wagon shops, two livery stables, and a brickyard. The fame of the great hunting grounds along the Kankakee River brought so many visitors that by 1882 two additional hotels had been established. Hebron was incorporated as a town in 1890 with a population that year of 689.

Postscripts: The McCune Inn, built in 1849 by James McCune, was Hebron's first hotel and is today the town's oldest building. It once served as a resting-place for people who came to hunt and fish in the great Kankakee Marsh. In 1970 the restored building, called the Stagecoach Inn, was opened to the public as a local history museum. The Panhandle depot was moved by the Hebron Historical Society in 1994 from the tracks to its current location behind the Stagecoach Inn. It now serves as a museum of railroad and local history.

Kouts

The town of Kouts is located on the rather flat Kankakee Outwash Plain less than four miles north of the Kankakee River. The soils in and around the town were laid down by meltwaters escaping from the glacier as it was forming the moraine. Nearby ditches and streams, such as Crooked Creek, still carry water from the moraine south to the Kankakee River.

In 1865 Bernard Kouts (originally Barnhardt Kautz) platted the town and established the town's first business adjacent to the new Chicago and Great Eastern Railway (Panhandle) line. The next year, a post office was established and H. A. Wright was named post-master.[5] Kouts's second rail line, the Chicago and Atlantic (Erie Lackawanna) was built in 1881.

In 1880 the St. Paul's German Evangelical Lutheran Congregation erected the first church building in Pleasant Township across the street from where St. Paul's new (1908) building is today. By 1890 the town had its post office, several stores, one church, a blacksmith, and two saloons. The population in 1900 was about 250. Kouts was incorporated as a town in 1921.

Ogden Dunes/Dune Acres/ Beverly Shores

The three residential communities of Dune Acres, Ogden Dunes, and Beverly Shores are built in the sand dunes immediately south of the present shoreline. Had Indiana's northern boundary not been moved north by ten miles when Indiana became a state in 1816, part of Ogden Dunes and all of Dune Acres and Beverly Shores would today still be a part of Michigan.

Each of the three communities extends from the lakeshore to about the South Shore Railroad. The building of the railroad in 1906–1908 increased awareness and interest in this lakeshore area, but it was the building of a highway that really made it possible for these three communities to get started.

Ogden Dunes was platted by Colin Mackenzie, in 1923, and named for landowner Francis Ogden. Two years later, it was incorporated as a town. A ski jump

THE DUNES HIGHWAY

It is no accident that the three lakeside communities of Dune Acres, Ogden Dunes, and Beverly Shores (as well as Dunes State Park) were all established in the 1920s. That was the decade in which the Dunes Highway was built.

This beautiful road between Gary and Michigan City was proposed in 1918 by the Dunes Highway Association, a group composed of representatives of northwest Indiana lakeside cities. Construction began in March 1922. The section from Michigan City to Baillytown followed the ancient Calumet Shoreline/Chicago–Detroit Stage Road and was easier to build than the western section, which crossed the Great Marsh (the former Calumet Lagoon). With great fanfare, the highway opened in November 1923. The only concrete highway in northern Porter County, it was immediately used by tourists, commuters, and cross-continental travelers. As the most direct route between Detroit and Chicago (as was the Chicago–Detroit stagecoach route ninety years earlier), it soon became the busiest highway in Indiana.

5. For one year the Kouts area was served by the Foster post office, which was located on the Baum's Bridge Road where it was crossed by the Panhandle Railroad. This has led to the misconception that Kouts was once called Foster.

Figure 145. The new Dunes Highway along the old Calumet Shoreline, ca. 1922. Note the sand dunes still present on the south side of the road. Calumet Regional Archives.

was built in 1927. Said to have the highest slide in the country, it was featured in a well-known South Shore advertising poster. Partly because of the South Shore's advertising, the ski lift attracted large crowds, but it was closed about six years later, a victim of the Great Depression. By 1950 there were more than 400 residents of the town.

Postscript: The Ogden Dunes Historical Society's Hour Glass Museum is located at 8 Lupine Lane.

Dune Acres was platted in 1923 just west of the proposed Indiana Dunes State Park and north of the old Bailly settlement. The community was planned by Gary school superintendent William A. Wirt, Arthur Melton, and other Gary residents as a lakeside residential area. Following an August 1923 election with nine votes in favor and none against, Dune Acres was incorporated as a town. Amenities such as a clubhouse and golf course were soon developed and helped give the new town its character. A small harbor was built into Lake Michigan, but a series of winter storms in 1927 washed it away. In the south part of the town is Cowles Bog, now part of the Indiana Dunes National Lakeshore.

Beverly Shores was planned by Chicagoan Frederick Bartlett, who purchased land east of Indiana Dunes State Park in 1927. He envisioned an elegant resort community with easy access via the South

MANY YEARS AGO . . .

"Within the tract now known as Ogden Dunes, my old friend, Tom Stearns . . . owned a tract of 80 acres. One day Tom came over to my place to buy two pigs at $2.00 a piece, he said he did not have the money to pay for them, but would give me the 80 acres for them. I told him to take the pigs home with him and pay me for them when he could get the money. This land sold a few years ago for about $800 per acre. Now I cannot raise enough pigs in ten years to purchase even a fifty-foot lot in those subdivisions in the Knobs.

It takes a pretty good prophet to fore-tell, long in advance, the events and conditions of the Calumet Region."

—Darus Blake, 1929

Shore Railroad to Chicago. Bartlett designed several subdivisions, constructed access roads, and built two South Shore stations (one still standing), a fashionable hotel and administration building on Broadway, and a country club with an 18-hole golf course. Keeping with the resort theme, Bartlett designed the buildings in a Mediterranean Revival style. Bartlett then enticed would-be buyers to ride the South Shore Railroad from Chicago to view his development.

In 1933, Frederick Bartlett sold his interests in Beverly Shores to his son Robert, who purchased and relocated several homes and other buildings from the just-closed Chicago World Fair. Six of these Century of Progress homes still stand. The investment paid off, and sales picked up. Within a few years Beverly Shores had many new homes, a post office, and a school. The town was incorporated in 1947.

Postscript: The Beverly Shores Historical Museum is located in the South Shore Depot on Broadway. The depot is on the National Register of Historic Places.

Figure 146. South Shore advertising poster: *Ski Meet: Ogden Dunes by South Shore Line* was a 1929 lithograph by Emil Biorn. Calumet Regional Archives.

Portage

The city of Portage extends today from Lake Michigan to the Tinley Moraine and contains all three of the lake's ancient shorelines. On the north side of the city, dunes of the Tolleston Shoreline can be found between the Little Calumet River and the present shoreline. The Little Calumet River flows through the lowland area that was once the site of the Calumet Lagoon (see Map 5). Burns Ditch was dug in 1926 through the High Tolleston Shoreline to connect the river with Lake Michigan.

The Calumet Shoreline passes through the city in a diagonal line just north of the Crisman area. From the B&O bridge to Willow Creek Road, it follows Melton Road (Route 20), although most of the sand dunes that once were part of this shoreline have been removed. The Calumet Shoreline can also be seen by the careful eye at the intersection of Interstate 94 and Crisman Road. (The

Figure 147. Beverly Shores Service Station. Indiana Dunes National Lakeshore collection.

expressway is down in the lake bottomland area, and Highway 20 is up on the shore.) Immediately south of this are the dunes of the Glenwood Shoreline, which extend from Garyton and the Crisman Elementary School area northeast toward the junction of Salt Creek and the Little Calumet. South of these sand hills is the low area that was Hobart Bay during the Glenwood phase of Lake Michigan (see Map 3). Portage High School is on the north slope of the Tinley moraine.

Beginning in 1837, part of the Calumet shoreline became the path of the Chicago–Detroit stagecoach route. Carley's Tavern, the first tavern or inn in Portage Township, was established in 1837 along this route (now Clem Road) where it crossed Willow Creek. A second and much more famous inn at the same location was the Old Maid's Tavern, run by Miss Holmes and Miss Rugar. Their inn reportedly had the neatest rooms, the most comfortable lodging, and the best food in the area.

Unfortunately, few roads in Portage today follow that old stagecoach route. One small segment is that part of Melton Road (Route 20) just east of the B&O overpass. This part of the highway was built on or just a bit south of the original road.[6] In places, Stagecoach Road in northwest Portage follows the approximate route of a road shown on several 1870 era maps. Stagecoaches used that old road, but it is impossible to determine just how much of the current Stagecoach Road is the same as that old route.[7]

For many years sand mining was big business in Portage Township. Historian George Garard reported in 1882 that "much sand is shipped from this township to Chicago, and it may be that in time this will be a fruitful source of wealth for the supply is almost limitless." At the Dune Park railroad station in 1889, the Lake Shore and Michigan Southern Railroad loaded and removed more than 300 cars of sand *every day*. During that year, this was the best paying freight station between Elkhart and Chicago.

Jacob and Lydia Wolf were among the earliest settlers of Portage Township, arriving in 1834. Jacob and Eleanor Blake arrived in 1836. As many of the Potawatomi Indians still lived in the area, Jacob Blake learned to speak the Potawatomi language. He and they were good neighbors. The first township election was held in the Wolfs' home in 1836 with twenty-nine male property owners casting votes.

---

6. Peter Youngman's article from the Historical Society of Ogden Dunes newsletter describes the early trails of the Portage/Ogden Dunes area. It is on the web page of the Historical Society of Ogden Dunes.

7. On old maps this road is shown to be much straighter than the current road—but then the early map makers often just marked the intersections of river and trails with their surveyed section lines and often simply estimated the location of rivers and trails between them.

Crisman was named for Benjamin and Elizabeth Crisman, who arrived in 1850, just before the Michigan Central Railroad was built in 1852. (The Crismans donated an acre of land for the Michigan Central depot.) In 1870, Mr. Crisman platted the village located at today's intersection of Crisman Road and Portage Avenue. The next year, when a post office was established in the village, their son Isaac, who had earlier established the first store in the area, became postmaster.

A four-room home north of the village (at Melton Road) was believed to have been an active station of the Underground Railroad. Each of the rooms is said to have had a trap door through which runaway slaves were harbored until the next night, when they would be taken to Michigan.

The B&O Railroad was built in 1874 and added to the community's growth. About twenty years later, the Wabash Railroad built its line. Both of these newer lines intersected the Michigan Central at Willow Creek Road.

In 1882, historian George Garard noted that Portage Township was known for its good school buildings. The first two-story brick Crisman School was built in 1879 and was soon considered the best school in the township. N. E. Yost was its teacher. It was later replaced by the buildings standing today. The smaller of the two schools was built in 1890; the larger went up in 1926.

McCool was located on McCool Road where the EJ&E and B&O Railroads crossed. Among its first settlers was Harrison Barnett. Other early residents were the McCool and Robbins families, both of whom established large dairy farms. When the B&O line was built in 1874, the McCools ensured the area's growth by donating a portion of their land for the depot. Soon up to 200 cans of milk were shipped daily to Chicago from the McCool station. Besides the depot, tower, and milk stand, McCool could also boast about eight houses and a general store/post office.

Garyton, next to the county line, was the site of an old Indian village. This community was established in 1912 when the Gary streetcar line was extended to Valparaiso. It was named after the nearby city of Gary in hopes of capitalizing on the growth of that booming and prosperous city. Its population grew, and it was the largest of the communities that later became part of Portage.

Figure 149. Benjamin and Elizabeth Crisman. Linda Kus, Crisman Elementary School.

The town of Portage, including Crisman, McCool, Garyton, and the lakeside community of Edgewater, was incorporated in 1959, the same year that Midwest Steel built its plant. Development of the lakeshore continued as Bethlehem Steel's first mills opened in 1964, and the Port of Indiana opened five years later. Portage became a city in 1967.

Postscript: Crisman School still stands at the corner of Crisman Road and Portage Avenue.

Porter/Burns Harbor

The towns of Porter and Burns Harbor extend from Lake Michigan, over the dunes of its current and ancient shorelines, to the flatter and fertile plain of the former Chesterton Bay. The Porter Beach area is built on Tolleston dunes of the Modern age. South of these dunes are the low-lying lands of the former Calumet Lagoon. Along the Dunes Highway (Route 12) is the Calumet Shoreline. South again (but only east of Wagner Drive) are the few visible Glenwood Dunes. (Bailly Drive North is in Glenwood dunes.)

In the center of Porter, and just inside the Burns Harbor limits, is the Lake Border Moraine extending roughly from south of the Calumet Dunes to the Little Calumet River. South of the moraine are the much flatter grounds of Chesterton Bay, a good-sized inlet off of Lake Michigan during its original Glenwood Stage. The original town of Porter is in this area.

The towns also lie along the old territorial and Indian boundary line. This line, marked today by Beam Street and Woodlawn Avenue, used to be the northern edge of the Indiana Territory. North of this line from 1805 to 1816 was Michigan territory.[8]

The story of Joseph and Marie Bailly, the first permanent settlers in the entire Calumet Area, appears in chapter 3. Also described there is an account of the stagecoach route on what is now the

8. For a history of the Indian Boundary, see chapter 3.

Dunes Highway. Settlement of the rich agricultural lands in Westchester Township began in 1834. In time the surrounding area attracted a number of Swedish immigrant farmers who founded the area's first church, the Augsburg Lutheran Church, in 1858.

In 1851, the Michigan Central built its line and established the first railway station in the Calumet Area. It was called Porter Station, or simply Porter. The town that grew up around this station (along today's Old Porter Road west of Mineral Springs Road) was also called Porter. So was the post office. However, within a year, when the Lake Shore and Michigan Southern Railroad built its line, the station was moved east to the intersection of the two sets of tracks so that it could serve both rail lines. The station building still had the Porter name over its door even though it was no longer at the old Porter location. In 1871, next to the relocated train station, Henry and Hannah Hageman laid out a town named for themselves.[9] Its post office was also named Hageman, but the railroad station was still called Porter.

Figure 150. Henry and Hannah Hageman. Westchester Public Library Archives and Dan Bruhn Photography.

Confusion reigned! The Porter post office was in the town of Porter Station, but the actual Porter rail station was a mile east in the town of Hageman. Passengers were confused, and freight deliveries were often made to the wrong location. Unfortunately for the Hagemans, the railroads continued to use the name Porter, and so within a few years the Hageman name was dropped. It has been preserved, however, in Hageman Avenue and the Hageman branch of the Westchester Public Library.

Unlike most other area town planners who designed towns with true north-south and east-west streets and avenues, Hageman designed his streets parallel to the Michigan Central tracks. The street closest to the tracks was called Front Street (of course, it fronted the tracks). It was later changed to Lincoln in honor of the president, whose funeral train had stopped in Porter on its way from Washington to Springfield, Illinois, in 1865.

The glacial clays in the Porter area were found to be suitable for brick making, and with the railroad nearby to carry bricks to distant customers, the first brickyard opened in 1871. Bricks were

9. Garard (in Goodspeed and Blanchard, 1882) and Ball (1900) state that the town was founded in 1872.

Figure 151. The old Porter Town Hall. Dan Bruhn Photography.

in great demand after the Chicago Fire, and the industry flourished. By 1884, there were eight brickyards in operation.[10] In the early 1890s more than 200 employees worked in Porter brickyards. In 1897 Indiana state geologist W. S. Blatchley noted that Porter had the largest pressed front brick factory in the state. Although the clay beds were thought to be inexhaustible, after only twenty-five years of mining, much of the best clay was extracted and many of the brickyards closed. The Hydraulic Pressed Brick Company was the last, biggest, and reportedly one of the finest brickyards in the country. It kept going until 1925. Other early industries utilized nearby sand to make glass and other clays to make china. With a careful eye, one can still see the sites of the old brickyards because the ground there is lower than the nearby roads. Yost Elementary School is at the site of one yard, and Hawthorne Park is at another.

A busy commercial district developed along Front (Lincoln) Street, and by 1880 the population of Porter was about 250. Porter was incorporated as a town in 1908. By 1910, its population had passed 500.

A modern town, Burns Harbor was incorporated as a town in 1967 with the aid of the Bethlehem Steel Company.

Postscript: The Bailly Homestead, the first permanent settlement in the entire Calumet Area, has been restored and is now operated by the Indiana Dunes National Lakeshore (see chapter 3). The Chellberg Farm is named for Anders and Johanna Kjellberg (later

10. Most of the Porter bricks went to rebuild Chicago. Others were used to build the Kalamazoo, Michigan, courthouse and other public buildings throughout the Midwest.

COMMUNITY BEGINNINGS

Anglicized to Chellberg), who came from Sweden in 1863 and worked for the Bailly family. In 1874 the Chellbergs established their own farm. The house now standing was built in 1884 with Porter brick. Not far from the Bailly Homestead, it is also operated by the National Park.

Figure 152. The Svenska Skola or Burstrom Chapel.

The Augsburg Svenska Skola (Burstrom Chapel) is a tiny church that was originally built as a tool shed for the Burstrom family. In 1880, the structure was moved to its current location on Oak Hill Road where it served first as a school, then as a Swedish language summer school, and finally as a chapel. The tower was added later.

Historical Tour of Porter, a pamphlet available at the Hageman Library, describes many of the old homes and storefronts in the oldest part of Porter.

Tassinong

Tassinong was once located on the Kankakee Outwash Plain, near the intersection of Baum's Bridge Road and Indiana Route 49, two miles north of Kouts. Its importance was due to its being on high ground north of the Kankakee marsh near the spot where the river was most easily crossed (at Baum's Bridge Road). The crossing, earlier known as Potawatomi Ford, was where George Eaton established a ferry in 1836. Pioneer hunter J. Lorenzo Werich noted that when the water was high, the river and marsh were one and a half miles wide even at that narrowest point.[11]

Tassinong is the site of one of the first known trading posts in the Porter–Lake County area. The importance of this site to Potawatomi culture and trade is well supported by the abundance of archaeological artifacts found there by Shirley Anderson, owner of the property. Some time before November 1824, U.S. Indian agent Alexander Wolcott authorized a temporary trading post at an Indian village called "Tay-say-eh-nong." According to Wolcott, Jacob Harsen and Leon Bourassa were licensed to trade with the Potawatomis there. In an 1827 census, the village of Tassinong is listed as having forty-seven Potawatomi residents.

Thus it was that Potawatomi Indians told the early settlers about

---

11. Werich noted that in 1849 Eaton built a toll bridge across the Kankakee—the first bridge upstream of Momence, Illinois—but that it burned down the following year. In 1857 a Mr. Sawyer built a bridge there, but high water and ice took it out the next spring. Then in the 1860s Enus Baum successfully built a bridge that stood for many years and gave the area its name.

the old trading post, which was gone by the mid-1830s. Surprisingly, nothing about the 1820s trading post was known to the early historians of the county. In 1882, historian George Garard suggested that perhaps there had been a French trading post there. He made no reference to the American post that was there only sixty years earlier.

,Tassinong's modern history is better known. Settlers started arriving in 1834, and a post office named Tassinong was established in 1838. By 1852, the year it was incorporated as a town, the little community had two stores, two blacksmith shops, a carpenter's shop, a tavern, and some shoemakers' shops. In 1855 a Presbyterian church was erected. However, in 1865 the Chicago and Great Eastern Railroad was built south of the village and a station erected at Kouts which prospered and grew instead of Tassinong. In 1900, Ball noted that it "can scarcely be called a village [anymore]." Soon afterward, the village ceased to exist. On June 12, 1960, a historical marker was placed at the site of this former little "shopping center of the prairie."

Tremont/Furnessville/Pines

The name Tremont is an Americanization of the French "Trois Monts" meaning three mountains. It is named for three of the highest dunes on the Indiana lakeshore, Mt. Tom, Mt. Holden, and Mt. Jackson. This small unincorporated area is located on the ancient Calumet Shoreline (Route 12, formerly the Chicago-Detroit stage route). In the 1830s, the Green Tavern was established on the Chicago-Detroit Road.[12] Nearby were the New City West post office and a cooper's shop. Although the Michigan Central Railroad added new life to much of the Calumet Area, it did put the stagecoach line out of business and with it the Green Tavern and the post office.

The early twentieth century changed the character of this remote area. In 1908, the South Shore Railroad was built alongside the Calumet Shoreline. It and the Dunes Highway in 1923 made transportation to and from the area much more convenient for families deciding to live "back of the dunes." After Indiana Dunes State Park was established in 1927, the South Shore's Tremont Station became an important stop on that line.

Furnessville is an unincorporated community alongside U.S. Highway 20 and the old Michigan Central Railroad. According to George Garard, the area was first called Murray's Side Track and

12. One of the three tallest dunes was originally named Mt. Green in honor of the Green family. In 1925, its name was changed to Mt. Jackson, honoring the governor of Indiana, who had arranged for the establishment of Indiana Dunes State Park.

later Morgan's Side Track—the first frame building being put up in 1853 by a Morgan family. Edwin and Louise Furness settled there in 1855 and opened a store in their basement the following year. They joined forces with the Morgans and established the lumbering firm of Morgan, Furness, & Co. Morgan's Side Track is also the name of what may have been the Calumet Area's first railroad, a road made of wooden rails with "trains" drawn by horses or mules. Morgan's Side Track Railroad stretched from Furnessville to Lake Michigan. Edwin Furness was responsible for a station being built alongside the Michigan Central tracks, and he was the first station agent. He also arranged for a post office to be established there in 1861 and so became postmaster. Not surprisingly the name of the community became Furnessville. The lumber business was an important industry with as many as three sawmills operating at one time. When the Morgan/Furness partnership broke up, Furness continued lumbering on his own.

Figure 153. Edwin and Louise Furness. From *History of Porter County, Indiana,* 1912.

A Society of Christians (Disciples) was established at Furnessville in 1869 by Rev. William Furness. A Methodist Society was also established. Both met in the local schoolhouse. Furnessville became somewhat famous in 1943 with the publication of *Dune Boy,* by naturalist Edwin Way Teale. The book is a collection of childhood stories of summers and vacations spent at his grandparents' farm not far from town. The book became an overnight success, and more than 100,000 copies were distributed to GIs serving in World War II. Teale Road, south of the Dunes Highway, is named for Furnessville's most famous son.

Pines is situated on the narrow strip of Calumet Shoreline dunes south of and parallel to Route 12. The town, located in Pine Township in the northeast corner of Porter County, was planned by William Schleman soon after the highway was built in 1922–23. It and the township were named after the great pine trees that once covered much of the area. Pines was incorporated as a town in 1952.

Postscript: The Furnessville Schoolhouse, built in 1886, now serves as a retail store. It sits across the street from the Furnessville Cemetery, which contains the graves of many of the early residents.

Valparaiso

The city of Valparaiso sits near the southeast edge of the Valparaiso Moraine near the area of its greatest relief. The gently sloping land

Figure 154. Thomas A. E. Campbell. From Goodspeed and Blanchard, 1882.

east of town is part of the Kankakee Outwash Plain and was formed by sand that was deposited by waters flowing off the glaciers. Salt Creek on the southwest side of the city flows northward, cuts through the moraine, and empties into the Little Calumet River at Portage. Southwest of and parallel to Salt Creek, Sievers Creek flows in the opposite direction, eventually emptying into the Kankakee River. The old Sauk Trail, which ran from Detroit to Rock Island, Illinois, once passed through Valparaiso.

Valparaiso and its environs have long utilized the moraine that bears its name. Uses have varied from industrial to recreational. At least four companies have mined clay and operated brickyards in the area. The 1885 *Valparaiso City Directory* lists two companies, both near the Nickel Plate Railroad. The 1922 *Handbook of Indiana Geology* lists two others. Recreational uses of the moraine include winter skiing down its steep hills and summer swimming, boating, and fishing in the many kettle lakes north of the city. Valparaiso has also used these lakes as a source of drinking water.

Valparaiso was platted alongside the Sauk Trail/LaPorte–Joliet Road about a mile west of an old Indian village called Chiqua's Town. Benjamin McCarty, who designed the town, later platted the town of Cedar Lake. Valparaiso's location was advantageous because it was not only along the old trail but also near the geographical center of the new Porter County. Intended from the beginning to be the county seat, it was first named Portersville. The first settlers in the area, arriving in 1834, were the families of Adam and Polly Campbell and Thomas and Margaret Campbell. (Campbell Street is named after them.) J. P. Ballard erected the first building on the site of the original village. In order to have a place to conduct county business, the first courthouse, a simple two-story frame building, was built in 1837.

Figure 155. Porter County Courthouse. Historical Society of Porter County Old Jail Museum.

According to Hubert Skinner (in 1876 Valparaiso's first historian), some sailors and marines who were spending the evening at Hall's Tavern suggested that since the county was named after Commodore David Porter, well known for a naval battle near the Chilean capital, Valparaiso, the new city's name should be Valparaiso. In any event, the city's name was changed. The fact that the name in Spanish means "Valley of Paradise" didn't bother the citizens of this hamlet atop the hills of the Valparaiso Moraine.

The little town grew. Stores and other businesses soon located near the new courthouse. The first churches established were First Baptist Church in 1837 and the Presbyterian and Methodist churches three years later. In 1838, the Porter County Library Association was formed. Probably the first lending library in the Calumet Area, this private organization had about 500 books that could be lent to members only. With a population of about 520, Valparaiso was incorporated as a town in 1851.

Valparaiso was late in entering the stagecoach era. In 1853, a stage route was established between Valparaiso and La-Porte. (See photograph in chapter 4.) The trip took five hours, and one could transfer at Westville to the stage that ran between Michigan City and Lafayette. A stage line connected Valparaiso with Calumet (now Chesterton) in 1854, and a year later the local mail carrier started taking passengers to Crown Point.

Figure 156. John Philip Sousa at the railroad station in Valparaiso. Sousa's band performed four times at Valparaiso's Memorial Opera House. Ajax Newservice, Inc.

The first railroad to serve the town was the Pittsburgh, Fort Wayne and Chicago (Pennsylvania) Railroad, which was built through town in 1858. With the new rail line completed into Chicago and the opening in 1859 of the new Valparaiso Male and Female College, the town expanded and prospered. Valparaiso was incorporated as a city in 1865.

In 1873, H. B. Brown purchased the Male and Female College and established the Northern Indiana Normal School, now Valparaiso University. In the early 1880s, two new rail lines were run through the city, spurring additional growth: the Grand Trunk in 1880 and the Nickel Plate in 1882. Also in 1882, the new county courthouse was built. Valparaiso grew quickly. In 1886, the city started pumping in drinking water from Flint Lake. By 1890, Valparaiso's population had increased to more than 5,000; by 1900, it surpassed 6,000.

Postscript: The 1882 county courthouse still stands in spite of a fire in 1934 that destroyed its interior. During reconstruction, the central tower was removed. The Memorial Opera House was built in 1893 by the Grand Army of the Republic in commemoration of the county's Civil War veterans. Its most recent renovation was completed in 1998. Sheriff's Home and Old Jail have served as the site for the Museum of the Historical Society of Porter County since

Figure 157. Memorial Opera House and Sheriff's Home. Historical Society of Porter County Old Jail Museum.

1975. The jail was built in 1871 at the back of the Porter County sheriff's residence, and both served their original function until 1973. Among its many artifacts, the museum has the bones of a mastodon found on a farm southeast of town.

Wheeler

The little community of Wheeler lies in the Tinley Moraine at the edge of what was called the Twenty Mile Prairie. Valparaiso's Thomas A. E. Campbell laid out the town in 1858, the year that the Pittsburgh, Fort Wayne and Chicago (Pennsylvania) Railroad was built through the area and a station was established. The main rail business was the shipping of milk. The town was named for one of the railroad's engineers. Within a year a general store, a saloon, and the Wheeler House had appeared. Four years later, they were joined by a blacksmith shop. George Longshore, one of the first residents; became the first postmaster.

The Nickel Plate Railroad was built in 1882, and even though it also established a station at Wheeler, the community has remained small.

LaPorte County can be said to be the natural entrance to the Calumet Area. It certainly was the historical entrance from the east. Its name means "the door," a reference to a break in the forests which in the early years allowed easy passage to the west. The Michigan Road, which extended from the Ohio River to Lake Michigan, was completed through LaPorte County in 1833. LaPorte County was created in 1832.

LaPorte

The city of LaPorte is located in the Kankakee Outwash Plain south of the Valparaiso Moraine. The area, located between the hilly and wooded lands to the north, and the Kankakee marshes to the south, was open, comparatively level, and thus considered suitable for agriculture by the earliest settlers. The location of several kettle lakes made the area a natural stopping place for Indian, European, and American travelers. The old Sauk Trail passed through LaPorte.

The first permanent residents of LaPorte were the families of Richard Harris, George and Elizabeth Thomas, and Wilson Malone, who settled there in 1830. LaPorte County was established in 1832, extending then from St. Joseph County all the way to the Illinois state line. That same year, the Andrew Brothers established a sawmill west of what would soon become the city of LaPorte. When the city was platted in 1833, it was named the new county's seat. The citizens lost no time in building a little courthouse, using bricks that were made on the premises. That same year the federal government opened a land office there, and thus it was to LaPorte that early settlers of all three lakefront counties of Indiana had to go in order to buy land.

In 1833, the First Methodist Episcopal Church of LaPorte was established. Two years later, LaPorte was incorporated as a town. In 1852, it became a city. In 1853 a stage route was established between LaPorte and Valparaiso. (See photograph in chapter 4.) One dollar bought a ticket for the 5:00 A.M. stage, which arrived in Valparaiso about 10:00. The return trip left at 1:00 P.M. and got its

Figure 158. Steamer on Pine Lake. LaPorte, with its fine lakes, was a wonderful place for Chicagoans to spend the weekend. LaPorte County Historical Society Museum.

passengers back to LaPorte by 6:30. For 50 cents, one could ride
to Westville, where one could then transfer to the stage that ran
between Michigan City and Lafayette.

The presence of the kettle lakes ensured that LaPorte would be
a location for lakeside summer homes. In the late nineteenth century, the Lake Shore and Michigan Southern Railway published a
pamphlet promoting the beauty of LaPorte and the ease with which
Chicagoans could get to the resort city. The line had fourteen trains
that made the two-hour trip every day, seven in each direction.

The lakes also gave LaPorte one of its most interesting industries, ice harvesting. By 1875 there were sixty icehouses in the
LaPorte area. Most of them were on Clear Lake, but Stone Lake,
Fish Trap Lake, and Pine Lake had some as well. At that time there
was more ice shipped out of the city of LaPorte than any other
location west of New York. Much of it went every winter to Chicago
on the same rail line that brought visitors to LaPorte resorts in the
summer.

By 1900, the population of LaPorte surpassed 7000. That year,
Timothy Ball noted that LaPorte had been called "unquestionably
the handsomest city in Indiana. Its streets are wide and well
shaded." It has long been known as the Maple City.

Postscript: The LaPorte County Courthouse was built of red
sandstone shipped from Lake Superior by boat to Michigan City
and then by rail to LaPorte. The third courthouse to stand at this

location, it was opened in March 1894. A few years later, Timothy Ball called it the "grandest temple of justice in northwestern Indiana." Inside the building is the cornerstone from the 1848 building. The LaPorte County Historical Museum is located across the street.

Michigan City

Michigan City is located where Trail Creek empties into Lake Michigan. Three of Lake Michigan's former shorelines cross the city, all parallel with today's shores. The Glenwood Shoreline is the widest, crossing Franklin Street at about Superior Street. Greenwood and St. Stanislaus Cemeteries are on Glenwood sand. The Calumet Shoreline extends from the State Prison to Trail Creek, barely noticeable crossing Franklin at about Ninth Street. Modern-age Tolleston dunes hug the current shoreline around Mt. Baldy. Farther south, the higher grounds of the gently undulating Lake Border Moraine can be found around the intersection of Indiana Highway 421 and Interstate 94. Michigan City is in the middle of dune country and at the site of what was once Indiana's largest sand dune, known as the Hoosier Slide because of its occasional avalanches (see chapter 6). Michigan City was the first town in Indiana to receive federal funding for a harbor on Lake Michigan.

Because the Potawatomi established trails along the ancient shorelines, several Indian trails passed through the Michigan City area. Parts of both the Lake Shore Trail and the Potawatomi/Calumet Beach Trail also served as stagecoach routes in the 1830s.

Early French voyageurs must have known about the Rivière du Chemin (Trail Creek) but left no written records of their visits. Father Jacques Marquette passed by in 1675 on his final trip along the lake and perhaps spent a day or two there. Pierre Durand, a Detroit fur trader, established a trading post alongside the creek in, or before, 1778. The post was operated by Jean Baptiste Point de Sable, a free black fur trader, and his Potawatomi wife, Catherine. Accused of being an American sympathizer, Point de Sable was arrested by British forces in 1779 and taken to northern Michigan; he may not have returned to the Trail Creek area.[13] According to historian George Brennan, Krueger Park was the site of the Revolutionary War battle described in chapter 3. A historical marker at the park marks this spot. (A similar marker at Dunes State Park marks that location as the site of the same battle.)

What is now Michigan City was in the Indiana Territory until 1805 when it was included in the new Territory of Michigan. It

---

13. Between 1784 and 1788, Point de Sable founded the settlement that became the city of Chicago.

Figure 160. Major Isaac Elston, founder of Michigan City. From Daniels, 1904.

then was returned to Indiana when Indiana was admitted to the Union in 1816. The Michigan City area was made available to settlers earlier than the rest of the Calumet Area because it was within the "Ten Mile Purchase" of land ceded by the Potawatomi in 1826.

In October 1830, the land containing the mouth of Trail Creek was purchased by Major Isaac Elston. Recognizing the potential of a city on the lake even though the area was uneven and marshy, Elston platted Michigan City in 1832.[14] He had great plans, and envisioned it, rather than Chicago, as the great metropolis on Lake Michigan. (Chicago then had a population of just 150 persons.) With plans for a major harbor to be built at the mouth of Trail Creek, Elston's city grew quickly. Settlers arrived, houses, hotels, and stores were built, and within two years the population of this new town was 715. (Chicago by then had grown to 1800 persons.)

The *Michigan City Gazette,* established in 1835, modestly described the area:

The advantages which this place possesses are manifold. Contiguous to us are the fertile and beautiful prairies with an adequate number of delightful groves, as well as an endless variety of the finest forest timber; and all these interspersed with streams. . . . Immediately upon the lake shore two huge bluffs rear their lofty heads as if on purpose to form in winter a rampart to protect us from the blasts that sweep along the lake, yet leaving a loop-hole through which we may peep at its angry surface.

Near the city, James Scott established a large flour mill, and soon found himself selling flour to settlers all through the Calumet Area. Customers are said to have come from as far west as Chicago and Joliet. When John Walker built the first sawmill in the township, residents of the new city were finally able to build houses of lumber rather than logs.

The Michigan Road, finished in 1833, connected Michigan City with Logansport in the Indiana "heartland." This road made it easier for Indiana settlers to move into the Michigan City area. It also provided a route for the new farmers to take wagonloads of produce to the city docks. In 1834 a schoolhouse was built and soon several churches served the area. Michigan City was incorporated as a town in 1836.

Work on a harbor was begun almost immediately, but without needed federal funds, progress was very slow. Warehouses were built on land, but boats had to load and unload while anchored out in the lake, and then only during periods of good weather. Nevertheless, beginning in 1837, Michigan City was the primary

14. For an eyewitness account of Elston's vision and salesmanship, see the vignette in chapter 4.

Figure 161. The 1858 Michigan City lighthouse.

grain market for northwest Indiana and in season saw up to forty oxcarts of grain arriving every day.

The first lighthouse, a forty-foot white brick and stone tower, was built in 1837. As more traffic and larger boats began to use the Michigan City harbor, a brighter light was needed. So in 1858, a larger brick and stone lighthouse was constructed.[15] It had a light visible on clear nights up to fifteen miles away. In 1871, with the new harbor finally completed, a second beacon was established on the east pier. It had a wooden elevated walkway that allowed the lighthouse keeper to get to it even in the worst storms. The new East Pier Lighthouse was built in 1904.

One of Michigan City's most noteworthy early citizens was Miss Harriet Colfax, who lived in the old lighthouse building and tended its lights for forty-three years. Miss Colfax, a strong but petite woman, had to maintain the facility, record weather and shipwrecks, and light the tower lanterns every night and extinguish them every morning during the shipping season. The walk out to the beacon on the east pier was often dangerous; more than once she was nearly swept off the pier by huge waves. She was thirty-seven in 1861 when she was offered the position, which then paid $350 a year. She retired in 1904 at the age of eighty.

In 1850, the Michigan Central Railroad laid its lines and established a station in Michigan City just two years after Chicago got its first rail line. In October of that year, the first train entered the town. The Monon Railroad arrived three years later. The promoters of the Monon, the first railroad to connect the Ohio River to Lake

15. Stone from Joliet was used for the foundation, and brick from Milwaukee was used for the walls. The first brickyard at nearby Porter would not open for another thirteen years.

Michigan, believed that Michigan City, not Chicago, would be the most promising port on Lake Michigan. It did not complete its line to Chicago until 1882.

By 1850, with a population of 996, Michigan City was the largest town in the Calumet Area. However, Chicago, incorporated as a town just three years before Michigan City, had nearly 30,000 citizens. That year, Congress appropriated some funds for the development of a harbor at Michigan City, but it was not until about 1870 that the harbor was finished. Chicago's growth was due primarily to its being named as the terminus of the Illinois and Michigan Canal, an enormous construction project that connected the waters of Lake Michigan to the Mississippi River. This canal resulted in Chicago becoming the destination point of the great railroads and thus the great city on the lake.

Two of the major exports in the late nineteenth century were sand and timber, both greatly needed by the city of Chicago and other growing localities. By 1900, with about 15,000 residents, Michigan City was still the largest community in northwest Indiana.

Postscript: In 1961, the city of Michigan City purchased the keeper's house (the old lighthouse) from the federal government after it was declared surplus property. The Michigan City Historical Society has turned this 1858 building into a museum. A replica of the old tower was added in 1973. The New Lighthouse, built in 1904, is now Indiana's only operating lighthouse.

Historic Michigan City churches form a dramatic component of the central city landscape. In alphabetical order, they are First Congregational, at Sixth and Washington, built in 1881, St. John's German United Evangelical Lutheran Church (later St. John's United Church of Christ), at Ninth and Franklin, built in 1867, St. Mary's Roman Catholic Church, at Tenth and Buffalo, with portions that were built in 1867, St. Paul Lutheran Church, at Ninth and Franklin Streets, built in 1876, and Trinity Church (Episcopal) at Sixth and Franklin, built in 1889.

Westville

Westville is located in the Kankakee Outwash Plain immediately southeast of the Valparaiso Moraine. Its first permanent residents were Miriam Benedict, her daughter Sarah, and her son-in-law, Indian trader Henly Clyburn, who settled there in 1829. A post office was established in 1842 with the name New Durham. The first store was opened in 1848; a blacksmith shop followed two years later. In 1851, the town was platted and named Westville. In 1853, the Louisville, New Albany and Chicago (Monon) Railroad was laid through town and a station was built. Westville was incorporated in 1864. The population in 1900 was 700.

Epilogue

Preserved Natural Areas

There are many preserved natural areas in the Calumet Area, some in private hands, others within park systems at the town, city, county, state, and federal levels. Much of the credit for the drive toward preserving natural areas belongs to a number of energetic organizations such as the Municipal Science Club and the Prairie Club of Chicago, the Nature Conservancy, the Save the Dunes Council, the Save the Dunes Conservation Fund, the Shirley Heinze Land Trust, Chicago Wilderness, and the Indiana Heritage Trust. In recent years, groups such as these, supported by civic, business, and industrial leaders, have formed partnerships that recognized the value of setting aside some lands not only for recreational and educational purposes but also literally for the improvement of the health of the planet.

The largest of these organizations, the Nature Conservancy, established in 1951, now operates the world's largest private system of nature sanctuaries. All of them (1,500 in the United States alone) safeguard imperiled species of plants and animals. The Illinois chapter was established in 1957; Indiana's chapter started two years later. The Conservancy uses nonconfrontational, market-based means to protect habitat areas. It accepts lands from donors and willing sellers. Some of its acquisitions, such as Gibson Woods, are then sold to public agencies or other private groups that can ensure protection.

Cook County Forest Preserves

In 1900, Chicago's Municipal Science Club first proposed that scenic areas of Cook County be set aside for public use and enjoyment. The next several years were spent in gathering support for the project. The Cook County Forest Preserves became a reality in 1914 when county citizens voted to create a series of preserves, thus ensuring that these areas would not be cleared or developed. Locations in the Calumet Area include:

- Calumet Woods at Riverdale and Blue Island and Eggers Grove on Wolf Lake
- Burnham Woods and Beaubien Preserve on the Grand and Little Calumet Rivers
- Paxton Avenue Prairie, Wentworth, Shabbona, and Clayhole Woods and the Sand Ridge Prairie and Nature Center along the Michigan City Road (High Tolleston Shoreline)
- Lansing, Glenwood, and Halsted Woods, and several other sites that make up a linear 4,200-acre series of preserves along North and Thorn Creeks
- Steger Woods, Sauk Trail Woods South, and Schuberts Woods along the Sauk Trail

The Indiana Dunes

One of the earliest groups to promote the preservation of natural areas was the Prairie Club of Chicago, which sponsored weekend outings to locations such as the Indiana Dunes. In 1913, this group even built a clubhouse in what was later to become the state park. In 1916, the National Dunes Park Association was created with the primary goal of establishing a national park along the Lake Michigan shoreline. Stephen Mather, the first director of the National Park Service, favored a dunes national park. But it would be fifty years before a national park would be established here, largely because of opposition by Porter County businessmen, who favored reserving the space for industry. In the meantime, the state moved ahead and established the Indiana Dunes State Park.

The park was proposed in 1920 by Richard Lieber, director of the Indiana Department of Conservation. His plan included preserving an eight-mile stretch of beach and dunes along Lake Michigan. Scaled down to about three miles of beach and about three and a half square miles (2,210 acres), it was established in 1927 at Waverly Beach. When state funds for purchasing the land were so

Figure 162. "Up to the top!" A Prairie Club outing at the Indiana Dunes. Calumet Regional Archives.

slow in coming that the success of the park was in jeopardy, William Gleason, superintendent of Gary's Illinois (United States) Steel Company and president of the National Dunes Park Association, convinced the steel company to make a generous donation of $250,000. The park was actively promoted and supported by the South Shore Railroad, which donated land for the entranceway and $25,000 toward the cost of building a resort hotel and bathhouse. The railroad often featured the scenery and activities at the park in its advertising posters. Chicagoans were, of course, urged to take the train to see the dunes.

The state park is at the site of Le Petit Fort, where many historians believe that a Revolutionary War skirmish was fought. The battle is commemorated by a historical marker near the park's main parking lot. (A similar marker at Michigan City's Krueger Park marks that location as the site of the same battle.) Two of the park's picnic shelters preserve the names of other earlier uses of this park land. City West Picnic Shelter gets its name from the grand city that was once proposed for the area, and Wilson Shelter is named after Wilson's Camp, where the Wilson Meat Packing Company of Chicago once had a clubhouse. The three tallest dunes in the park are Mt. Tom, probably named for Tom Brady, who was captured at the battle at the nearby Petit Fort, Mt. Holden, named for Edward J. Holden, president of the Prairie Club of Chicago, and Mt. Jackson, named for Indiana governor Ed Jackson. Holden and Jackson were both active supporters of movements to preserve the character of the Indiana Dunes.

Figure 163. The Bathing Pavilion at Indiana Dunes State Park under construction, 1929. Westchester Public Library Archives and Dan Bruhn Photography.

Indiana Dunes National Lakeshore, established in 1966, is composed of approximately 15,000 acres. It is a unique national park in that it is located in an urban, industrialized region and is composed of several distinct parcels separated by residential and industrial areas. After a century of study, beginning with University of Chicago botanist Henry Cowles's work in 1899, more than 1,445 plant species have been found in the park. This wealth of plant species is exceeded in only two other national parks, the Great Smoky Mountains and Grand Canyon, both of which are much larger than the Lakeshore. Within the park boundaries are the Lake Michigan shoreline and sand dunes, as well as expansive marshes, bogs, and fens. Miller Woods and the Douglas Environment Center in Lake County are also a part of the national park, as are the Bailly Homestead and the Chellberg Farm in Porter.

The establishment of a National Lakeshore in northwest Indiana was a divisive subject in the 1960s. As some groups argued for preservation of the dunes, others argued against it.

In 1916, Stephen Mather, the first director of the National Park Service, called the Indiana dunes "admittedly wonderful and inherently distinctive," and stated that "a large section of this dune region should be preserved for all time." He proposed the creation of Sand Dunes National Park.

When Senator Paul Douglas began his campaign to establish a national park in the dunes, poet Carl Sandburg wrote to him saying, "Those dunes are to the Midwest what the Grand Canyon is to Arizona and the Yosemite to California. They constitute a signature of time and eternity; once lost, the loss would be irrevocable."

Others, however, believed differently. The following is the April 1966 testimony of the Portage Town Board president: "The area in question on the southern shore of Lake Michigan is a highly strategic one which if left to develop its natural potential will return rich rewards in the form of jobs and economic strength. . . . I cannot and will not stand idly by and watch our economic birthright be snatched away. A National Lakeshore here can have no other effect than to jeopardize, frustrate, and seriously curtail the development which will otherwise take place here in the next few generations."

Because Lake Michigan's water is such a valuable resource, the Indiana Dunes are located in the center of an area in which commercial, industrial, residential, and recreational uses compete for space. One quarter of American steel and most of the Calumet Area's electricity is made in close proximity. In addition, several highways and rail lines run alongside and through the parks. Eight million people live within a day's drive of these parks. Professor Mark Reshkin has called the Indiana Dunes a

Figure 164. Henry Chandler Cowles in the Indiana Dunes, 1913. Calumet Regional Archives.

prototype for *urban* national parks. He noted that natural land management within the Indiana Dunes area may very well demonstrate whether or not scientific and aesthetically valuable areas can be preserved and sustained in heavily industrialized urban areas of the world.

The park is also the location of the Indiana Dunes Environmental Learning Center at Camp Good Fellow, an extended-stay center for schoolchildren and adults. It is run by a private/public partnership including the National Park Service. Participants usually spend three days and two nights at the center. This gives participants more time to learn about the dunes region and to study its environment than if they had visited the dunes for only a few hours.

Other Calumet Area Preserves

At 548 acres, the Hoosier Prairie in Griffith is the largest virgin prairie tract remaining in Indiana. Now a state nature preserve, it is owned and managed by the Indiana Department of Natural Resources. Within its borders are 546 species of native plants, 43 of which are rare in Indiana.

The 100-acre Gensberg-Markham Prairie is one of four prairies making up the Indian Boundary Prairies in and near Markham that are managed by the Nature Conservancy, Northeastern Illinois University, and the Natural Land Institute.

Thornton Fractional North High School (Superior Street) Prairie contains savanna, sand prairie, wet prairie, and sedge meadows on its thirty-three acres. The prairie is a ridge and swale remnant north of the High Tolleston Shoreline. An Illinois Natural Inventory site, it has 300 species of plants.

Gibson Woods, a 178-acre preserve north of 163rd Street in Hessville, contains an oak savanna on a dune and swale topography that was once very common in northwestern Indiana and southeastern Cook County. This park consists of Michigan Central Railroad land that was never developed. In 1980, the Nature Conservancy purchased the property and sold it to the Lake County Parks and Recreation Department.

Bieker Woods and Heritage Park, owned and managed by the Munster Department of Parks and Recreation, are on the ancient Calumet Shoreline at the site of the 1837 Gibson Inn and 1845 Brass Tavern/Stallbohm Inn. Helen Kaske Bieker, granddaughter of innkeepers Johann and Wilhelmina Stallbohm and a member of the Save the Dunes Council, steadfastly refused to give up this valuable land until 1976, when she agreed to sell it to the town. Within the park today is the restored Kaske House, now on the National Register of Historic Places.

Carlson Oxbow Park in Hammond is an eighty-five-acre woods and wetland area nestled between Interstate Highway 80/94 and the Little Calumet River. It was a former dumping ground that was cleaned up and transformed into a city park in 1998.

The Richardson Wildlife Sanctuary is on a 3.7-acre parcel of land on the Lake Michigan shoreline that was not subdivided when adjacent Dune Acres was founded in 1923. Established by Flora Richardson in 1958, it is operated by a private, nonprofit organization that supplies schools and interested groups with information about ecology and natural history—especially information about the Indiana Dunes.

Coffee Creek Watershed Preserve is a 167-acre parcel of land within Coffee Creek Center, a planned residential community east of Indiana Highway 49 in Chesterton. The preserve, donated in June 2001 by the Lake Erie Land Company to the Coffee Creek Water-

HENRY COWLES, FATHER OF AMERICAN ECOLOGY

Cowles Bog, at the National Lakeshore, in 1965 became Indiana's first federally designated Natural Landmark. The bog was named for Dr. Henry Chandler Cowles, a botanist from the University of Chicago whose research in the Indiana Dunes and Blue Island areas resulted in his concept of plant succession. Cowles recognized that plant societies change over time.

The Indiana Dunes area was perfect for his research because of the lack of urban development and the proximity of its three ancient shorelines to each other and to the current shoreline. Because each of the shorelines increased in age as one moved southward and upward to the Tolleston, Calumet, and Glenwood Shorelines, the landscapes on and between them increased in age, too. Thus Cowles was able to study different-aged landscapes all within a very short distance. Cowles is often referred to as the "Father of American Ecology."

shed Conservancy, has been restored to something akin to a pre-settlement landscape, and many native plants have been reestablished. In addition, more than five miles of walking trails have been built. The Coffee Creek Center itself was designed to reverse the trend toward urban sprawl by concentrating development while permanently setting aside the high-quality natural areas.

Taltree Arboretum opened in October 2001. A 360-acre collection of restored prairies and wetlands, oak savannas, and gardens south of U.S. 30 in Porter County, it has an outreach program whereby its staff visits schools and teaches concepts in environmental studies.

The Nature Conservancy properties can be found in all four Calumet Area counties. Among these properties are the Indian Boundary Prairies in Markham, the Ivanhoe Dune and Swale in northwestern Gary, and the Moraine Nature Preserve in Porter County.

The Shirley Heinze Land Trust properties have been protected since 1981 when the Fund was established. Since then, the Fund has purchased more than 700 acres of environmentally important wetlands, prairies, and dunelands in the Lake Michigan Watershed of Northwest Indiana. Among them are the Cressmoor Prairie in Hobart, Seidner Dune and Swale in Hammond, the John Merle Coulter State Nature Preserve in Portage, and Ambler Flatwoods east of Michigan City.

The Indiana Heritage Trust was established in 1992. Administered by the Indiana Department of Natural Resources, it purchases land with funds raised by the selling of environmental license plates. The Trust also supports environmental organizations such as the Shirley Heinze Land Trust; its funds were used to help purchase the four preserves described above. Other local projects have included the Grand Kankakee Marsh in south Lake County, the Moraine Nature Preserve in Porter County, and Camp Red Mill in LaPorte County, which contains the headwaters of the Little Calumet River.

Glossary

Bog: Waterlogged ground with acidic peaty soil, often too soft to support heavy objects. Example: Pin Hook Bog near Michigan City.

Devonian: A period of geologic history; the fourth period of the Paleozoic Era.

Dolomite: A sedimentary rock, similar to limestone, composed primarily of the mineral of the same name. Thornton Quarry rock is dolomite.

Dune: A hill of sand made by blowing wind. Some dunes are just a few feet high, whereas others are more than 100 feet high. The largest Indiana dunes are near the current or ancient shorelines of Lake Michigan. Many small dunes exist near the Kankakee River.

End moraine: A band of hills formed at the furthest extent of a glacial advance. Also called a terminal moraine. Examples include the Valparaiso and Tinley/Lake Border Moraines. A glacier may form an end moraine each time it advances and retreats.

Erratics: Boulders that have been moved from their original location and found elsewhere, often scattered throughout moraines. (Hundreds of Calumet Area erratics have been moved again by residents of the area and placed at the ends of their driveways.)

Fen: A geographical feature characterized by wet land with alkaline, neutral, or slightly acidic soil, often too soft to support heavy objects. Cowles Bog in the Indiana Dunes is really a fen. (Compare to Bog)

Freshet: A river with a high water level caused by heavy rains or melting snows.

Glacier: A moving, or formerly moving, mass of ice formed from compacted snow.

Gradient: The slope of a river, stream, or a land surface.

Igneous rock: Rocks such as granite and basalt formed by the solidification of magma.

Jurassic: A period of geologic history; the middle period of the Mesozoic Era.

Kettle lake: A lake formed by the melting of a large mass of ice that had fallen from a glacier onto, and perhaps buried by, glacial till. Examples include Flint and Pine Lakes.

Lake Chicago: A name that once referred to former stages of Lake Michigan.

Lacustrine plain: A rather flat landscape that was once the bottom of a lake. Depending upon the depth of the lake, whether it had wave action, and how quickly the water was drained from it, lacustrine plains may have sandy or clay soils with sand and perhaps gravel along their edges. The Calumet Lacustrine Plain is the rather flat area between Lake Michigan and the Valparaiso and Lake Border Moraines.

Metamorphic rock: A type of rock that has been altered by heat, pressure, or chemical activity. Examples include slate and marble.

Moraine: A geographical feature composed of materials that were deposited by a glacier. Two common types of moraine are ground moraine and end moraine.

Outwash plain: A plain composed of materials that were washed away from a glacier. The Kankakee Outwash Plain is the flat sandy area south of the Valparaiso Moraine.

Pleistocene: A period of geologic history; the first of the two epochs of the Quaternary Period. The Great Ice Age occurred during this epoch.

Sand bar: An underwater ridge of sand built up close to the water's surface.

Scarp: A steep slope. There is a scarp just north

of Ridge Road (the Calumet Shoreline) that extends from Munster to Glen Park (Gary).

Sediment: Solid material that has been moved from its place of origin by water, ice, or air and has settled upon the ground. Most soils in the Calumet Area are composed of sediments.

Sedimentary rock: A type of rock that has been formed by the accumulation and hardening of sediment. Sedimentary rocks include sandstone, limestone, dolomite, coal, and shale.

Shoal: A shallow place in a river, lake, or sea.

Silurian: A period of geologic history; the third period of the Paleozoic Era.

Spit: A peninsula or long ridge of sand, often with gravel, near the edge of a lake or sea built by its waves.

Succession: The change over time of the population of plants and animals that can live in a particular area. Dr. Henry Cowles's work in the Indiana Dunes led to his theories about succession.

Swale: A geographic depression, often wet. Sometimes called a slough.

Till: Unsorted material that had been carried and deposited by a glacier.

Till plain: A ground surface (usually gently undulating) made of till that was deposited as a glacier was receding. Sometimes called ground moraine.

Wisconsin Age: The period during which the last major ice advance occurred.

Bibliographic Essay

The preparation of this work largely involved gleaning materials written by geologists and local historians. Of special usefulness for a work such as this is Lance Trusty's book, *The Calumet Region: A Master Bibliography*.

This section is written for those readers who would like to read more about certain topics as well as researchers who will want to know where I found particular information. A copy of this manuscript with footnotes has been deposited at the Calumet Regional Archives at Indiana University Northwest in Gary.

Geologic maps were among the prime sources of information about the geology of the area. Bretz published a very detailed set of maps of the area in 1955. Schneider and Keller's map of 1970 was useful because it spanned the entire Calumet Area. Brown, Bleuer, and Thompson's 1996 map was much appreciated because of its scale and its inclusion of the latest interpretations of landforms. Of great use were the specially created maps by geologist Steve Brown, who superimposed for me the data of the Brown, Bleuer, and Thompson map onto 7½-minute topographic maps. Scores of on-site checks were then made to determine how much evidence was readily visible.

The remainder of this section gives the major sources of information for each chapter and section.

PROLOGUE

Cannon, Loring, and Robb; Cowles, 1917; Engel; Franklin and Schaeffer; Gravier; Marquette; Meyer, 1945; Moore; and personal communications with John Swenson and Paul Petraitis, 2002.

1. SEAS, SEDIMENTS, AND GLACIAL ICE

"The Rock-Recorded History": Ehlers; Gray 1987; Hartke, Hill, and Reshkin; Hill, Carr, Hartke, and Rexroad; Kluessendorf and Mikulic; Volp; and Willman.

"The Formation and Spread of Glaciers": Clarke; Ehlers; Hough; and Milankovitch.

"Divisions of the Pleistocene Ice Age": Chamberlin, 1894, 1895, and 1896; Ehlers; Hansel and Johnson; and Richmond and Fullerton.

"Moraines, Kettle Lakes, and the Kankakee Outwash Plain": Bayless et al.; Blatchley; Bretz, 1939 and 1955; Brown, Bleuer and Thompson; Bushnell; Chamberlin, 1883; Colman et al.; Ehlers; Hansel and Johnson; *History of Porter County;* Leverett, 1897 and 1899; Post; and personal communications with Steve Brown, Timothy Fisher, and Ardith Hansel.

2. WATER AND WIND

The contributions of the earliest and current geologists as well as some local historians were used in the writing of this chapter. They were the works by Ball, 1873; Bannister; Garard; Levette; Rieck and Winters; Robinson, 1847; Shepard; Thompson, Fraser and Hester; and Tinkham.

"Ancient Shorelines and Beaches of Lake Michigan": Ball 1884; Bretz 1943 and 1955; Chrzastowski, Pranschke and Shabica; Chrzastowski and Thompson, 1992 and 1994; Cole; Colman, et al.; Cressey; Fisher; Fryxell; Goldthwait; Hansel et al.; Hansel and Mickelson; Hartke, Hill, and Reshkin; Hough; Leverett, 1897; Moore; Schneider; Schneider and Reshkin; Shepard; Thompson, 1992; Thompson and Baedke; Thompson, Fraser and Hester; Thwaites and Bertrand; Wilson; and the Works Projects Administration (WPA).

"The Grand and Little Calumet Rivers": Brennan; Brown, 1999; Fryxell; Moore; and personal conversation with Paul Petraitis, 2003.

3. THE CALUMET AREA BEFORE 1833

Introduction: Andreas; Ball, 1900; Blatchley; Brock; Eenigenburg, 1941; Goodspeed and Blanchard; Jackson; Meyer 1956, Moore; Mumford; Robinson, 1847; and Whitaker.

"Native American Occupation": Allouez; Ball, 1873 and 1900; Blake, 1927; Briggs, circa 1930c, Cannon, Loring, and Robb; Edmunds; Gray, 1989; *History of Porter County, Indiana;* Howat; Kaquados; Kellar; Knotts; Meyer, 1945 and 1954; Mitchell; Moore; Quimby; Patterson, 1934; Scharf; Slapin and Seale; Struever and Holton; Tanner; and Weatherwax.

"French Exploration and the Fur Trade": Ball, 1884, Brennan; Butterfield; Danckers and Meredith; Deale; Donnelly; Eccles; Edmunds; Esarey; Goodspeed and Blanchard; Kenton; Marquette in Thwaites; Moore; Parkman; Spicer, 2000b; Swenson, 2000a; and Volp.

"The British Period": Alvord; Danckers and Meredith; Kinnaird; Moore; and Teggart.

"The Northwest Territories": Andreas; Ball, 1900; Cannon, Loring, and Robb; Danckers and Meredith; Gray, 1989 and 1998; Hubbard; Lane, 1978, Meyer, 1954 and 1956; Mitchell; Pierce; U.S. Northwest Territory Celebration Commission; and Wellington. Rep. Findley's comments were reprinted by Wellington.

"The Last Trading Posts": Bowers, 1922; Clemensen; Danckers and Meredith; Howe; Swenson, 2000b; and Wolcott.

4. THE PIONEER AND STAGECOACH PERIOD

Powell Moore's 1959 *The Calumet Region* was an important resource for this chapter. His footnoting and bibliography led me to many primary sources of information. State geologist Blatchley's 1897 report was a great source of information about land use. This report also contained several of the photographs of the landscape. Each of the four counties in the Calumet Area had histories written before and near the turn of the nineteenth century and these contain a wealth of information. They were by Andreas, Ball, Cannon, Loring, and Robb, Daniels, Goodspeed and Blanchard, Howat, and Packard.

Introduction: Andreas (including Butler's quotation); Ball, 1873; Blake, 1927; Blatchley; Bowers, 1922 and 1929; "Beginnings on a River," *Chicago Tribune* web site, 1999; Knotts; Quaife; Meyer, 1956; Moore; Pierce; Robinson, 1847; and Waterman.

"Stagecoach Routes and Taverns": Andreas; Ball, 1873 and 1900; Blake, 1929; Cook and Jackson; Gibson; Howat; Howe; "Hammond Girl Is in Fire Peril," *Lake County Times* (Hammond, Ind.), November 4, 1909; Lester, 1923; Luther in Ball, 1884; Martineau; Meyer, 1956; Moore; Packard; Robinson, 1847; Rowlands; and Trusty, 1984.

"Squatters": Ball, 1873; Daniels; Goodspeed and Blanchard; Howat; Moore; and Robinson, 1847.

"Transportation": Ball, 1900 and 1904; Gleason; Howat; Martineau; Robinson, 1847; Watt; Work Projects Administration; and personal conversations with my grandmother, Katie Koedyker, circa 1962.

"Housing": Ade; Austin and Patton; Ball, 1900; Brennan; Eenigenburg, circa 1941, and Woods, 1938.

"Mills, Blacksmith Shops, and Cooperages": Ball, 1904; Blake, 1929; Briggs, 1930a; and Maple, Applegate and Backus.

"Farming": Woods, 1938.

"Mineral Springs": Cook and Jackson; Garard; *History of Porter County;* and Moore.

"Dream Cities of the Calumet Area": Bowers, 1929.

Conclusion: Personal conversations with Larry McClellan and Paul Petraitis, 2002–03.

5. RAILROADS AND EVERYDAY LIFE

"The Coming of the Railroads": Andreas; Ball, 1884, 1900, and 1904; Brennan; Cohen and McShane; Cook and Jackson; Corliss; *History of Porter County;* Levette; Middleton; Moore; Simons and Parker; and Watt.

"Eyewitnesses to History": Blake, 1929; Carr; Eenigenburg, 1935; Gibson; Kaske; Forsyth; Hill; Ooms; Pearson, 1954; Reese; Schoon, Dick J.; Schoon, Jacob J.; Schrage; and Woods, 1938.

"Octave Chanute and Human Flight in the Dunes": Crouch and Moore.

6. ALTERING THE LANDSCAPE

Opposing Viewpoints were quoted by Lane, 1978.

"Logging": Ball, 1873; Cook and Jackson; Garard; Moore; Packard; and Robinson, 1847.

"Sand Mining": Ball, 1900; Bieber and Smith; Bretz, 1955; Cressey; Franklin, and Schaeffer, 1983; Gleason; *Lake County Star,* in Moore; Gibson; Levette; Melton; Moore; Munger; Willman; WPA; and personal communications with Bunty MacDonald.

"Clay Pits, Borrow Pits, and Brickyards": Austin and Patton; Blatchley; and personal conversations with Marvin Jacobs and Roger Wiers.

"Designed Residential Landscapes": Lakes of the Four Seasons.

"Canals, Dams, Ditches, and Levees": *Blue Island;* Briggs, ca 1930b; "That Canal Project." *Chesterton Tribune,* May 28, 1908; Christianson, 2001; Esarey; Gray, 1998; Meyer, 1945; "Canal to Wabash: The Improvement Company Is Quietly at Work." *Michigan City Evening Dispatch,* December 3, 1903; Owen; Reshkin; Trusty, 1982; Woods, 1938; and personal conversation with Paul Petraitis, 2002.

"Expanding into the Lakes": Cressey; Indiana Department of Natural Resources, 1979; and the Midwest Region National Park Service web site.

"Ports on Lake Michigan": Andreas; Ball, 1900; Gray, 1998; and Moore.

PART THREE

The geologic maps referred to above were of great use for the introductory paragraphs in this section of the book. Population figures were accessed from Ball, 1900, and the U.S. Bureau of the Census.

7. COOK COUNTY COMMUNITIES

The primary source of information for early history included in this chapter was Andreas's *History of Cook County*. In most cases, material since 1884 was provided by local history books.

"Blue Island/Calumet Park": Andreas; *Blue Island: An Illustrated Review;* Cook, 1998; *Genealogical and Biographical Record of Cook County;* Meyer, 1954; and Volp.

"Calumet City/Burnham": *Calumet City Centennial Celebration;* Cook, 1998; the *Diamond Jubilee Historical Record;* and McClellan, 1998.

"Chicago Heights/South Chicago Heights/Ford Heights": Andreas; Beatson; Beeson; *Chicago Heights Centennial; Chicago Heights Centennial Celebration; Looking Back to Look Forward;* Mikulic and Kluessendorf; Morris; and personal communication with Larry McClellan.

"Dolton/Riverdale": Andreas; Cook, 1998; *Dolton, 1892–1976;* McClellan, 1998; Wiers; and Zimmerman.

"Glenwood": André; Andreas; Carlson; Tolman; and personal communications with Larry McClellan.

"Harvey/Dixmoor/Phoenix": Andreas; *City of Harvey Golden Jubilee.*

"Hazel Crest/East Hazel Crest": Peattie; Rocke, Ross, and Breslin.

"Hegewisch": Andreas; Gibson; Kunert; Lester, 1922; and Meyer, 1954.

"Homewood/Flossmoor": Adair and Sandberg; Andreas; Bretz, 1939; Hinko; Senior; Wagner; and personal conversation with Jim Wright, 2003.

"Lansing/Lynwood": Andreas; *First Reformed Church Centennial; Lans-Cent-Orama;* and *Lansing Centennial Album.*

"Markham/Posen/Robbins": Beaudette-Neil; Cook, 1998; Haymore; and McClellan, 2000.

"Morgan Park/Beverly/Washington Heights": Andreas; Chicago Fact Book Consortium.

"Roseland/Pullman/Kensington/West Pullman": Andreas; Chicago Fact Book Consortium; Dedmon; Historic Pullman Foundation web site; Rowlands; Van Hinte; and personal communications with Paul Petraitis, 2002.

"Sauk Village": Andreas; *Chicago Heights Centennial Celebration; Saint James Church,* and Thompson, 1920.

"South Chicago (Calumet)/South Deering/The East Side": Andreas; "Down in South Chicago: What Chicago Gained along the Calumet by Annexation." *Chicago Tribune,* August 11, 1889; Clifford and Clifford; *East Side Centennial Commemoration;* Kijewski, Brosch, and Bulanda; Lester, 1923, Mikulic and Kluessendorf; and personal communications with Rod Sellers and Paul Petraitis, 2002.

"South Holland": Blanchard; Cook, 1966; Eenigenburg, 1935 and 1941; Ettema; Lucas; and Van Hinte.

"Steger": Cook, 1998.

"Thornton": Andreas; Beaudette-Neil; Bretz, 1943; Cook, 1998; and Meyer, 1954.

8. LAKE COUNTY COMMUNITIES

Sources of information for early history included Goodspeed and Blanchard's 1882 history, Ball's four histories, and the reports of the Old Settlers Association of Lake County. Moore's history and Elin Christianson's 2001 publication were great resources because they were so well documented.

"Cedar Lake/Lake Dalecarlia": Ball, 1884; Belman; Christianson, 2001; Duff; Howat; Lane, 1997; Robinson, 1847; and the WPA.

"Crown Point": Ball, 1873 and 1900; Belman; and Robinson, 1847.

"Dyer": Ball, 1873 and 1900; Moore; Protsman; *Town of Dyer Bicentennial Book.*

"East Chicago": Cannon, Loring, and Robb; East Chicago Public Library; Howat; McKinlay; Moore; LeVan; Morris; and Whiting Savings and Loan Association.

"Gary": Baker; Ball, 1900; Bennett; Cannon, Loring, and Robb; Cohen; "Scene at D.A.R. Unveiling Services Marking Site of Old Gibson Inn." *Gary Post Tribune,* June 30, 1923; Gleason; *Guide to Glen Park;* Howat; Lane, 1978; Lane and Cohen; Lester, 1923; Millender; Moore; Schaeffer and Franklin; and the WPA. (See also Miller and Tolleston.)

"Griffith": Baker and Carmony; Ball, 1900; *A Brief History of the Griffith-Highland United Methodist Church;* and *Seventy-five Years of Growing Together.*

"Hammond": Andreas; Ball, 1873; Bowers, 1929; Cannon, Loring and Robb; Dabertin; Howat; Moore; Trusty, 1984; and personal communications with Dorothy Humpfer Zacny and Suzanne Long. (See also Hessville.)

"Hessville/Gibson Station": Baker; Ball, 1873; Belman; Howat; Hess; Housty; "Kittie Gibson," *Lake County Times* (Hammond, Ind.), December 27, 1907; Moore; Simons and Parker; and Trusty, 1984.

"Highland": Ball, 1900; Douthett.

"Hobart/Ainsworth": Ball, 1873 and 1900; Blatchley; Christianson, 1980, 2001; Clemens and Collins; Demmon; Dudley; Moore; Pleak; and personal communications with Elin Christianson.

"Lake Station, Liverpool, and New Chicago": Ball, 1873; Blake, 1929; Cannon, Loring and Robb; Christenson; Christianson, 2001; Goodspeed and Blanchard; Patterson, 1929; Robinson, 1847; WPA; and personal conversation with Paul Petraitis.

"Leroy": Baker and Carmony; Ball, 1900; Goodspeed and Blanchard; and Keene.

"Lowell": Ball, 1873, 1900, and 1904; Brownell; *One Hundredth Anniversary of the Church of Christ, Lowell, Indiana;* Dwyer; Garard; Goodspeed and Blanchard; *History of the First United Methodist Church of Lowell, Indiana;* Lowell Historical Society web site; *Saint Edward Parrish;* Schmal; and WPA.

"Merrillville": Ball, 1873; Clemens and Collins; Denta; Robinson, 1847; Woods, 1975; and the WPA.

"Miller's Station": Ball, 1873; Howat; Lane, 1978; Moore; Pearson, 1970; Spicer, 2000a and 2000b, and Thompson, 1951.

"Munster": Austin and Patton; Ball, 1884 and 1900; Cannon, Loring, and Robb; Lester, 1923; "Hammond Girl Is in Fire Peril," *Lake County Times* (Hammond, Ind.), November 4, 1909; Luther; and Trusty, 1982.

"Ross": Ball, 1873 and 1900; and Woods, 1938.

"St. John": Ball, 1873 and 1900; Goodspeed and Blanchard; "Church Returns to Home," *Hammond Times,* May 28, 1974; Tuley; and Woods, 1938.

"Schererville/Hartsdale": Ball, 1873 and 1900; Jonas; and personal communications with Art Schweitzer.

"Tolleston": Ball, 1873; Borman; Cannon, Loring, and Robb; "Tolleston Gun Club Now Passing." *Gary Post Tribune,* May 15, 1908; Lane, 1978; Moore; Rump; Starr; Schoon and Schoon; *Tolleston "Old-Settlers" Centennial.*

"Whiting": Ball, 1900; Cannon, Loring, and Robb; Dabertin; Ford; Moore; Putnam; and the Whiting Savings and Loan Association.

"Winfield/Palmer": Garard; Gibbs; "History of Winfield"; and Weiler.

9. PORTER AND LAPORTE COUNTY COMMUNITIES

The primary source of information for early history of Porter County were Goodspeed and Blanchard's work and the 1912 *History of Porter County* (re-printed by the Porter County Historical Society). Another valuable source of information were the *Duneland Notes,* newsletters of the Duneland Historical Society. They are held both by the Westchester Public Library and the Calumet Regional Archives.

"Boone Grove": Ball, 1900.

"Chesterton/Crocker": Cannon, Loring, and Robb, *Chesterton Centennial;* Garard; and *History of Porter County.*

"Hebron": *Century of Progress;* Garard; *Hebron United Presbyterian Church Centennial; Methodist Episcopal Church Centennial; United Methodist Church, Hebron;* and Shults-Gay.

"Kouts": Baker and Carmony; Ball, 1900; Garard; *Kouts Is Five in Score; St. Paul Lutheran Church.*

"Ogden Dunes/Dune Acres/Beverly Shores": Ball, 1900; Baker and Carmony; *Beverly Shores Golden Jubilee;* Cannon, Loring, and Robb; Cook and Jackson; *Dune Acres;* Moore; and Slupski.

"Portage": Briggs, circa 1930c; Garard; Goodspeed and Blanchard; Lane, 1991; Moore; Patterson, 1929; and Youngman, 1997.

"Porter/Burns Harbor": Ahrendt; Ball, 1900, Blatchley; Briggs, circa 1930b; Garard; Miller; and Porter Centennial.

"Tassinong": Anderson; Ball, 1900; Finney; Garard; Meyer, 1935; Werich; and Wolcott.

"Tremont/Furnessville/Pines": Briggs, circa 1930c; Cook and Jackson; Garard; and Meyer, 1945.

"Valparaiso": Ball, 1900; Goodspeed and Blanchard; *Handbook of Indiana Geology; History of Porter County, Indiana;* Shults-Gay; and Skinner.

"Wheeler": Goodspeed and Blanchard; and Hardesty.

"LaPorte": Ball, 1900; Daniels; *History of Porter County;* Lake Shore and Michigan Southern Railroad; LaPorte County Historical Society web site; Packard; Maple, Applegate and Backus; and personal communications with Jim Rogers and Fern Schultz.

"Michigan City": Ball, 1900; Brennan; Clifford and Clifford; Cottman; Daniels; Packard; Roberts and Jones; Simons and Parker; and Swenson 2000b.

"Westville": Ball, 1900; and Daniels.

EPILOGUE

Blatchley; Cottman; Lane, 1991; Mather; Meyer, 1945); Nature Conservancy web site; Pavlovic and Bowles; Reshkin; Shirley Heinze Land Trust web site; Sullivan; and Waldron.

Works Cited and
Suggestions for Further Reading

Adair, Anna B., and Adele Sandberg. 1968. *Indian Trails to Tollways: The Story of the Homewood-Flossmoor Area.* Homewood, Ill.: Fremouw Press.

Ade, John. 1911. *Newton County.* Indianapolis: Bobbs-Merrill.

Ahrendt, William J. 1975. "A Swedish Heritage: History of Burstrom Chapel." Brochure. Chesterton, Ind.

Allouez, Claude-Jean. [1667] 1917. "Father Allouez's Journey to Lake Superior." In Louise Phelps Kellogg, ed., *Early Narratives of the Northwest, 1634–1794.* New York: Scribner's.

Alvord, Clarence W. 1908. "The Conquest of St. Joseph, Michigan, by the Spaniards in 1781." *Missouri Historical Review* 2: 195–210.

Anderson, Shirley. September 1975. "Tassinong." Duneland Historical Society newsletter, *Duneland Notes.*

André, L. Aumund. 1987. *Glenwood: Boys and Dogs Have Right of Way.* Glenwood, Ill.: Glenwood Press.

Andreas, Alfred T. 1884. *History of Cook County, Illinois: From the Earliest Period to the Present Time.* Chicago: A. T. Andreas.

Austin, George S., and John B. Patton. 1972. "History of Brick Manufacture in Indiana." *Proceedings of the Indiana Academy of Science* 81: 229–37.

Baker, J. David. 1976. *The Postal History of Indiana.* Louisville: Leonard H. Hartmann.

Baker, Ronald L., and Marvin Carmony. 1975. *Indiana Place Names.* Bloomington: Indiana University Press.

Ball, Timothy H. 1873. *Lake County, Indiana, from 1834 to 1872.* Chicago: J. W. Goodspeed.

———, ed. 1884. *Lake County, Indiana, 1884: An Account of the Semi-Centennial Celebration of Lake County, September 3 and 4, with Historical Papers and Other Interesting Records Prepared for This Volume.* Crown Point, Ind.: Lake County Star Press.

———. 1900. *Northwestern Indiana from 1800 to 1900.* Chicago: Donohue and Henneberry.

———. 1904. *Encyclopedia of Genealogy and Biography of Lake County, Indiana, with a Compendium of History, 1834–1904.* Chicago: Lewis.

Bannister, Henry M. 1868. "Geology of Cook County." In A. H. Worthen, *Geology and Palaeontology,* 3: 239–56. Springfield: State Journal Steam Press.

Bayless, E. Randall, Leslie D. Arihood, William C. Sidle, and Noel B. Pavlovic. 1999. *A Study of Natural and Restored Wetland Hydrology.* Fact Sheet 104-99. Indianapolis: U.S. Geological Survey.

Beatson, J. W. 1897. *The Pioneer.* Chicago: H. W. Machlan.

Beaudette-Neil, E. Palma. 1921. *Thornton Township, Cook County, Illinois: A Brief Sketch of the Township's Prominent Men and Industrial Establishments and a Few Interested near Boundary Line.* Hammond, Ind.: Neil.

Beeson, F. S. 1938. "Industrial and Labor Survey, 1890–1937: Chicago Heights, Illinois." Manuscript housed at the Chicago Heights Public Library.

"Beginnings on a River." 1999. *Chicago Tribune.* http://chicago.digitalcity.com/150th/moments/intro3.html. Accessed September 19, 1999.

Belman, W. C. 1924. "Early Schools and Teachers of Lake County." In James W. Lester, ed., *Historical Records of the Lake County Old Settler and Historical Association of Lake County, Indiana.* Crown Point, Ind.: n.p.

Bennett, Ira E. 1915. *History of the Panama Canal: Its Construction and Builders.* Washington, D.C.: Historical.

Beverly Shores Golden Jubilee. 1983. Brochure. Beverly Shores, Ind.

Bieber, C. L., and Ned M. Smith. 1952. *Industrial Sands of the Indiana Dunes.* Bulletin no 7. Bloomington: Indiana State Geological Survey.

Blake, Darus P. 1927. "Darus P. Blake." In Thomas H. Cannon, Hanibal H. Loring, and Charles J. Robb, eds., *History of the Lake and Calumet Region of Indiana Embracing the Counties of Lake, Porter, and LaPorte.* Indianapolis: Historians Association.

———. 1929. "Early Days in Lake and Porter Counties." In Lake County Historical Association, *History of Lake County,* vol. 10. Gary, Ind.: Calumet Press.

Blanchard, Rufus. 1881. *Discovery and Conquests of the North-west, with the History of Chicago.* Wheaton, Ill.: R. Blanchard.

Blatchley, Willis S. 1897. *Geology of Lake and Porter Counties, Indiana.* Department of Geology and Natural Resources of Indiana, 22nd annual report. Indianapolis: William B. Burford.

Blue Island: An Illustrated Review of Its Leading Industries, Churches, Schools, Societies, Officials, Businessmen, and Citizens. 1915. Brochure. Blue Island, Ill.

Borman, Frank. 1922. Untitled essay in J. W. Lester, ed., *Papers by Various Hands,* housed at the Gary Public Library. Reprinted in 1934 as "Reminiscences of Tolleston," in Old Settler and Historical Association of Lake County, *History of Lake County XI.* Crown Point, Ind.: Lake County Star Press.

Bowers, John O. 1922. *The Old Bailly Homestead.* Gary, Ind.: n.p.

———. 1929. *Dream Cities of the Calumet.* Gary, Ind.: Calumet Press.

Brennan, George A. 1923. *The Wonders of the Dunes.* Indianapolis: Bobbs-Merrill.

Bretz, J Harlen. 1939. *Geology of the Chicago Region, Part I—General.* Bulletin no. 65. Urbana: Illinois State Geological Survey.

———. 1943. *Chicago Areal Geologic Maps.* Supplement to Bulletin no. 65, *Geology of the Chicago Region.* Reprint, Urbana: Illinois State Geological Survey, 1955.

———. 1955. *Geology of the Chicago Region, Part II—The Pleistocene.* Bulletin no. 65, part 2. Urbana: Illinois State Geological Survey.

A Brief History of the Griffith-Highland United Methodist Church. n.d. Griffith, Ind.: Griffith-Highland United Methodist Church.

Briggs, William A. ca. 1930a. "Mills in Porter County." *Duneland Notes,* July 1967.

———. ca. 1930b. "Some Early History of Chesterton and Porter." *Duneland Notes,* April 1973.

———. ca. 1930c. "Taverns, Our First Hotels in Early Porter County." *Duneland Notes,* August 1968.

Brock, Kenneth J. 1997. *Birds of the Indiana Dunes.* 2nd ed. Michigan City, Ind.: Shirley Heinze Environmental Fund.

Brown, Steven E. 1999. "Geologic History of the Little Calumet and Grand Calumet Rivers." Unpublished notes.

Brown, Steven E., N. K. Bleuer, and Todd A. Thompson. 1996. *Geologic Terrain Map of the Southern Lake Michigan Rim, Indiana.* Bloomington: Indiana Geological Survey.

Brown, Steven E., and Todd A. Thompson. 1995. *Geologic Terrains of the Chicago 30 × 60 Minute Quadrangle in Indiana.* Bloomington: Indiana Geological Survey.

Brownell, Lillian Hughes. 1934. "Lowell." In Old Settler and Historical Association of Lake County, *History of Lake County,* vol. 11. Crown Point, Ind.: Lake County Star Press.

Bushnell, Thomas M. 1927. "Physiography of the Kankakee Region." *Proceedings of the Indiana Academy of Science* 37: 141–42.

Butterfield, Consul Willshire. 1881. *History of the Discovery of the Northwest by John Nicolet in 1634.* Port Washington, N.Y.: Kennikat Press.

Calumet City Centennial Celebration. 1993. Calumet City, Ill.: Centennial '93 Committee.

"Canal to Wabash: The Improvement Company Is Quietly at Work." *Michigan City Evening Dispatch,* December 3, 1903.

Cannon, Thomas H., Hanibal H. Loring, and Charles J. Robb, eds. 1927. *History of the Lake and Calumet Region of Indiana Embracing the Counties of Lake, Porter, and LaPorte.* Indianapolis: Historians Association.

Carlson, Frieda. ca. 1976. "Hickory Bend/Glenwood." http://www.lincolnnet.net/users/lrglanhs/history/1976.htm. Accessed November 1998.

Carr, Drusilla. 1921. "Mrs. Drusilla Carr Tells of Early Days at Miller Beach." Manuscript housed at the Gary Public Library, Gary, Ind.

Century of Progress [of Hebron], 1890–1990. 1990. Hebron, Ind.: n.p.

Chamberlin, Thomas C. 1883. "Preliminary Paper on the Terminal Moraine of the Second Glacial Epoch." *Report of the Director of the United States Geological Survey.* Washington, D.C.: U.S. Geological Survey.

———. 1894. "Glacial Phenomena in North America." In James Geikie, *The Great Ice Age and Its Relation to the Antiquity of Man,* 3rd ed., pp. 724–55. London: E. Stanford.

———. 1895. "The Classification of American Glacial Deposits." *Journal of Geology* 3: 270–77.

———. 1896. "Nomenclature of Glacial Formations." *Journal of Geology* 4: 872–76.

Chesterton Centennial, 1852–1952. 1952. Pamphlet. Chesterton, Ind.: n.p.

Chicago Fact Book Consortium. 1980. *Local Community Fact Book: Chicago Metropolitan Area.* Chicago: University of Illinois at Chicago.

Chicago Heights Centennial, 1892–1992. 1992. Brochure. Chicago Heights, Ill.

Chicago Heights Centennial Celebration, 1833–1933. 1933. Brochure. Chicago Heights, Ill.

Christenson, Susan, ed. 1976. *From Lake Station to East Gary.* East Gary, Ind.: East Gary American Revolution Bicentennial Commission.

Christianson, Elin B., ed. September 27, 1980. *Hobart History Advocate.* Hobart, Ind.: Hobart Historical Society.

———. 2001. *Lake County Communities, Past and Present.* Hobart, Ind.: Hobart Historical Society.

Chrzastowski, Michael J., Frank A. Pranschke, and Charles W. Shabica. 1991. "Discovery and Preliminary Investigations of the Remains of an Early Holocene Forest on the Floor of Southern

Lake Michigan." *Journal of Great Lakes Research* 17: 543–52.

Chrzastowski, Michael J., and Todd A. Thompson. 1992. "Late Wisconsinan and Holocene Coastal Evolution of the Southern Shore of Lake Michigan." In *Quaternary Coasts of the United States: Marine and Lacustrine Systems*. SEPM Special Publication no. 48, pp. 397–413.

———. 1994. "Late Wisconsinan and Holocene Geologic History of the Illinois-Indiana Coast of Lake Michigan." *Journal of Great Lakes Research* 20: 9–26.

"Church Returns to Home." *Hammond Times,* May 28, 1974.

City of Harvey Golden Jubilee. 1941. Brochure. Harvey, Ill.: Harvey Association of Commerce.

Clarke, G. K. C. 1987. "Fast Glacier Flow: Ice Streams, Surging and Tidewater Glaciers." *Journal of Geophysical Research* 92: 8835–41.

Clemens, Janette M., and Deborah Collins. 1976. *A Pictorial History of Merrillville*. Merrillville, Ind.: Merrillville Ross Township Historical Society.

Clemensen, A. 1975. "Evaluation of Historic Resources at Bailly Homestead." Manuscript housed at the Indiana Dunes National Lakeshore, Porter, Ind.

Clifford, Mary Louise, and J. Candace Clifford. 1993. *Women Who Kept the Lights*. Williamsburg, Va.: Cypress Communications.

Cohen, Ronald D. 1990. *Children of the Mill: Schooling and Society in Gary, Indiana, 1906–1960*. Bloomington: Indiana University Press.

Cohen, Ronald D., and Stephen G. McShane. 1998. *Moonlight in Duneland: The Illustrated Story of the Chicago South Shore and South Bend Railroad*. Bloomington: Indiana University Press.

Cole, Kenneth L. 1986. "A Twocreekan Spruce Forest at the South End of Lake Michigan." In Ardith K. Hansel and W. Hilton Johnson, *Quaternary Records of Northeastern Illinois and Northwestern Indiana*. Champaign: Illinois State Geological Survey.

Colman, S. M., J. A. Clark, L. Clayton, A. K. Hansel, and C. E. Larsen. 1994. "Deglaciation, Lake Levels, and Meltwater Discharge in the Lake Michigan Basin." *Quaternary Science Reviews* 13: 879–90.

Cook, Marlene. 1998. *Portals in Time: A Guide to Suburban Heritage*. Homewood, Ill.: South Suburban Heritage Association.

Cook, Richard A. 1966. *A History of South Holland, Illinois*. South Holland, Ill.: South Holland Trust and Savings Bank.

Cook, Sarah Gibbard, and Robert S. Jackson. 1978. *The Bailly Area of Porter County, Indiana: The Final Report of a Geo-historical Study Undertaken on Behalf of the Indiana Dunes National Lakeshore*. Evanston, Ill.: Robert Jackson and Associates.

Corliss, Carlton J. 1950. *Main Line of Mid-America*. New York: Creative Age Press.

Cottman, George S. 1930. *Indiana Dunes State Park: A History and Description*. Publication no. 97. Indianapolis: Department of Conservation, State of Indiana.

Cowles, Henry Chandler. 1899. "The Ecological Relations of the Vegetation on the Sand Dunes of Lake Michigan." *Botanical Gazette* 27: 95–117, 167–202, 281–302, 361–91.

———. 1917. Quoted in Stephen T. Mather, *Report on the Proposed Sand Dunes National Park, Indiana*. Washington, D.C.: Department of the Interior.

Cressey, George B. 1928. *The Indiana Sand Dunes and Shore Line of the Lake Michigan Basin*. Geographic Society of Chicago Bulletin no. 8. Chicago: University of Chicago Press.

Crouch, Tom D. 1992. "Octave Chanute." Brochure prepared in cooperation with the National Park Service, Indiana Dunes National Lakeshore. Washington, D.C.: Government Printing Office.

Dabertin, David M. 1995. *Walk-able, Ride-able Whiting and Robertsdale*. Hammond, Ind.: Wild Onion Press.

Danckers, Ulrich, and Jane Meredith. 2000. *A Compendium of the Early History of Chicago to the Year 1835 When the Indians Left*. Menomonee Falls, Wis.: Inland Press.

Daniels, E. D. 1904. *A Twentieth-Century History and Biographical Record of LaPorte County Indiana*. Chicago: Lewis.

Deale, Valentine B. 1939. "The History of the Potawatomi before 1722." Ph.D. diss., University of Notre Dame.

Dedmon, Emmett. 1953. *Fabulous Chicago: A Great City's History and People*. New York: Atheneum.

Demmon, A. M. 1934. "Hobart Pioneers." In Old Settler and Historical Association of Lake County, *History of Lake County*, vol. 11. Crown Point, Ind.: Lake County Star Press.

Denta, Elaine, ed. 1991. *A Pictorial History of Merrillville*. Revision of a booklet of the same title by Janette M. Clemens and Deborah Collins. Merrillville, Ind.: Merrillville Ross Township Historical Society.

Diamond Jubilee Historical Record Commemorating the 75th Anniversary of the Dolton, 1892–1976. 1976. Brochure. Dolton-South Holland Junior Woman's Club.

Donnelly, Joseph P. 1968. *Jacques Marquette, S.J., 1637–1675*. Chicago: Loyola University Press.

Douthett, Mabel. 1934. "Highland." In Old Settler and Historical Association of Lake County, *History of Lake County*, vol. 11. Crown Point, Ind.: Lake County Star Press.

"Down in South Chicago: What Chicago Gained along the Calumet by Annexation." *Chicago Tribune,* August 11, 1889.

Dudley, Marion, ed. 1997. *Hobart Sesquicentennial, 1847–1997*. Hobart: City of Hobart.

Duff, John. 1965. "50 Years of Rest-A-While, 1915–1965." In *Cedar Lake Bible Conference Grounds 50th Anniversary.* Pamphlet. Cedar Lake, Ind.

Dune Acres, 1923–1973. 1973. Brochure. Dune Acres, Ind.

Dwyer, Cornelia. 1924. "Early History of Lowell and Vicinity." In James W. Lester, ed., *Historical Records of the Lake County Old Settler and Historical Association of Lake County, Indiana.* Crown Point, Ind.: n.p.

East Chicago Public Library. 2000. "East Chicago Church Chronology." Manuscript housed at the East Chicago Public Library.

East Side Centennial Commemoration: History and Progress of East Side. 1951. Brochure. Chicago.

Eccles, William J. 1998. *The French in North America.* East Lansing: Michigan State University Press.

Edmunds. R. David. 1978. *The Potawatomis: Keepers of the Fire.* Norman: University of Oklahoma Press.

Eenigenburg, Harry. 1935. *The Calumet Region and Its Early Settlers.* Reprint, Chicago: Arrow Printers, 1998.

———. ca. 1941. "The Settlement of the Calumet Region." Reprinted in Henry S. Lucas, *Dutch Immigrant Memoirs and Related Writings.* Seattle: University of Washington Press, 1955.

Ehlers, Jürgen. 1996. *Quaternary and Glacial Geology.* Chichester: Wiley.

Engel, J. Ronald. 1983. *Sacred Sands: The Struggle for Community in the Indiana Dunes.* Middletown, Conn.: Wesleyan University Press.

Esarey, Logan. 1970. *A History of Indiana from Its Exploration to 1850.* Indianapolis: Hoosier Heritage Press.

Ettema, Ross K. 1976. *From the Land of Windmills and Wooden Shoes: Early Dutch Settlers of South Holland, Thornton, Lansing, and Dolton, Illinois.* South Holland, Ill.: n.p.

Finney, Arthur A. June 1960. "Site of Tassinong: A Dedication of a Marker at That Location." *Duneland Notes.*

First Reformed Church Centennial, 1861–1961. 1961. Lansing, Ill.: Centennial Committee.

Fisher, Timothy G. 1999/2000. Geology of the Grand Calumet River Region. *Proceedings of the Indiana Academy of Science* 108/109: 11–18.

Ford, Clara Eggers. 1934. "Pioneer Days of Robertsdale, Whiting, Berry Lake." In Old Settler and Historical Association of Lake County, *History of Lake County,* vol. 11. Crown Point, Ind.: Lake County Star Press.

Forsyth, Oliver O. 1911. "Oliver Forsyth's Account." In Whiting Savings and Loan Association, *Whiting City Almanac and Cook Book.* Chicago: Hammond Press, W. B. Conkey.

Founding of Calumet City, 1893–1968. 1968. Brochure. Calumet City, Ill.

Franklin, Kay, and Norma Schaeffer. 1983. *Duel for the Dunes: Land Use Conflict on the Shores of Lake Michigan.* Urbana: University of Illinois Press.

Franquelin, Jean-Baptiste Louis. 1688. "Carte de l'Amerique Septentrionale." n.p.

Fryxell, F. M. 1927. *The Physiography of the Region of Chicago.* University of Chicago Local Community Research Committee, Chicago Commonwealth Club. Chicago: University of Chicago Press.

Garard, George A. 1882. Chapters in Weston A. Goodspeed and Charles Blanchard, *The Counties of Porter and Lake.* Chicago: F. A. Battery.

Genealogical and Biographical Record of Cook County, Illinois. 1894. Chicago: Lake City.

Gibbs, Mrs. A. H. 1934. "Winfield Township." In Old Settler and Historical Association of Lake County, *History of Lake County,* vol. 11. Crown Point, Ind.: Lake County Star Press.

Gibson, Henrietta Combs. 1922. "Reminiscences of Mrs. Henrietta Gibson." Quoted in J. W. Lester, "Pioneer Stories of the Calumet," *Indiana Magazine of History* 18: 166–71.

Gleason, W. P. 1922. "The Gary Works of the Illinois Steel Company." In J. W. Lester, ed., *Papers by Various Hands,* vol. 1, p. 315, housed at the Gary Public Library.

Goldthwait, James W. 1907. "The Abandoned Shorelines of Eastern Wisconsin." *Wisconsin Geology and Natural History Survey Bulletin* 17: 61–62.

Goodspeed, Weston A., and Charles Blanchard. 1882. *The Counties of Porter and Lake.* Chicago: F. A. Battery.

Gravier, Jacques. 1696. "Dictionary of the Algonquin Illinois Language." Manuscript housed at the Watkinson Library, Trinity College, Hartford, Conn.

Gray, Henry. 1987. Introduction to reprint of David Dale Owen, *A Geological Reconnaissance and Survey of the State of Indiana in 1837 and 1838.* Department of Natural Resources Geological Survey Bulletin no. 61. Bloomington: Indiana State Geological Survey.

Gray, Ralph D. 1989. *The Hoosier State: Readings in Indiana History.* Bloomington: Indiana University Press.

———. 1998. *Public Ports for Indiana: A History of the Indiana Port Commission.* Indianapolis: Indiana Historical Bureau.

Green, Silas E. 1924. "Jerusalem or East Tolleston: A Town Founded on the Site of Gary." Manuscript housed at the Gary Public Library.

Guide to Glen Park. 1952. Gary, Ind.: Illustrated Guide.

"Hammond Girl Is in Fire Peril," *Lake County Times* (Hammond, Ind.), November 4, 1909.

Handbook of Indiana Geology. 1922. Publication 21. Indianapolis: Department of Conservation, State of Indiana.

Hanna, Paul R., I. James Quillen, and Gladys L. Potter. 1940. *Ten Communities.* Chicago: Scott, Foresman and Company.

Hansel, Ardith K., and W. Hilton Johnson. 1992. "Fluctuations of the Lake Michigan Lobe during the Late Wisconsin Subepisode." *Sveriges Geologiska Undersokning* 81: 133–44.

Hansel, Ardith K., and David M. Mickelson. 1988. "A Reevaluation of the Timing and Causes of High Lake Phases in the Lake Michigan Basin." *Quaternary Research* 29: 113–28.

Hansel, Ardith K., David M. Mickelson, Allan F. Schneider, and Curtis E. Larsen. 1985. "Late Wisconsinan and Holocene History of the Lake Michigan Basin, Quaternary Evolution of the Great Lakes." Edited by P. F. Karrow and P. E. Calkin. Special Paper no. 30. St. John's, Nova Scotia: Geological Association of Canada.

Hardesty, A. G. 1876. *Illustrated Historical Atlas of Porter County, Indiana.* Valparaiso, Ind.: A. G. Hardesty.

Hartke, E. J., J. R. Hill, and M. Reshkin. 1975. *Environmental Geology of Lake and Porter Counties, Indiana—An Aid to Planning.* Environmental Study no. 8. Bloomington, Ind.: Department of Natural Resources, Geological Survey Special Report 11.

Haymore, Tyrone. 2001. "The Story of Robbins, Illinois." Brochure. Robbins, Ill.

Hebron United Presbyterian Church Centennial. 1937. Booklet. Hebron, Ind.: Hebron United Presbyterian Church.

Hess, Alys. 1929. "Hessville and Joseph Hess." In Lake County Historical Association, *History of Lake County,* vol. 10. Gary, Ind.: Calumet Press.

Hill, Mrs. J. L. 1929. "Reminiscences." Paper read at the Old Settlers meeting of 1928. Reprinted in Lake County Historical Association, *History of Lake County,* vol. 10. Gary, Ind.: Calumet Press.

Hill, John R., Donald D. Carr, Edwin J. Hartke, and Carl B. Rexroad. 1979. *Geology as a Contribution to Land Use Planning in LaPorte County, Indiana.* Bloomington, Ind.: Department of Natural Resources, Geological Survey Special Report 14.

Hinko, Michael J. 1976. *History of Homewood.* Homewood, Ill.: Richard D. Irwin.

Historic Pullman Foundation. 2000. http://members .aol.com/PullmanIL. Accessed November 5, 2000.

An Historical Look Back "To Our Past 25 Years." 1991. Crown Point, Ind.: Lakes of the Four Seasons Property Owners Association.

History of Augustana Lutheran Church. 1996. Hobart, Ind.: Augustana Lutheran Church.

History of Porter County, Indiana: A Narrative Account of Its Historical Progress, Its People, and Its Principal Interests. 1912. Chicago: Lewis.

History of the First United Methodist Church of Lowell, Indiana. 1999. Booklet. Lowell, Ind.: Lowell Methodist Church.

"History of Winfield." 1970. In *Reports and Papers,* vol. 12. Crown Point, Ind.: Historical Association of Lake County.

Hough, Jack L. 1958. *Geology of the Great Lakes.* Urbana: University of Illinois Press.

Housty, Leana. 1990. "Joseph Hess: The Founder of Hessville." In *Lake County Heritage.* Dallas: Curtis Media Corporation.

Howat, William F. 1915. *A Standard History of Lake County, Indiana, and the Calumet Region.* Chicago: Lewis.

Howe, Frances. 1907. *The Story of a French Homestead in the Old Northwest.* Columbus, Ohio: Nitschke Brothers.

Hubbard, Gurdon S. 1818. Papers housed at the Chicago Historical Society.

Indiana Department of Natural Resources. 1979. *An Inventory of Man-made Land along the Indiana Shoreline of Lake Michigan.* Technical Report no. 304. Indianapolis: Indiana State Planning Services Agency.

———. 1999. *Early Peoples of Indiana.* Indianapolis: Indiana Department of Natural Resources.

Jackson, Marion T., ed. 1997. *The Natural Heritage of Indiana.* Bloomington: Indiana University Press.

Jonas, Richard. 1991. *History of the Crossroads: 125th Anniversary, Schererville, 1866–1991.* Schererville, Ind.: Schererville Historical Society.

Kaquados, Simon. 1920. "Customs." Quoted in Publius V. Larson, "The Potawatomi." *Wisconsin Archeologist* 19: 41–115.

Kaske, Wilhelmine Stallbohm. 1934. "Early Days in Munster." In Old Settler and Historical Association of Lake County, *History of Lake County,* vol. 11. Crown Point, Ind.: Lake County Star Press.

Keene, Minnie. 1970. "History of Leroy." In Historical Association of Lake County, Indiana, *Reports and Papers,* vol. 12. Crown Point, Ind.: Historical Association of Lake County.

Kellar, J. H. 1983. *An Introduction to the Prehistory of Indiana.* 2nd ed. Indianapolis: Indiana Historical Society.

Kenton, Edna, ed. 1954. *The Jesuit Relations and Allied Documents: Travels and Explorations of the Jesuit Missionaries in North America (1610–1791).* New York: Vanguard Press.

Kijewski, Marchia, David Brosch, and Robert Bulanda. 1972. *The Historical Development of Three Chicago Millgates: South Chicago, East Side, South Deering.* Chicago: Illinois Labor History Society.

Kinnaird, Lawrence. 1932–33. "The Spanish Expedition against Fort St. Joseph in 1781: A New Interpretation." *Mississippi Valley Historical Review* 19: 173–91.

"Kittie Gibson." *Lake County Times* (Hammond, Ind.), December 27, 1907.

Kluessendorf, Joanne, and Donald G. Mikulic. 1997. *Teacher's Guide to Thornton Quarry.* n.p.

Knotts, A. F. 1929. "Indian Trails, Towns, and Mounds in Lake County." In Lake County

Historical Association, *History of Lake County,* vol. 10. Gary, Ind.: Calumet Press.

Kouts Is Five in Score—Ready for a Hundred More. 1965. Centennial brochure. Kouts, Ind.

Kunert, William. 1922. "Early Days in Lake County." Quoted in J. W. Lester, "Pioneer Stories of the Calumet," *Indiana Magazine of History* 18: 173–76.

Lake County Historical Association. 1929. *History of Lake County,* vol. 10. Gary, Ind.: Calumet Press.

Lake Shore and Michigan Southern Railroad. 1884. *LaPorte, Indiana, and Its Lakes: A New Summer Resort.* Cleveland: Forman.

Lane, James B. 1978. *City of the Century: A History of Gary, Indiana.* Bloomington: Indiana University Press.

———, ed. 1991. *A History of Portage, Indiana.* Steel Shavings, 20. Gary: Indiana University Northwest.

———, ed. 1997. *A History of Cedar Lake, Indiana.* Steel Shavings, 26. Gary: Indiana University Northwest.

Lane, James B., and Ronald D. Cohen. 1983. *Gary: A Pictorial History.* Norfolk, Va.: Donning.

Lans-Cent-Orama. 1954. Lansing Historical Society brochure. Lansing, Ill.

Lansing Centennial Album, 1893–1993. 1993. Lansing, Ill.: Lansing Historical Society.

LaPorte County Historical Society. 2000. http://www.lapcohistsoc.org/history.htm. Accessed September 3, 2000.

Lester, J. W. 1922. "Pioneer Stories of the Calumet." *Indiana Magazine of History* 18: 166–76.

———. 1923. "Part of Historic 40-Acre Tract, Site of First Tavern and White Man's Dwelling Now Occupied by Froebel High School." Manuscript housed at the Gary Public Library.

——— (a.k.a. Ni-gan-quet). 1924. "Lake Indians Visit the Camp Sites of Their Ancestors." In James W. Lester, ed., *Historical Records of the Lake County Old Settler and Historical Association of Lake County, Indiana.* Crown Point, Ind.: n.p.

LeVan, Rose G. 1968. *East Chicago Diamond Jubilee Record.* East Chicago, Ind.: n.p.

Leverett, Frank. 1897. *Pleistocene Features and Deposits of the Chicago Area.* Chicago: Chicago Academy of Sciences, Bulletin II.

———. 1898. "Raised Beaches of Lake Michigan." *Transactions of the Wisconsin Academy of Sciences, Arts and Letters* 7: 177–92.

———. 1899. *The Illinois Glacial Lobe.* Monographs of the United States Geological Survey, vol. 38. Washington, D.C.: Government Printing Office.

Levette, G. M. 1874. "Report of Observations Made in the Counties of DeKalb, Steuben, LaGrange, Elkhart, Noble, St. Joseph and LaPorte." In E. T. Cox, *Fifth Annual Report of the Geological Survey of Indiana, Made during the Year 1873.* Indianapolis: Sentinel.

Lincoln Highway Association. 1935. *The Lincoln Highway: The Story of a Crusade That Made Transportation History.* New York: Dodd, Mead.

Looking Back to Look Forward, 1843–1993: The First Presbyterian Church of Chicago Heights, Illinois. Chicago Heights, Ill.: Historical Book Committee, 1993.

Lowell Historical Society. 2002. http://www.lowellpl.lib.in.us/history.htm. Accessed December 12, 2002.

Lucas, Henry. 1955. *Dutch Immigrant Memoirs and Related Writings.* Seattle: University of Washington Press.

Luther, James H. 1884. "History of Northern Lake County." In Timothy H. Ball, *Lake County, Indiana, 1884: An Account of the Semi-Centennial Celebration of Lake County, September 3 and 4 with Historical Papers and Other Interesting Records Prepared for this Volume.* Crown Point, Ind.: Lake County Star Press.

McClellan, Larry. August 30, 1998. "Burnham's growth shaped by steel and the Calumet." *The (Tinley Park, Ill.) Star.*

———. February 27, 2000. "World's Fair beginning leads to Robbins' world-wide notice." *The (Tinley Park, Ill.) Star.*

McCord, Shirley S. 1970. *Travel Accounts of Indiana, 1679–1961.* Indianapolis: Indiana Historical Bureau.

McKinlay, Archibald. 1988. *Twin City: A Pictorial History of East Chicago, Indiana.* Edited by Tony Lillis. Norfolk, Va.: Donning.

Maple, G. B., George Applegate, and Edith J. Backus. n.d. "History of LaPorte Industries." Manuscript housed at the LaPorte County Historical Society Museum.

Martineau, Harriet. 1836. "Travels in and around Michigan, 1836." *Michigan History* 7 (1923): 49–99.

Material Service Corporation. "This Is the Thornton Quarry." Undated brochure. Thornton, Ill.

Mather, Stephen T. 1917. *Report on the Proposed Sand Dunes National Park, Indiana.* Washington, D.C.: Department of the Interior.

Melton, Arthur P. 1931. "Early Recollections of Gary." In J. W. Lester, ed., *Papers by Various Hands,* vol. 1, p. 279, at the Gary Public Library. Parts were reprinted in Powell Moore, *The Calumet Region: Indiana's Last Frontier.* Indianapolis: Indiana Historical Bureau, 1959.

Methodist Episcopal Church Centennial. 1935. Booklet. Hebron, Ind.: First Methodist Episcopal Church.

Meyer, Alfred H. 1935. "The Kankakee Marsh of Northern Indiana and Illinois." *Papers of the Michigan Academy of Science, Arts, and Letters* 21: 359–96.

———. 1945. "Toponomy in Sequent Occupance Geography, Calumet Region, Indiana-Illinois." *Proceedings of the Indiana Academy of Science* 54: 142–59.

———. 1954. "Circulation and Settlement Patterns of the Calumet Region: First Stage of Occupance—The Pottawattomie and the Fur Trader." *Annals of the Association of American Geographers* 44: 245–74.

———. 1956. "Circulation and Settlement Patterns of the Calumet Region of Northwest Indiana and Northeast Illinois: The Second Stage of Occupance—Pioneer Settler and Subsistence Economy, 1830–1850." *Annals of the Association of American Geographers* 46: 312–56.

Middleton, William D. 1999. *South Shore: The Last Interurban.* Rev. ed. Bloomington: Indiana University Press.

Midwest Region National Park Service, Department of the Interior. 1998. Calumet Ecological Park Feasibility Study. http://www.lincolnnet.net/environment/feasibility/calumet2.html. Accessed December 12, 2002.

Mikulic, Donald G., and Joanne Kluessendorf. 1999. *The Classic Silurian Reefs of the Chicago Area.* Illinois State Geological Survey Guidebook 29. Champaign: Illinois State Geological Survey.

Milankovitch, Milutin. 1941. "Kanon der Erdbestrahlung und seine Anwendung auf das Eiszeitenproblem." *Koniglich Serbische Akademie Belgrad,* Special Publication 133.

Millender, Dolly. 1967. *Yesterday in Gary: A Brief History of the Negro in Gary, 1906–1967.* Gary, Ind.: n.p.

Miller, Martha. 1982. *The Chellberg Family/The Chellberg Farm.* Chesterton, Ind.: Millar Publications.

Mitchell, Gary. 2001. "Potawatomi Stories." http://www.ku.edu/~kansite/pbp/books/mitch/gm04_euro.html. Accessed December 12, 2002.

Moore, Powell A. 1959. *The Calumet Region: Indiana's Last Frontier.* Reprint, with an afterword by Lance Trusty. Indianapolis: Indiana Historical Bureau, 1977.

Morris, Jack H. 1993. "Inland Steel at 100: Beginning a Second Century of Progress." Chicago: Inland Steel Industries.

Mumford, Russell E. 1997. "Wings across the Sky: Birds of Indiana." In Marion T. Jackson, *The Natural Heritage of Indiana.* Bloomington: Indiana University Press.

Munger, Elizabeth M. 1969. "Michigan City's First Hundred Years." Manuscript housed at the Michigan City Public Library. (Published in 1990 by the Michigan City Historical Society.)

Nature Conservancy. 1999. http://nature.org/. Accessed December 12, 2002.

Nelson, Kim. 1986. "Glacigenic Sediment of the Kankakee Outwash Plain and Valparaiso Morainic System, Northern Indiana." In Ardith K. Hansel and W. Hilton Johnson, *Quaternary Records of Northeastern Illinois and Northwestern Indiana.* Champaign: Illinois State Geological Survey.

One Hundredth Anniversary of the Church of Christ, Lowell, Indiana. 1942. Booklet. Lowell, Ind.: Church of Christ.

Ooms, Delia. 1966. "Sunday—When I Was Young." Family newsletter.

Owen, David Dale, and J. G. Norwood. 1852. *Report of a Geological Survey of Wisconsin, Iowa, and Minnesota, and Incidentally of a Portion of Nebraska Territory.* Philadelphia: Lippincotte, Grambo.

Owen, Richard. 1862. *Report of a Geological Reconnaissance of Indiana.* Indianapolis: H. H. Dodd.

Packard, Jasper. 1876. *History of LaPorte County, Indiana, and Its Townships, Towns, and Cities.* LaPorte, Ind.: S. E. Taylor.

Parkman, Francis. 1905. *LaSalle and the Discovery of the Great West.* Boston: Little, Brown.

Patterson, Arthur E. 1929. "Lake Station." In Lake County Historical Association, *History of Lake County,* vol. 10. Gary, Ind.: Calumet Press.

———. 1934. "The Pottawatomie Trail of Lake County." In Old Settler and Historical Association of Lake County, *History of Lake County,* vol. 11. Crown Point, Ind.: Lake County Star Press.

Pavlovic, Noel B., and Marlin L. Bowles. 1996. "Rare Plant Monitoring at Indiana Dunes National Lakeshore." In W. L. Halvorson and G. E. Davis, eds., *Science and Ecosystem Management in the National Parks.* Tucson: University of Arizona Press.

Pearson, Esther. November 1970. "The History of Miller." *Duneland Notes.*

Pearson, Mrs. George. 1954. "Time Marches On." In *Lans-Cent-Orama* (pamphlet). Lansing, Ill.

Peattie, Donald Culross. 1930. *Flora of the Indiana Dunes.* Chicago: Field Museum of Natural History.

Pierce, Bessie Louise. 1937. *A History of Chicago.* New York: Alfred A. Knopf.

Pleak, Mariam J. ca. 1947. *A Short History of Hobart.* Hobart, Ind.: Hobart Gazette.

Porter Centennial 1951. Pamphlet. Porter, Ind.

Porter on Parade: Being a Brief History of the Founding of Porter and a Record of Its Citizens, Past and Present. 1959. Porter, Ind.: Porter Centennial.

Post, Thomas W. 1997. "The Central Flatlands." In Marion T. Jackson, ed., *The Natural Heritage of Indiana.* Bloomington: Indiana University Press.

Protsman, Gladys G. 1962. *The Dyer Union Church and Sunday School.* Dyer, Ind.: n.p.

Putnam, Jennie E. 1934. "Pioneering in Whiting." In Old Settler and Historical Association of Lake County, *History of Lake County,* vol. 11. Crown Point, Ind.: Lake County Star Press.

Quaife, Milo M. 1923. *Chicago's Highways Old and New: From Indian Trail to Motor Road.* Chicago: D. F. Keller.

Quimby, George Irving. 1960. *Indian Life in the Upper Great Lakes 11,000 BC to AD 1800.* Chicago: University of Chicago Press.

Reese, Henry. 1911. "A Talk with Henry Reese." In

Whiting Savings and Loan Association, *Whiting City Almanac and Cook Book*. Whiting, Ind.: n.p.

Reshkin, Mark. 1987. "The Natural Resources of the Calumet: A Region Apart." In *Sand and Steel: The Dilemma of Cohabitation in the Calumet Region*. Gary: Indiana University Northwest.

Richmond, G. M. and Fullerton, D. S. 1986. "Summation of Quaternary Glaciations in the United States of America." *Quaternary Science Reviews* 5: 183–196.

Rieck, Rocjard L., and Harold A. Winters. 1981. "Frank Leverett: Pleistocene Scholar and Field Worker." *Journal of Geological Education* 29: 222–27.

Roberts, Bruce, and Ray Jones. 1994. *Great Lakes Lighthouses: Ontario to Superior.* Saybrook, Conn.: Globe Pequot Press.

Robinson, Solon. 1834. Quoted in Shirley S. McCord, ed., *Travel Accounts of Indiana, 1679–1961*. Indianapolis: Indiana Historical Bureau, 1970.

———. ca. 1840. Quoted in Weston A. Goodspeed and Charles Blanchard, *The Counties of Porter and Lake*. Chicago: F. A. Battery, 1882.

———. 1847. "History of Lake County, 1833–1847." *Lake County Star,* September 8, 15, and 22. Reprinted in Lake County Historical Association, *History of Lake County*, vol. 10. Gary, Ind.: Calumet Press, 1929.

Rocke, Verva Coleman, Lucile Ross, and Ileane Breslin. 1990. *Living in Hazel Crest, 1890–1990*. Hazel Crest, Ill.: n.p.

Rowlands, Marie K. 1949. "Down an Indian Trail in 1849: The Story of Roseland." *Calumet Index,* serial beginning June 20. Reprint edited by Paul Petraitis and Ross and Peggy Ettema, Palos Heights, Ill.: Dutch Heritage Center, Trinity Christian College, 1987.

Rump, A. 1934. "Tolleston and the Calumet Region." In Old Settler and Historical Association of Lake County, *History of Lake County*, vol. 11. Crown Point, Ind.: Lake County Star Press.

Saint Edward Parrish, Lowell, Indiana, 1870–1995. 1995. Booklet. Lowell, Ind.: Saint Edward Church.

Saint James Church: Sauk Village, Illinois, 1962–1987. 1987. Columbia, S.C.: Saint James Church.

Saint Paul Lutheran Church, 1880–1980. 1980. Kouts, Ind.: Saint Paul Lutheran Church.

"Scene at D.A.R. Unveiling Services Marking Site of Old Gibson Inn." *Gary Post Tribune,* June 30, 1923.

Schaeffer, Norma, and Kay Franklin. 1984. "Industry versus Preservation." In *The Indiana Dunes Story.* Reprint, Michigan City, Ind.: Shirley Heinze Environmental Fund, 1997.

Scharf, Albert F. 1903. "Indian Villages of Chicago and Cook County." Manuscript housed at the Chicago Historical Society.

Schmal, Richard C. 1988. "The History of Lowell." http://www.lowellpl.lib.in.us/s1988jan.htm. Accessed December 12, 2002.

Schneider, Allan F. 1968. "History of a Morainal Gap at Valparaiso, Indiana." *Geological Society of America Special Paper 115, Abstracts from 1967,* 398–99.

Schneider, Allan F., and Stanley J. Keller. 1970. *Geologic Map of the 1° × 2° Chicago Quadrangle, Indiana, Illinois, and Michigan, Showing Bedrock and Unconsolidated Materials*. Bloomington, Ind.: Indiana Geological Survey.

Schneider, Allan F., and Mark Reshkin. 1982. "Identification of the Twocreekan Substage in Indiana." Abstract. *Proceedings of the Indiana Academy of Science* 91:347.

Schoon, Dick J. 1966. "Special Days—Years Ago." In an unpublished family newsletter.

Schoon, Jacob J., Sr. 1966. "Typical Workdays as a Youth." In an unpublished family newsletter.

Schoon, Kenneth J., and Margaret S. Schoon. 1981. *Portraits of a Ridge Family: The Jacob Schoons.* Munster, Ind.: n.p.

Schrage, Henry. 1921. "From Section Hand to Bank President." Manuscript housed at the Gary Public Library.

Senior, Barbara. ca. 1987. *We Would Like You to Know Our History*. Homewood, Ill.: First Presbyterian Church of Homewood, Illinois.

Seventy-five Years of Growing Together: The History of the People of Griffith, Indiana. 1979. Griffith, Ind.: Griffith Diamond Jubilee Committee.

Shepard, Charles U. 1838. "Geology of Upper Illinois." *American Journal of Science* 34: 134–37.

Shirley Heinze Environmental Fund. 2001. http://www.heinzefund.org. Accessed December 12, 2002.

Shults-Gay, D. H. "After 1917." In *One of the Earliest Authentic Histories of Porter County, Indiana, from 1832 to 1876*. Valparaiso, Ind.: n.p.

Simons, Richard S., and Francis H. Parker. 1997. *Railroads of Indiana*. Bloomington: Indiana University Press.

Skinner, Hubert M. 1876. *History of Valparaiso from the Earliest Times to the Present*. Valparaiso, Ind.: Normal.

Slapin, Beverly, and Doris Seale. 1992. *Through Indian Eyes: The Native Experience in Books for Children*. Philadelphia: New Society.

Slupski, Janice. 1999. "The Glory Days of the Dunes Highway." *Singing Sands* 19, no. 4: 5.

Spicer, Steve. 2000a. "Miller History: Native Americans and Early Exploration." http://www2.crown.net/sspicer/miller/hist_na.html. Accessed December 12, 2002.

———. 2000b. "Marquette Park—Miller's little jewel on the lake." http://www2.crown.net/sspicer/miller/park.html. Accessed December 12, 2002.

Starr, Oliver, Jr. "The Gibson Inn." *Gary (Ind.) Post Tribune,* October 30, 1955.

Struever, Stuart, and Felicia Holton. 1979. *Koster:*

Americans in Search of Their Prehistoric Past. Garden City, N.Y.: Anchor Press/Doubleday.

Sullivan, Jerry. n.d. *Chicago Wilderness: An Atlas of Biodiversity.* Chicago: Chicago Region Biodiversity Council.

Swenson, John F. 2000a. "Chicago: Meaning of the Name and Location of Pre-1800 European Settlements." In Ulrich Danckers and Jane Meredith, *A Compendium of the Early History of Chicago to the Year 1835 When the Indians Left.* Menomonee Falls, Wis.: Inland Press.

————. 2000b. "Jean Baptiste Point de Sable: The Founder of Modern Chicago." In Ulrich Danckers and Jane Meredith, *A Compendium of the Early History of Chicago to the Year 1835 When the Indians Left.* Menomonee Falls, Wis.: Inland Press.

Tanner, Helen Hornbeck. 1987. *Atlas of Great Lakes Indian History.* Norman: University of Oklahoma Press.

Taylor, Arthur B. 1926. "Obadiah Taylor." Paper presented to the Lake County Historical Society. In *Lake County Heritage.* Dallas: Curtis Media Corporation.

Teggart, Frederick J. 1911. "The Capture of St. Joseph, Michigan, by the Spaniards in 1781." *Missouri Historical Review* 5: 214–28.

"That Canal Project." *Chesterton Tribune,* May 28, 1908.

Thompson, Joseph J. 1920. *The Archdiocese of Chicago: Antecedents and Development.* Des Plaines, Ill.: St. Mary's Training School Press.

Thompson, Ruth. 1951. *The Chapel of the Dunes 50th Anniversary.* Gary, Ind.: n.p.

Thompson, Todd A. 1992. "Beach-Ridge Development and Lake-Level Variation in Southern Lake Michigan." *Sedimentary Geology* 80: 305–18.

Thompson, Todd A., and Steve J. Baedke. 1995. "Beach-Ridge Development in Lake Michigan: Shoreline Behavior in Response to Quasi-Periodic Lake-Level Events." *Marine Geology* 129: 163–74.

————. 1997. "Strand-Plain Evidence for Late Holocene Lake-Level Variations in Lake Michigan." *Geological Society of American Bulletin* 109: 666–82.

Thompson, Todd A., Gordon S. Fraser, and Norman C. Hester. 1991. *Lake-Level Variation in Southern Lake Michigan: Magnitude and Timing of Fluctuations over the Past 4,000 Years.* Bloomington: Indiana State Geological Survey.

Thwaites, F. T., and Kenneth Bertrand. 1957. "Pleistocene Geology of the Door Peninsula, Wisconsin." *Geological Society of American Bulletin* 68: 831–79.

Thwaites, Reuben Gold, ed. 1966. "Voyages of Marquette." Ann Arbor, Mich.: University Microfilms. A reprint of *Travels and Explorations of the Jesuit Missionaries in New France, 1610–1791,* vol. 59 (Cleveland, Ohio: Burrows Brothers, 1900).

Tinkham, Reland. August 23, 1831. Unpublished letter housed at the Chicago Historical Society.

"Tolleston Gun Club Now Passing." *Gary Post Tribune,* May 15, 1908.

Tolleston "Old-Settlers" Centennial, 1851–1951. 1951. Gary, Ind.: n.p.

Tolman, Lynne. 2000. http://www.majortaylor association.org. Accessed December 12, 2002.

Town of Dyer Bicentennial Book. 1976. Dyer, Ind.: Senior Citizens Club of Dyer.

Trusty, N. Lance. 1982. *Town on the Ridge: A History of Munster, Indiana.* Hammond, Ind.: Regional Studies Institute, Purdue University Calumet.

————. 1984. *Hammond: A Centennial Portrait.* Norfolk, Va.: Donning.

————. 1985. *The Calumet Region: A Master Bibliography.* Hammond, Ind.: Regional Studies Institute.

Tuley, William T. 1987. *St. John, Indiana: 150 Years, 1837–1987.* Schererville, Ind.: Minuteman Press.

United Methodist Church, Hebron, IN, 1835–1985. 1985. Booklet. Hebron, Ind.: First Methodist Episcopal Church.

U.S. Bureau of the Census. Census Returns for Lake County, Ind., 1850, 1860.

U.S. Northwest Territory Celebration Commission. 1937. *History of the Ordinance of 1787 and the Old Northwest Territory.* Marietta, Ohio: U.S. Northwest Territory Celebration Commission.

Van Hinte, Jacob. 1985. *Netherlanders in America: A Study of Emigration and Settlement in the Nineteenth and Twentieth Centuries in the United States of America.* Grand Rapids, Mich.: Baker Book House.

Volp, John H. 1935. *The First Hundred Years 1835–1935: Historical Review of Blue Island, Illinois.* Blue Island, Ill.: n.p. Reprint, Salem, Mass.: Higginson Book Company, 2001.

Wagner, Susan F. 1974. "A History of the Village of Flossmoor, 1851–1974." Flossmoor Historical Committee brochure. Flossmoor, Ill.

Waldron, Larry. 1998. *The Indiana Dunes.* n.p.: Eastern National.

Waterman, A. N. 1908. *Historical Review of Chicago and Cook County.* Vol. 1. Chicago: Lewis.

Watt, William J. 1999. *The Pennsylvania Railroad in Indiana.* Bloomington: Indiana University Press.

Weatherwax, Paul. 1941. "The Indian as a Corn Breeder." *Proceedings of the Indiana Academy of Science* 51: 13–21.

Weiler, Mrs. Albert. 1970. "History of Palmer." In Historical Association of Lake County, Indiana, *Reports and Papers,* vol. 12. Crown Point, Ind.: Historical Association of Lake County.

Wellington, Raynor G. 1914. *The Political and Sectional Influence of the Public Lands, 1828–1842.* n.p.: Riverside Press.

Werich, J. Lorenzo. 1920. *Pioneer Hunters of the Kankakee.* n.p.

Whitaker, John O., Jr. 2002. "Mammals of the Grand

Calumet River Region." *Proceedings of the Indiana Academy of Science,* 108/109: 122–44.

Whiting Savings and Loan Association. 1911. *Whiting City Almanac and Cook Book.* Chicago: Hammond Press, W. B. Conkey.

Willman, H. B. 1971. *Summary of the Geology of the Chicago Area.* Circular 460. Urbana: Illinois State Geological Survey.

Wilson, L. R. 1932. "The Two Creeks Forest Bed, Manitowoc County, Wisconsin." *Wisconsin Academy of Sciences Transactions* 27: 31–46.

Wolcott, Alexander. 1824. "Alexander Wolcott Jr. to Tipton, November 19, 1824." In Nellie Armstrong Robertson and Dorothy Riker, *The John Tipton Papers,* vol. 1: *1809–1827.* Indianapolis: Indiana Historical Bureau, 1942.

Woods, Bruce. 1975. "Bartlett Woods: The Grand Old Man of Lake County." Paper presented to the Lake County Historical Society. Reprinted in *Lake County Heritage.* Dallas: Curtis Media Corporation.

Woods, Sam B. 1938. *The First One Hundred Years of Lake County, Indiana.* n.p., n.d.

Works Projects Administration. 1939. *The Calumet Region Historical Guide.* Gary, Ind.: Garman.

Youngman, Peter. October 1997. "Old Trails of Ogden Dunes and Vicinity." *Hour Glass* 5, no. 10.

Zimmerman, Jacob F. 1938. "History of Incorporated Municipalities of Thornton Township." Manuscript housed at the Library of the South Suburban Historical and Genealogical Society, South Holland, Ill.

Index

KENNETH J. SCHOON is a professor of science education in the School of Education and associate dean of education at Indiana University Northwest. He came to IUN in 1990 after teaching middle and high school science for twenty-two years. Dr. Schoon is a board member of the Indiana Dunes Environmental Learning Center, Munster Parks and Recreation, and Indiana Science Olympiad and an active participant in the Historical Community of Northwest Indiana. In this book he combines three primary interests: geology, history, and the Calumet Area of Indiana and Illinois.

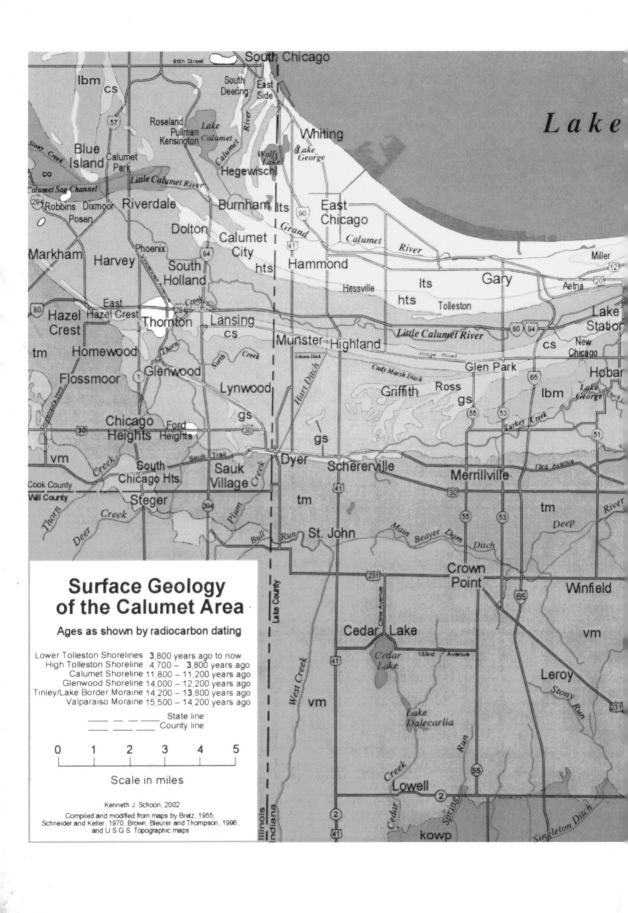

Surface Geology of the Calumet Area

Ages as shown by radiocarbon dating

Lower Tolleston Shorelines **3,800** years ago to now
High Tolleston Shoreline 4,700 – 3,800 years ago
Calumet Shoreline 11,800 – 11,200 years ago
Glenwood Shoreline 14,000 – 12,200 years ago
Tinley/Lake Border Moraine 14,200 – 13,800 years ago
Valparaiso Moraine 15,500 – 14,200 years ago

——————— State line
– – – – – – County line

0 1 2 3 4 5
Scale in miles

Kenneth J. Schoon, 2002

Compiled and modified from maps by Bretz, 1955,
Schneider and Keller, 1970; Brown, Bleurer and Thompson, 1996,
and U.S.G.S. Topographic maps